Praise for Perfectly Paired

"It is rare indeed to read a memoir of such transparency and honesty. It was not Bonny's plan to fall madly in love with a Brother in the religious life. She decided to not be fearful of love and immersed herself in the journey at a depth that goes beyond measurement. She also reveals the growth she experienced from grief, and how she learned to become unafraid of death. This masterful work inspired me with its kaleidoscope of courage, humor and compassion."

—Gerald G. Jampolsky, M.D. bestselling author of *Love is Letting Go of Fear, Forgiveness: The Greatest Healer of All* and over 20 additional titles. Founder, Attitudinal Healing. https://www.ahinternational.org/

"A memoir of grief, love and life reentry, Bonny Meyer takes the reader inside her life with a mesmerizing voice you can hear through the pages.

For anyone who loved and lost, *Perfectly Paired* will walk with you to the depths of loyalty and intimacy bridging the past and present with wine, adventure and love for life.

Grab some tissues and step into Bonny's big life before, during and after loss. You will forever be changed."

—Christina Rasmussen, bestselling author of *Second Firsts* and *Where Did You Go?*

"The story, the writing, and the energy of love from every page made it impossible for me to put the book down. It is a beautiful, beautiful book filled with passion, great story telling, deep insight, unbridled joy as well as tragedy and heartbreak. I loved every page and feel that this book will make a significant contribution to people's experience with love and their capacity to open to it.

This is a book for lovers. This is a book for people who long for love. This is a book for everyone. It is beautifully written, and it carries the reader gracefully through the mountains and valleys of opening oneself fully to love and to be loved. I give it my highest recommendation."

—Lynne Twist, author of *The Soul of Money: Transforming Your Relationship with Money and Life.* Founder and President, Soul of Money Institute, and Co-Founder of the Pachamama Alliance. https://soulofmoney.org/ https://www.pachamama.org/

"If you're interested in how the sweat, faith and genius of a few heartful people transformed the orchards and dairy farms of the Napa Valley into one of the greatest wine-making regions in the world, this book is for you. If you're interested in the spiritual alchemy that can transform lead to gold, can draw four cards on a bad hand and end up with a royal flush, or can find love everywhere and in everything and transform grief into a new life, this book is also for you."

—Don Joseph Goewey, former Director of the Center for Attitudinal Healing and author of *The End of Stress, Mystic Cool,* and *Fishing for Fallen Light.*

"At times heart-wrenching but always heart-touching, Meyer's courageously candid memoir of her passions personal and professional deserves to be read by anyone searching for meaning. She delivers at the same time a lively page in the storied history of Napa. This tale is uplifting for wine-lovers, and lovers, period."

—Stephen O'Shea, historian and author of *The Alps: A Human History from Hannibal to Heidi* and *Beyond and Sea of Faith: Islam and Christianity in the Medieval Mediterranean World.*

"Meyer takes us on a captivating journey into passion as she bravely and tenderly recounts the life she shared (and continues to share) with her now deceased husband and her God, proving that life and love are eternal. Part memoir, part relationship guide, part grief counseling book, this is a heart-expanding tale for anyone who wants to know the depths of real love."

—**Karen Brailsford**, author of *Sacred Landscapes of the Soul.*

Perfectly Paired

The Love Affair Behind Silver Oak Cellars

Perfectly Paired

The Love Affair Behind Silver Oak Cellars

Bonny Meyer

Cover Design by Charles McStravick, One Rocket Media
Back Cover Photography by Rick Bolen
Book Design by Holly C. Meyer,
The Creativity Ninja
Published in the United States by Meyer Family Enterprises, LLC
www.mfenterprises.com
This book was typeset in Big Caslon, Big Caslon with 10 degree slant, and
Coneria Script Demo used as display typefaces

Printed and bound in the United States by Kingery
First Edition
ISBN: 978-1-7343283-0-1

Permission to reproduce lyrics to "You Are So Beautiful"
granted by Hal Leonard

Dedication

I dedicate this book to my children; Chad, Matt, and Holly, their partners Aimee, Karen, and Hany, and my grandchildren; Justin, Sidney, Lily, Dana, and Cooper. The wisdom and stories within are the most precious legacy I can give you.

I dedicate this book to my beloved, Justin. Without him there would be no stories to tell.

I dedicate this book to my readers, that together we come to know we are all capable of extraordinary relationship and can rise beyond grief and death into an expanded life filled with light, connection, and a sense of fulfillment.

Table of Contents

Perfectly Paired

The Love Affair Behind Silver Oak Cellars

Bonny & Justin Meyer

Prelude

For decades, people have been telling me that I should write the story of how my husband Justin and I met, fell in love, and created the famed Napa Valley winery Silver Oak Cellars. Friends who admired our deep connection and love for one another called it special and rare. They said we were "perfectly paired" like herb-crusted rack of lamb and a bottle of Silver Oak Cabernet. Some knew that Justin had been a Christian Brother and wanted to know the story of how he decided to leave the monastic life. Be it winery or relationship, they wanted to be let in on the secrets of our success.

Then a remarkable confluence of events convinced me that I should share the story. Within the space of a week, three different men with disparate life stories confessed to me that they felt they had never really been in love, had never really given themselves to another. They had all married and been happy enough for a while. Then when things started to fall apart, they found the candor that comes with tragedy, and confessed to me. They each felt they had never really loved in the first place. In fact, they all said they thought they were broken somehow, and that made them incapable of loving.

It felt as if every cell within my body shouted "No!" We are born loving beings. Every infant looks up at her mother with unbridled love and devotion. Everyone is capable of love, and more than that, everyone deserves a beautiful and precious loving relationship. My friend Mary Kay Bigelow, a brilliant and gifted marriage and family therapist, made what she felt was a fundamental discovery years ago. Every person she counseled who had been married and divorced realized they had gotten exactly what they had wanted, but nothing more. In retrospect, they came to realize their marriage allowed them some limited success: to be with a beautiful woman, to be taken care of by a powerful man, to finally move out of their parent's home, to have children... The list goes on.

Subconsciously, they had all assumed that wonderful, happily-ever-after romance would automatically follow the wedding ceremony.

It didn't and it doesn't.

So why is it that what we are born to do, what we long for most, seems so elusive and so rare?

My friend and celebrated author Dr. Jerry Jampolsky says, "Love is letting go of fear." Is that it? Do we hold back because we are afraid of losing ourselves? The irony is that when we hold back and take comfort in playing a role or being strategic in our relationships because we think we are unlovable, we lose track of ourselves. We mask our true self that longs to be present in relationship. Thus, we will indeed be unavailable for love. How can another person love us when it feels to them that we are not really there? If we are afraid of being vulnerable, being exquisitely intimate, then we will never experience the gifts of ecstasy. Being afraid of loving is tantamount to being afraid of living.

I am a student of Dr. Brené Brown's work on vulnerability. She has mapped the attributes of people who live deep, fulfilling lives and relationships. She has also charted the unconscious strategies we use to block happiness and deep connection. She found that vulnerability was the fundamental quality common to all the people who were successful at living a happy life. Compelled by what she found, she embarked upon a personal transformation to become more vulnerable.

As my story unfolded in these pages, I realized that alchemical transformation was a common thread woven through the love, the wine, the loss, the reconnection, and the resurrection in my life.

Alchemy occurs when something ordinary is transformed—through chemical reaction, fire, fermentation or some other means—into something extraordinary.

Wine has been a symbol of alchemy from the beginning of human history. Grapes grow wild just about everywhere in earth's temperate climates. When grapes are crushed to release their juice, wild yeasts on the skins naturally start a fermentation process that turns the juice into wine. This is magical enough. Add to this centuries of careful cultivation of meticulously chosen grape varieties. Then perform the dozens of little things that a viticulturist does to a vine: pruning it, tying it, training it, thinning it, making sure there is some stress but not too much. The resulting grapes are no longer ordinary. Now give those grapes to a master enologist who ferments the juice at exactly the right temperature; cultivates maceration (juice contact with grape skins and seeds) to extract the perfect amount of color and tannin; separates the juice from the solids at the right moment; ages the wine in carefully chosen oak barrels; and finally lets it rest in bottles for the right amount of time. Now you have the nectar of the gods in your glass! Build a business around that, and you have the alchemical magic of Silver Oak, the renowned winery Justin and I founded with our financial partner, Ray Duncan.

Intimate committed love relationships are alchemical too. It is all too common for couples to have ordinary relationships which they complain about, put up with, and distance themselves from. All that effort, when what we long for is to become one with the other, to dissolve our disturbing human sense of separation. Every marriage and committed relationship offers the perfect opportunity, the ultimate crucible, for personal transformation. When couples put their fears and egos aside and dive into that crucible, when they let the fire burn the illusion of separation, an extraordinary relationship can emerge.

My extraordinary love affair with Justin was alchemy.

Our alchemical love affair infused Silver Oak Cellars and our wines with romance. Good business sense alone cannot account for the phenomenal success and loyalty Silver Oak enjoyed. Our love, our commitment to each other and to making the best Cabernet Sauvignon possible, no matter what, created memorable experiences for those who tasted and enjoyed our wines. Over the thirty years we ran Silver Oak, we received hundreds of accounts of marriage proposals, anniversaries honored, and mountains climbed that were celebrated with Silver Oak Cabernet. There was definitely a special kind of heart-warming magic in our wine.

In the alchemy of collaboration, we are partners; each contributing our unique gifts and talents toward a common goal. The vintners of the Napa Valley did this. They took an industry that had been content to produce ordinary generic wine for over a century and together determined they would help each other excel. Their generosity toward one another was the love, the fire, the catalyst that raised Napa Valley to the extraordinary level of quality and regard the region enjoys today.

Grief is likewise alchemical. Those who dive into the deep, dark, black well of grief discover that grief breaks their hearts open and immolates their spirits, allowing a phoenix to arise. I found the courage for this dive. Grief had its way with me, ultimately transforming me.

In every indigenous shamanic tradition that I have learned about, the initiates must metaphorically die. They are buried alive, they leap from a mountain top, take powerful medicinal plants that can just as easily heal them as stop their heart or drive them insane. This fierce initiation is viewed as a requirement for a life of service. It is the crucible of alchemy. If they survive, they will have embraced death, looked it in the eye and conquered the ultimate human fear. From this place, they are capable of anything. No longer fearing death unleashes ultimate potential and ultimate power. I know this alchemy intimately because I have come close to dying more than once, and I am no longer afraid.

It is my fervent hope that you will find within my life stories your own passion and power; the courage to commit, to take risks, and to love profoundly. Everyone is born a worthy and consummate lover. My wish for you is that you begin to know this and find your way to what you have been longing for. I share my stories of struggle that you may find, within yourself, your own resilience. Nothing can stop an inner sense of peace, power, love, and joy once these have been ignited within our hearts and souls.

I invite you into the magic and mystery of the powerful love affair that gave birth to extraordinary Cabernet and transcended grief. May this alchemical journey lead you to the magic that already lies within you.

Love,

Bonny
Oakville, Winter, 2020

The Holy Longing

Johann Wolfgang von Goethe

Tell a wise person, or else keep silent,
For those who do not understand will mock it right away.
I praise what is truly alive,
What longs to be burned to death.

In the calm water of the love-nights,
Where you were begotten, where you have begotten,
A strange feeling comes over you
When you see the silent candle burning.

Now you are no longer caught
In the obsession with darkness,
And a desire for higher love-making
Sweeps you upward.

Distance does not make you falter,
Now, arriving in magic, flying,
And, finally, insane for the light,
You are the butterfly and you are gone.

And so long as you haven't experienced this:
To die and so to grow,
You are only a troubled guest
On the dark earth.

Chapter One

Bonny & Justin Meyer, Lower Blue Lake, CA, August 6, 2002

August 6, 2002

The love of my life is slipping out of my arms.

On a gorgeous day by a pristine mountain lake, unfathomable gravity tugs my husband, Justin, out of my embrace and takes him down to the ground.

There was no warning. There is no time for thought. I go to my knees and blow into his mouth with long, full exhalations, then push hard on his chest, hoping against hope he will start breathing again. Hoping he will show some movement. Some sign of life.

When I am exhausted with the effort and shaky from the adrenalin coursing through my body, I ask Ruggero, Justin's dear friend, if he can take over. Ruggero kneels down next to Justin's body across from me, lovingly looks at his friend and begins to administer chest compressions in a steady, rapid rhythm.

I get to my feet, watching Justin and Ruggero, hoping against hope. And then I hear the sound: a peculiar, rattling exhale coming from the depths of my husband's body. Somehow I know the meaning of that sound. Whatever life force was left in him has ridden that exhale right out of his body.

Slowly I back away, shaky on my feet but never taking my eyes off Justin. Ruggero continues to try to force his lungs to breathe and heart to beat. Someone has called for an ambulance, but up here in the Sierra Nevada mountains it will have to come from a distant town on two-lane roads. The local heroes will not reach us in the nick of time. The drama unfolding in front of me will not wait.

I become aware of myself, sitting on the top of a picnic table and able to see everything: Justin lying still, Ruggero focused and pushing hard on his chest and breathing into his mouth without stopping. Somewhere nearby, Ruggero's wife Gina and other picnickers keep a measured distance. They do not assist Ruggero, or comfort me. It seems they do not even move. Are they waiting for me to become frantic, to rage or cry?

In this eerie stillness of shock and disbelief, I know intellectually that the worst I could imagine is happening before my eyes. But something stronger than my mind keeps me focused on Justin. His face, always naturally ruddy, begins to take on some unnatural patches of purple. First his nose, then his cheeks. Now the bystanders take a couple of steps back, separating themselves from death by a pretty lake on a summer day.

I want the ambulance to arrive, but not because anyone can save Justin now. The extravagant physical effort of CPR already feels morbid, a travesty. Nevertheless I force myself to return to Justin's side to relieve Ruggero. We don't need to speak. We wordlessly agree we will not stop our efforts until we are assured by an emergency professional that Justin is dead. After a while I feel exhausted again, but now it is not solely from the physical effort. I can feel my emotions backing up inside, threatening to overload. My body feels heavy, like Justin's did from one moment to the next, as if my life force exited in the same moment as did his. I look up at Ruggero. He understands. He takes over again.

Finally, the ambulance arrives. I say to the attendant, "Please tell us that he is dead so we can stop." His look means I have said something strange, perhaps even suspicious. Not the usual greeting from the wife of someone who has just died.

He walks over to where Justin lies. Ruggero, Gina and I watch carefully, holding our breath. It takes only a moment to confirm that Justin is indeed dead.

Everything alters. What was surreal is now a fact, a routine medical event that turns my beloved over to administrative processes. I feel like I have been hit by a sledgehammer, too crushed to cry.

Our efforts to revive Justin have forced some saliva out of his mouth and onto his face. With moistened paper towels I carefully clean Justin's face, taking my time and attending to every fold of skin, his ears, his eyes, carefully washing his face and neck. I run my hand over his bald forehead and close-cropped hair. I prolong the process until I feel the others around me, silently waiting. Finally, I stand up and back away.

Justin has belonged to me in music, life, romance, marriage, parenthood, business, phenomenal success... Now he belongs to the ambulance man. He summarily squats down, grabs the bottom of Justin's grey t-shirt, and raises it up so that it covers his face. This is another shock, like a gut punch in its intensity. With Justin's face covered, he is transformed from my beloved into a faceless corpse.

The ambulance attendant and Ruggero carefully maneuver Justin's body onto a stretcher and then to the ambulance. I stop them before they slide him inside. Tenderly I lift Justin's shirt from his face and take it in my hands. It is still warm. I kiss him many times over, smoothing his skin, brushing his closed eyes with my lips. Finally, it is time for the ambulance to take him away. As I watch it pull away, a realization hits my heart like a hammer: I will never touch or lay my eyes on Justin again.

And so, a new journey begins. Though I am deep in grief and physically fragile, the memories of what has come before contain the fire and grace that will sustain me.

Wanting to Run

I slide into the front passenger seat of Ruggero's Jeep, where Justin had been sitting on the drive to the lake earlier. It is the first of countless times that I will take Justin's place, in arenas too numerous and various to recognize now. As we head back to Ruggero and Gina's house, they encourage me to spend the night with them before I return home to Napa Valley. But they cannot persuade me. I want to be with my children. I need to tell them about their father.

At the house I quickly shove my things into a duffle bag. As I prepare to do the same with Justin's things, I stop and stare at them. They have no owner now. He won't need these pants, this toothbrush, this beautiful sweater I gave him... My awareness shifts to a bulky object in my pocket. It is Justin's wallet, filled to overflowing with the essential and the precious. He doesn't need this anymore either. Catching myself in reverie, I remind myself that I must keep moving if I am going to get out of the Sierras before sundown.

As soon as I am in the car, it floods with memories of the day before, when Justin and I had driven up to visit Ruggero and Gina. The car itself is a cascade of memories: a BMW convertible Justin gave me for my 50th birthday. Driving up into the mountains, we had reveled in the sense of freedom that comes with the feeling of wind in our hair. We had breathed in the fresh air and the stunning mountain vistas as we made our way over Echo Summit and Carson Pass, descending into Alpine County on the east side of the mountains.

Now I am driving west through the mountains, not east. My passenger is Gina, not Justin. Ruggero follows close behind in the Jeep. They have decided that it is not safe for me to travel alone. Perhaps they consider me emotionally fragile. In reality I feel mightily determined. I make my way up Highway 89 to the summit then down Highway 50 to the west, into the sun, top down, jaw set, tears in my eyes. Gina asks me how I am feeling, and I tell her I am feeling like a mama bear absolutely possessed by an imperative to protect her cubs.

Nevertheless, a strange thing starts happening as the miles fly by. My eyes are repeatedly drawn into the conifer forests of deep green that line the highway. Every time I see a dirt road or half-abandoned track that cuts through the green curtain, I imagine a remote little cabin, some sanctuary of stillness far from civilization. I could stay there for months, years maybe. I could be alone to cry and curse and scream my heart out.

I am mystified by this urge as I race toward Napa to be with my children. The temptation to veer off the highway is fierce. But then I see Gina, looking straight ahead, focused on the highway. Or I look in the rearview mirror and see Ruggero following close behind us. The two of them are energetically holding me to the road.

My sons Chad and Matt and their wives have been told to meet me at my home later that evening. But they don't know yet why. I need to look into their eyes when they learn about Justin.

Still fresh in my mind are phone conversations with all three children early that morning. Justin had followed the conversation with keen focus, without joining in. He could tell from my side of the conversation that everyone was fine and happy. Now I am flooded with remorse. If I had insisted that he take the phone as well, his children would have had the gift of one last conversation with him.

An even earlier conversation comes back to me, during the drive into the mountains the day before. Justin had sensed anger in me and asked why. I was frustrated that he would not restrict his diet to keep his diabetes in check, and told him so.

His response had cut me to the core. "Don't you know me by now, after all these years? Don't you know that I love to eat and drink whatever I want and enjoy what I want? I would rather do that than be careful. I'm going to die at some point, and I would rather enjoy every minute than eat nothing but a bunch of rabbit food!"

That took the heat right out of my frustration. Indeed, Justin had always been that way; savoring every morsel and minute of life. Careful was not part of his personality or approach to life. I glanced over at him, feeling deep love and admiration for his honesty.

"Yes, I know you," I had told him.

Silence pregnant with deep connection had filled the rest of our drive. Now I am grateful for that conversation. It would have been a terrible burden if I had been holding myself away from him, in anger, when he died.

I look to my right again, into the deep woods. The cool green forest calls to me. My life as I knew it is over. It ended the moment Justin's heart stopped. Now I want to run away from everyone and everything, hide from everyone I know, hide even from my children as I rush to meet them.

I arrive home to find Chad, Matt, and their wives just driving up to the house. When they realize that Justin is not with me, they immediately ask why. I suggest we sit on the sofa together. After we are all settled, I close my eyes and take a long breath before telling them quietly how their father has died that afternoon. I tell them about being with Gina and Ruggero and having a picnic lunch by the lake. I tell them about how much fun we were having, until Justin got shaky on his feet...

Ruggero chimes in and tells about our lunch of cold pasta with a bottle of Zinfandel. He is lamenting that Justin's last meal was cold pasta because Ruggero forgot his propane stove. He is sad also that Justin, known as the King of Cabernet, had to drink Zinfandel for lunch. "We should have been drinking Silver Oak!"

Then I tell them how Ruggero and I needed to help Justin walk, and how he slipped to the ground like a rag doll, his legs no longer able to hold him, his heart no longer beating.

When there is no more to say, nothing feels real or right, as if our world has just shifted on its axis. But slowly it sinks in. Chad and his wife Aimee have news of their own – she is pregnant with her first child, shortly after their honeymoon. This joyful announcement morphs into agony as Chad cries out, "Our baby will never know his grandfather!"

Matt keeps staring at me, hard. He knows that I have a rare form of cancer. I am still recovering from major surgery at the beginning of summer. After learning he has lost one parent, Matt seems already afraid he will lose the other.

Early the next morning, Ruggero drives me and Chad to the airport in San Francisco to pick up my daughter Holly and my niece Vanessa. They have been on a cross-country road trip and rushed home at the news of Justin's death. When they finally descend the escalator, Holly is clutching a tear-stained pillow. We embrace in a blurring field of grief and disbelief. Time stops. Waves of emotion course through our entwined bodies.

At some point the others reach in through the fog. Holly and Chad hug and cry together. With tender sadness I embrace Vanessa. Ruggero, despite having lost his best friend, is the most practical of us all, keeping an eye out for the girls' luggage and then shepherding us home.

Touching In

That evening, I am tenderly tucking Holly into my bed on the side Justin has always occupied. I am sitting on the edge of the bed stroking her hair, comforting her, when a pebble strikes the floor.

There is only one place it can come from: a niche in the adobe wall of our master bedroom, about ten feet from where I am sitting on the bed. Years before I had placed a small fountain in the niche, which includes pebbles for the water to splash onto, creating natural music. Somehow one of these pebbles has propelled itself through the air and landed at my feet.

Holly and I catch our breath, startled. Then we look up at each other, wordlessly asking, "Did you see what I saw?" We both stare down at the mysterious pebble again. But the second time we raise our eyes to each other, it is not in surprise. Holly's expression softens as she says in a small voice, "Hi, Daddy."

After a while, I pick up the pebble and hand it to her. We sit there trying to think of another explanation for a pebble flying across the room. We can't. All we can surmise is that it must be Justin's way of saying that he is here with us.

Eventually I walk around the bed to the other side and climb in next to Holly and hug her tight. Despite the flying pebble of re-assurance, it is a restless, grief-filled night.

The next morning, the hair dryer goes off in the bathroom without anyone touching it or using it.

Our king-size bed sits up against a room divider that separates the bedroom from the bathroom. There is a counter on the bathroom side with a double sink. Just inches from where Holly's head lies on the pillow is Justin's sink, and next to it is the hair dryer with a magnetized base for the nozzle that blows the hot air. Pull the nozzle away from the base and it goes on. Put it back and the hair dryer shuts off.

While I had always considered this pretty clever, Justin hated the thing. He was always bumping into it with his elbow, causing the hair dryer nozzel to pop off its base, then buzz loudly and dangle until he caught it and replaced it to stop the infernal noise.

Now, the morning after the mysterious flying pebble landed at my feet, the hair dryer has fallen and started buzzing all by itself. When I put it back on the magnetic base it doesn't turn off. Nothing I do turns it off. But when I give up and turn to leave, it stops of its own accord.

But that is not the end of it. The hair dryer seems to have acquired some kind of awareness or intention. When Holly or I walk into the bedroom, it goes on for a little while then stops. A close friend staying with me in the house notices a pattern. When I am feeling particularly bereft, the hair dryer goes wild. As I calm down, it settles down to a purr, and then stops.

We begin to wonder if the pebble and hair dryer incidents are somehow related, directed and controlled in some mysterious way by Justin. It seems impossible, but one thing keeps challenging my disbelief: What a classic example of Justin's wry sense of humor that would be, comforting me with that silly hair dryer he hated so much.

Chapter Two

Brother Justin Meyer playing his homemade banjo and Bonny Smith playing a guitar the night they met at Dr. Harold and Helen Olmo's home

No, I Was Never a Nun

It was a natural question, but it always amused me. People would learn that I married a monk, and ask if I had been a nun.

Monks and nuns becoming husbands and wives sounds like an oxymoron, but it began to occur frequently in the 1960s as more people questioned traditions and institutions of all kinds. Catholic religious orders, in particular, experienced a mass exodus from which they have never recovered. Just in my own circle, a number of former teachers and current friends made the journey from a religious life into married life.

I did not. But I came close.

My childhood years were fairly typical of the post-war 1950s. Though neither of my parents finished college, they both put a high value on education and had aspirations that their children would get university degrees. They grew up in Dearborn, Michigan, where both their fathers worked for Ford Motor Company. Grampa Smith ran Henry Ford's bank; Bompa Gassett, my mother's dad, was an inventor who helped develop early technologies for radio, television and airplane flight for Ford. One of those technologies is the instrument landing system still in use today, allowing airplanes to land safely at night or in low visibility using a combination of radio frequencies and light. Regardless of their status or role at Ford, or what they had accomplished, people from Dearborn carried the manners and ways of people from a small, provincial company town.

Eager for adventure, my father followed a college professor to Central America to collect specimens for study at the University of Michigan one summer. He liked it so much that he stayed when the fall semester started. Thus he found himself in Panama when World War II broke out. He was quickly conscripted by the U.S.

government to work in the Canal Zone. Except for contracting malaria, my father had a much better experience during the war than most everyone else. As a civilian, he got hazard pay and weeks of time off. He used that time to explore the jungles of Panama and Guatemala, his machete becoming his most prized possession.

When he finally returned after the war, he looked for Isabelle Gassett, the girl he had fallen in love with as a 17-year-old. Though they had each written to the other during the intervening years, their letters were never delivered. So my father was both relieved and excited when he found that Isabelle was in good healty—and unmarried. Soon they married in a simple ceremony, with borrowed wedding clothes. Then they packed their few possessions into my father's car and headed to California for their honeymoon, and never returned. Must have been something about those Michigan winters.

My siblings and I, Baby Boomers all, grew up in what is now known as Silicon Valley. Back then, the prune and apricot orchards that blanketed the gentle slopes bordering San Francisco Bay were giving way to new subdivisions. Los Altos was a sleepy little town along the railroad tracks in Santa Clara Valley, where San Franciscans had come for generations to escape their cold, grey summers shrouded in heavy fog. At the edges of Los Altos there were still orchards and grapes, along with row crops of every kind. We called them "truck farms" because they fed the local community and San Francisco—always called "The City"—40 miles to the north. Santa Clara had been named "Valley of the Heart's Delight" by the Native Americans who lived there. Along with its deep, fertile soils came temperate weather: moderate rainfall, sunny summer days and mild winters without frost.

The children in my neighborhood grew up running free, playing in the adjacent field until it was covered by trays of drying prunes and apricots in late summer. Even then, we would sneak out to help ourselves to a handful of sweet, half-dried fruit. Mothers made apricot pie and apricot jam, and the children harvested prunes for spending money. When we got tall enough, we cut "cots"—apricots—for 50 cents a tray: lofty wages in those days.

I loved being outdoors and playing sports, so I was quickly termed a tomboy. My summer days were usually spent at the local elementary school, participating in all manner of recreation programs. I enjoyed leadership and teaching as a teenager and became the youngest employee of the Santa Clara County school district, running summer recreation programs at elementary school campuses when I was only 15 and 16 years old.

Like my brothers and sister, I attended public schools through junior high. But when it came time to go to high school, my mother suggested I might want to attend the all-girls Catholic high school in Mountain View run by Sisters of the Holy Cross. She knew how frustrated I had been in junior high when students were disrespectful to teachers, resulting in chaos in the classrooms. I allowed that I would try Holy Cross, but I also secured a promise from my parents that if I didn't like it, I could transfer to the town's secular high school after a year.

As it turned out, I thrived. It was essentially a competitive college prep school, which energized me. Our teachers were a mixture of nuns and lay women. They generally were bright, fun and light-hearted, so they were easy to admire and emulate. The Sisters in particular were well-educated and relatively broad-minded. Their mother house at St. Mary's College was in South Bend, Indiana, across the street from and associated with the University of Notre Dame.

In addition to the school's curriculum, culture and educators, I loved being at an all-girls school where I felt totally free to be, well, all girl. Students could sit cross-legged on the hallway floor talking with each other, be silly in class, ask the craziest questions and never be concerned about how we were seen by boys. I could take leadership roles, excel at math, compete in sports and not be seen as too athletic or "brainy." I love to sing, and led "hootenanny Masses" at church on Sundays. Students at Holy Cross wore uniforms, so the only wardrobe choice each morning was whether to wear a navy blazer or a blue sweater. I'd iron my white blouse collar and run out the door.

When I was in my junior year, I dated a boy named Mike who was a senior at St. Francis, the boy's Catholic school down the road. He was quite romantic in his way. He particularly liked to draw floor plans of the future home we would live in. What was most curious about this is that he was also determined to join the Congregation of the Holy Cross—a celibate order. So, after graduation, he headed off for his orientation and serious religious studies. We kept in touch—though he had to pretend I was his cousin.

Maybe he was the one who inspired me. Maybe it was my teachers. Maybe it was the spirit of peace and light-heartedness that pervaded the school. Perhaps it was all of these. During my senior year, I decided to become a nun. By April, I had applied to the Sisters of the Holy Cross and had been accepted.

By June, I changed my mind. I simply decided I loved men and wanted a family too much to be happy with a celibate life. At graduation, the names of girls headed for the convent were announced to the assembly. Mine was not one of them. A hundred wondering faces turned in my direction. It was delicious.

First Meeting

I started college in the fall of 1967, attending the University of California at Davis, in California's central valley. A month into the first term I got an invitation to a dinner party at a professor's house. I didn't know the hosts or any of the guests beside the young man who invited me. But after four weeks of dorm living, being in a professor's house and eating a home-cooked meal sounded like heaven.

The invitation came from Norm, a senior. We had met during my first week at the university, when I had gone to Newman Center, home of the campus' Catholic ministry, to volunteer my services as a musician. Norm was nice and we became friends. Now he was inviting me into a whole new world.

The previous year, he had lived with Professor Harold Olmo, his wife Helen, and another UC Davis student known as BJ, short for Brother Justin. While Norm had since moved to an apartment in town, BJ was still living with the Olmos. The dinner was a celebration of his 29th birthday.

The Olmos lived in a rambling farmhouse outside of Davis, down a gravel road next to Putah Creek. By the late 1960s, Harold was a world-renowned viticulturist and grape breeder. On his property was a walnut orchard and acres of tomatoes but no vineyard. I came to find out that Dr. Olmo spent his time in the university campus vineyards, green houses and off-campus research stations. He had no need, or time, for a vineyard of his own.

Norm took me into the Olmo home the way the family entered, through the garage. My whole body relaxed as I was engulfed with the sights, sounds and aromas of a happy family home. In the kitchen, I met three generations of the Olmo family: Dr. Olmo's wife Helen, their kids Jeanne and Paul, and Helen's mother, known as "GG." I offered to help set the table and was directed to a large china cupboard which held service for fifty. Clearly the Olmos loved hosting dinners for friends and students. The dining room table was covered with an elegant, hand-embroidered Italian lace tablecloth. The dinner plates were made of fine china and were complemented by beautiful stemware.

When Harold offered me a glass of wine, I hesitated only a moment before accepting. I had turned 18 less than a month before, but everyone drank wine in the Olmos' house. Fruit of the vine, nectar of the gods, staple food of Italians. And Dr. Olmo had the most interesting wine collection: a crazy mix of experimental varieties, good cheap red and fine older vintages. This evening we were drinking wines from the Christian Brothers winery. They had been made and blended by BJ and his mentor, America's most famous winemaker at the time, Brother Timothy.

I had just taken a couple sips of delicious Christian Brothers wine when Brother Justin himself walked into the kitchen. His husky, athletic form filled the doorway, but his enthusiasm, round face and friendly smile were instantly disarming. I had expected him to be dressed in a black robe like the nuns at my high school. But instead he was wearing a knit shirt with blue stripes and grey trousers. With his larger-than-life presence he would have been intimidating in all black. But this way he felt approachable and fun-loving.

Like me, BJ was studying at UC Davis. There the similarities ended. He had come to the university at age 26, with a previous college degree in economics and three years as a high school teacher behind him. He then completed a second bachelor's degree, this time in viticulture, the science of grape growing. But the persuasive Dr. Olmo had convinced him to stay another year for a master's degree in viticulture. So at 29, BJ was not a wide-eyed young student but a winemaker and grape grower honing his technical skills.

Sitting next to Norm, I fully enjoyed BJ's birthday dinner with the Olmo family. I felt relaxed and welcome, participating in the playful conversation around the dining room table. Dinner was delicious and plentiful. Helen was an excellent natural cook, unlike my mother who specialized in casserole recipes she found in the daily paper. My excitement also included a little secret: I had stashed my guitar behind my dining chair. Norm had suggested I bring it because BJ played the banjo. So I knew there was music ahead.

As dinner wound down and it became time for BJ's birthday cake, I brought out my guitar. His eyes immediately lit up as I led everyone in "Happy Birthday." Then he went to his room to grab his banjo. Obviously handmade, his long neck instrument was crafted in the same style as the one played by famed folksinger Pete Seeger.

There at the dining table BJ and I launched into some folk songs we both knew while the men savored cigars and everyone sipped the last bit of wine in their glasses. Now focused on BJ, I matched his strums and chord changes. The two of us quickly became swept up in the music, delighted by our complementary voices and effortless harmony. We decided to move to the family room and continue playing, to the eager assent of everyone else.

Brother Justin and I played and sang together for hours that night. We were both fans of folk music, particularly the Kingston Trio and Peter, Paul and Mary. When one song ended, one of us quickly suggested the next. We easily wove our voices together in harmony, picking up the next verse whenever one of us slipped behind or forgot a lyric. Norm and the Olmo family all joined in on familiar choruses. By the time the night had ended, BJ and I each knew we had found a fun-loving kindred spirit and fellow musician.

As I put away my guitar, the Olmos encouraged Norm to bring me again sometime soon. My heart leaped at this possibility. This had been the most warm, welcoming, delightful night I had enjoyed since my arrival at the university.

As Norm drove me back to my dorm room, we quietly talked about the evening full of family, celebration and song. Had BJ been just another man and not a professed Christian Brother, Norm might have been a little jealous at all the attention I riveted on him as we sang. As it was, Norm enjoyed the music and the evening as much as I had. For my own part, it never occurred to me to entertain any feelings toward Brother Justin other than pure friendship. I had been around celibate nuns, monks and priests in religious orders, and had even considered joining the Sisters of the Holy Cross, so I was very familiar with their vows of chastity, poverty, and obedience.

A couple of weeks after that, just before Thanksgiving break, Norm asked me to marry him. I sincerely told Norm I would give his proposal serious thought, that I had enjoyed the time we had spent together and looked forward to more. When I got home to my parents' house for Thanksgiving, I told my mother about his proposal. As we sat in our family room in front of the fire, she asked me if I loved him. I said I liked Norm well enough and considered the marriage proposal a real compliment. I went on to say it was important for me to get to know him better before any thought of marriage. Besides, I intended to get my college degree. I had no intention of settling for an "MRS degree" as some girls did, just a few months or a year into their university studies.

That was before Norm's past came rushing back into the present, changing the destinies of those around him.

Saved by Synchronicity

Norm and I continued to date after Thanksgiving, but something strange was happening. This man who was keenly interested in me, who just weeks before had asked me to marry him, was becoming more distant. I was doing my best to keep up with my coursework and prepare for finals. He appeared not to focus on his classes; I suspected he was not studying much, if at all. Initially very kind and sweet, he had developed an edge of impatience and anger which I found confusing.

Things went from confused to disturbed when I received a couple of phone calls from the police department in the middle of the night, just to "check on me" and "see if I was safe." The voices were reassuring but the questions were alarming. Apparently Norm was the reason for the calls; he told the police that someone was threatening me. But

I had received no such threats. I began to wonder if Norm himself had threatening feelings toward me.

Then, in the middle of final exam week, Helen Olmo called to tell me that Norm had been admitted to the university health center as an inpatient. That meant he was seriously ill in some way. So as soon as I finished my chemistry final later that day, I went to see him.

When I walked into his room, he was lying in bed dressed in a hospital gown. I came up to the bed intending to give him a kiss, but his eyes stopped me in my tracks. His face was a picture of thinly veiled rage. The man who had asked me to marry him less than a month before was angry, argumentative, blaming, vengeful, threatening. I stood my ground and tried to calm him down, but nothing worked. Something had changed, but I could not discover what it was. I began to feel the urge to bolt out the door.

Just then, the door was blocked by the large, athletic form of Brother Justin, carrying a couple of heavy textbooks under one arm. He too had just come from a final exam and, like me, had swung by to visit Norm. I was relieved to have him there, because he quickly had a calming effect on Norm – and on me. The three of us talked for another 20 minutes or so, and then I felt it was a good time for me to go. BJ picked up his books and escorted me out.

As we walked down the health center corridor, I felt so many conflicting emotions. How could a man who proposed to me suddenly come to revile me? Brother Justin must have read the inner turmoil in my silence, because he spoke up with a gentle yet surprising proposal: Would I like to go get a Coke?

I accepted immediately, eager to hold on to his comforting presence a little while longer. He drove us to a Dairy Queen off Russell Boulevard that had seen better days. It was an unusually warm afternoon in mid-December so we found two stools at the outside counter where we could have a private conversation. When our Cokes arrived, I almost fell off my seat when Brother Justin pulled money out of his pocket and paid. Whenever I had gone out for an ice cream or casual meal with nuns from my school, it was always on me. Nuns don't have money. But this monk had ready cash in his pocket. It was a double delight, to be treated by someone I never imagined would do so.

After some minutes of conversation, it dawned on me that Brother Justin wasn't just socializing, or giving a confused freshman some comfort. He had something to tell me. I gave him the space to do that, and it wasn't long before a strange tale came tumbling out. Norm had lived with the Olmos the previous year by special arrangement, after being diagnosed and treated for manic-depressive disorder. Those involved thought it would be better for him to live with a family rather than on his own, and they were right. Norm did well in the Olmos' warm, caring environment. That's why he had been allowed to move into his own apartment for his final year of college. When he started to date me, his family and friends felt even more confident, BJ explained. People thought I was such a nice girl. Norm was going to be just fine.

I stared at BJ, eyes wide first with sudden understanding, then with fury. "Who knew?" I demanded. His answer shocked me: the Olmos, the Newman Center pastor, the school, the police, BJ himself. Everyone but me, the unwitting innocent in a crazy play everyone else was watching. A rush of anger and betrayal coursed through me like electricity. I already understood human psychology well enough to know that finding a nice girl doesn't make a man's mental illness disappear.

BJ apologized for his own part, and then for everyone else who was involved. He apologized for their misguided hope and misunderstanding of Norm's illness. He apologized for leaving me vulnerable and potentially in harm's way. This calmed my outrage enough so that I could explain my side of the story.

I told BJ how Norm had asked me to marry him right before Thanksgiving, but then seemed to do nothing but sleep for a week. This was followed by an apparent manic impulse when he picked me up one evening to go to Sacramento to purchase a drum set, an errand that kept us up pretty much all night and made me struggle the next day to stay awake in class. I told him about the puzzling phone calls from the police. And the way Norm had raged at me in the health center earlier that afternoon.

BJ listened compassionately, letting me pour everything out. By the time our glasses were empty, I felt like I had matured a couple of years. I was also grateful for the amazing synchronicity of Brother

Justin showing up in Norm's hospital room when he did. I felt calmer, but also more uncertain. Would I ever see any of them again—Helen and Harold Olmo, BJ, or Norm? I was certainly not anxious to see Norm anytime soon. But the Olmos? BJ? Losing their friendship and hospitality would be hard.

I finished my final exams and headed home for Christmas vacation. There was a new year just around the corner. I would come back to Davis in January as if for the first time, when winter descended to chill the city, farms and fields that had once seemed so warm and welcoming.

Chapter Three

Justin Meyer

Honoring His Memory

The day after Justin's death I spoke to the media and answered questions with all the patience and clarity I could muster. The disconnect between their hunger for news and my hunger to escape it made me want to scream. It was easier to call friends and colleagues so they would know what had happened before they read it in the newspapers.

Justin's closest friends took on the task of informing others in our extended circle of friends, vintners, and community members. I had called Jaime in Hawaii, and he had reached out to other friends who were part of the TS Restaurant group. Jaime and Bill Haywood rounded up a few more TS veterans, and I vividly remember them walking through my front door in Napa Valley without knocking, their arms overflowing with groceries. Their upbeat generosity soon got me laughing despite what was happening in my heart. In short order they took over my kitchen and, for days, provided soul-nourishing meals for the steady flow of relatives, friends and other well-wishers who came to the house.

In between greeting people, accepting condolences, and performing the duties of a surviving spouse, I kept thinking about running away into the arms of a deep green forest.

Justin died on a Tuesday. The memorial service was planned for the following Saturday, at Silver Oak Cellars, the winery we had founded, built to prominence, and retired from so recently. It was generous of the owners to make the winery available to me, but returning there on Saturday was particularly poignant: it was just a week after the winery's 30th anniversary celebration which Justin and I had attended as a couple.

We planned a private funeral Mass at our church for family and close friends before the memorial service. We told only a few people about the Mass, but the memorial announcement was in the newspapers and word of the church service flowed quickly through the local wine industry.

Friends and close relatives filled our house that Saturday morning. I don't recall now exactly who was there, nor do I remember who drove us to the church. I was focused on one thing that morning: Holly and I had decided to open the service by leading the congregation in a musical, call-and-response version of the "Our Father" prayer. I carried my 12-string guitar with one hand and had Holly's hand in the other. Somehow, we would get through this together.

As we arrived at the church, I felt enveloped in a deep fog of emotion, making it difficult to concentrate on the simplest task. I could tell that the building was full to overflowing, but that didn't matter. Just get through the song.

When we stood up and faced the congregation, I sensed that Holly too was full of feeling. Her voice was soft at first, but in the reverential silence it was clear and pure. "Our Father..." she began. "Our Father..." the congregation chimed back. "Who art in heaven ... who art in heaven ... hallowed be thy ... hallowed be thy name." That first refrain brought tears to my eyes, and pulled us forward with more strength and courage. "Thy kingdom come ... Thy kingdom come ... thy will be done ... thy will be done" all the way to the end, "are yours forever ... yours forever more." The next thing I remember is walking out of the church and into the embrace of a long-time friend who said me I looked incredibly beautiful in a tragic sort of way. Indeed.

Our entourage went back to the house, and I went directly to bed. I needed time alone before facing a much larger crowd at the memorial. It seemed only minutes later that I was summoned for the drive to Silver Oak. On the grounds next to the main building was a huge open-sided tent, filled with chairs facing a small stage at one end. Justin and I had supervised the placement of just such a tent many times, after Silver Oak's famous "release day" became a national event. So as I walked down the aisle to the front row, past fellow vintners, friends and Silver Oak fans, I didn't have to count the crowd to know that around 2000 souls had come together to honor Justin. When I reached my seat, my eyes welled with tears. Laid there by someone, with exquisitely whimsical thoughtfulness, were a Hawaiian lei and a piece of Doublemint chewing gum, Justin's favorite.

Our son, Chad, was the master of ceremonies. Focused and poised, he seemed so much like a younger version of his father, to whom he now offered personal tribute with grace, wit and presence of mind. I was so proud and grateful. Then I stood up.

I could hear gasps and whispers around me. Apparently, people had not expected the stricken widow to address them. But I had something important to say.

Knowing that Judaism has a deep tradition around death and grieving, certainly richer than what I had experienced as an American Catholic, I had called a Jewish friend. She described various traditions that resonated with me, and one that felt particularly profound: When a father dies, the sons are expected to take on and embody the best character traits of their father. In this way, both they and the world continue to benefit from the departed's life and legacy.

This struck a chord so deep, I decided that I would do it myself. I sat in deep reverie about Justin, someone I knew so well for so long that I didn't have to think about his best qualities—they were just who he was. Slowly and surely, certain qualities emerged as fundamental to all the others. Embodying his best qualities meant being more courageous, generous, and stepping into leadership more fully in ways that would benefit my family and the world.

Now, at Justin's memorial, it was time to become that person. My first act of living more boldly, becoming the "Justin within," was to invite each person at the memorial to do as I had done: choose to carry his values and qualities forward within themselves.

My strong sense of purpose was belied by my body, which wobbled as I started up the steps to the podium. It was just days after Justin's death. Helping hands got me up the stairs. Then I looked out over the crowd and felt their love and admiration for Justin... and for me. This realization gave me the strength to speak deliberately as I read aloud my intention: "To go forth honoring Justin by being more genuine and generous, living boldly with personal integrity, unpretentious self-confidence, and joyful humor."

After a moment's pause, I continued. "I invite you to likewise search your hearts, find what you most admired in Justin, and carry those qualities forward from today onward, as the most precious way to honor him and his life that has touched us all."

After I finished, Chad introduced a long stream of close friends who shared reflections and told stories, a surprising number of which I had not heard. Sitting there, I realized, with a sense of wonder that this man who I knew so well and loved so intimately had a much larger life than I could ever have experienced. Every individual had their own unique relationship with him, and their own personal and precious stories.

Once all the speakers had finished, the friends and admirers who came to honor Justin that day turned to each other to share their own stories. They laughed, cried, chewed Doublemint, ate ice cream cones and remembered.

Justin had taken some flying lessons as a Christian Brother because the idea of being a pilot excited him—and the Brothers had a company plane. When Chad expressed interest in flying at twelve, Justin purchased a Cessna 206 and resumed flight instruction. He found a man named Deke at the Napa Airport, who had just hit mandatory retirement age after a career flying Boeing 747s for United Airlines. Deke was delighted to have a student and a reason to be up in the sky again. After teaching Justin how to fly his 206, he later taught Chad how to fly the Piper Cub we later gave him. When Silver Oak became big enough to need a company plane and successful enough to afford one, Deke became our pilot and flew us in our Aerostar turboprop to wine events everywhere west of Denver. More than that, over the years, Deke became a family friend who loved Justin like a brother.

For the memorial, Deke organized an honor for Justin that only pilots can offer and fully understand: an overflight of Silver Oak with the "missing man" formation. This took place shortly after the formal memorial program was finished, so that the crowd would be outside the tent and able to see the sky. As the drone of aircraft engines approached, faces turned to the heavens. Bob Little lifted his bugle and slowly began to play taps. Now five airplanes appeared overhead, glistening in the afternoon sun, looking beautiful and regal in a perfect V formation. Then Deke, flying Justin's 206, peeled off, alone, and headed due west. The squadron of shimmering planes was now missing a man. The pain in my chest grew more intense, then moved up to my throat. My hand reflexively went there to keep myself from crying out. Tears spilled down my face as Justin's Cessna headed towards the Mayacamas Mountains and into the sunset. His plane slowly disappeared from view, much as Justin had disappeared from our lives.

Our sons clung to their wives while Holly and my girlfriends huddled around me protectively. We were arm in arm when a hundred white doves were released. They made two wide circles above us and then, in a rush of silence, they were gone.

The Dark Sets In

When the memorial was over, the wine industry people went home, local friends and associates left, and distant relatives departed. A few close friends stayed on for a bit. But eventually they left too. Jaime and Bill and the others from Hawaii left as a group to return to their lives and work. I was so grateful they had lingered. Their food, teasing and laughter helped my heart feel just a bit lighter. I still vividly remember feeling both love and trepidation as they headed down the driveway.

Everyone went back to normal life. But there was no normal for me to return to. Instead, there was darkness which stole into my heart and would not dissolve. I did not sleep, but neither was I awake. I would toss and turn in bed, the nights feeling interminable. My mental fog became even more dense and though there was much to do, I got little accomplished.

The yearning to run away was more powerful than ever. It took more and more effort to resist it. It was a stand-off, without a winner.

I was invited to dinner but did not accept. I was invited to lunch and didn't go. I yearned to die so I could be with Justin. This was an ache so deep, a hundred thousand first-love longings pale by comparison. I would go to bed, stare at the ceiling and think: Up, up, up ... I want to be up there with you, my love. My heart throbbed with a pain that nothing could touch, that no one could soothe.

Yes, the hair dryer went off nearly every time I walked into our bedroom. I was thus reminded daily of Justin and his invisible presence. Yes, the notes and letters of condolence kept coming. Yes, my house was full of beautiful orchids that so many people had sent.

I still wanted to die.

I began to imagine that I could will my cancer to come back – and claim me this time. It would be there for me if I really wanted it, if I wished for it hard enough. Or I could stop eating and drinking, and just wither away. Death did not seem so distant or so difficult. The more I thought about this, the more tempting it became.

Nights were the worst. Tossing and turning, going over and over our last day together. The picnic in the mountains, Justin's last rattling exhale when Ruggero was pushing on his chest. How I knew he was dead then. His purple-blotched face that I washed and kissed. The drive home.

I also relived the memories and pain of my cancer surgery. How I had awakened from the anesthetic to find half a dozen tubes coming out of unnatural places. How I had been completely opened up, hands deep inside my abdomen searching everywhere for cancer. The doctors had disturbed all the connective tissue around my organs, lifted them, washed them, and then placed them back inside me according to some approximate geography. I could not escape the feeling of having been thoroughly violated. The surgical scar, still bright and angry, ran from above my navel down to my pubis.

These memories kept spinning and spinning, fueled by my restlessness, becoming waking nightmares.

Then I would remember the scared look in my children's eyes. They could see how fragile I was, how untethered. They had just lost their father; they did not want to lose me too. So I would steel myself and carry on.

Bathed in Him

Justin is to be cremated, up in the mountains where he died. I ask our children if they want to see his body before he is immolated. They do not, though Holly wants him to be dressed in his favorite outfit for the cremation. Together we pick out a pair of shorts and a beautiful blue Hawaiian shirt to match his deep blue eyes. These go off to the crematorium, along with instructions. All is in order, yet nothing is as it should be.

Eight days after the memorial, Deke arrives. Justin's beloved friend and company pilot has flown his ashes back to me. As he places the box in my hands I see the tears in his eyes. "He flew all the way home with me in the right seat," Deke says. The right seat —that's code for the co-pilot's seat. That brings tears for me too, remembering how much the two of them loved flying together. Deke kept Justin as close as he could on their journey home, and now, so will I.

The 6-inch square cardboard box is much smaller than I have imagined. Justin was such a big man, 230 pounds, broad-shouldered and strong as an ox. I look down at the box and I wonder how all of him can possibly fit in there. But the heavy weight of it startles me too. People always refer to remains as "ashes." This is definitely not a box of ashes.

Justin had spent the past year designing, directing, and supervising the building of a wine cave near our house. It was set into the hillside just beyond the circular driveway outside the front door. Every day for months, he sat on a bench by the door watching the huge cave-drilling machine as it bore first a main corridor then two more tunnels fanning out from the large, high-ceilinged circular room in the center. The result was a grand Y formed deep into the earth. The mixture of rock and soil was perfect for a wine cave, and the curved walls and ceiling were finished with gunite to make sure there was a seamless interior surface. The floor was covered with compacted crushed granite.

I had designed the wall sconces and found a stunning chandelier to hang from the high ceiling above the center room. Justin had carefully designed black metal wine racks which line the cave corridor walls. He filled them with his life's work: bottles of Silver Oak Cabernet Sauvignon. Special racks lined the center room to display impressive large bottles holding six, 12, and 18 liters of wine. In the center of this room under the chandelier stands a beautiful round table, hand-crafted from a black walnut tree. I had commissioned it for Justin, as a surprise.

The cave was finished just in time for Chad and Aimee's wedding, now a month in the past. The ceremony had been held in the center room. Everyone was moved by this dramatic space deep in the earth. Now I have another ceremony in mind.

After saying an emotional "good-bye" to Deke, I go inside the house and take a large, oversized brandy snifter off the wine glass rack. My mind is burning with the image of Justin consumed by flame. Even my skin feels hot. I hold my breath as I slowly open the cardboard box. There he is. Beach sand. Dusty grey beach sand.

I exhale and pour Justin into the snifter. I take the snifter in both hands and lift it with the same reverence as wine is raised in church at Mass. A few moments later I am at the massive redwood door to the wine cave. When I open it, the earthy mustiness of the cave immediately fills my nostrils and cools my burning body. I adjust the sconces so that they glow with just enough light to guide me forward.

After closing the door behind me, I deeply inhale the pungent smell of earth mixed with wine and listen to the deep silence. Then I hear my soft footfalls on the crushed granite floor, as I slowly step to the center, into the womb of Mother Earth. I place the snifter on the table close to me. Again, deep silence descends. My beloved and I have been reunited. We are alone together in the near-dark, as we were for those thousands of nights. The moment has come.

I remove my clothes, feeling the cool air embrace me everywhere. Naked, I dip my hands into the snifter and feel him there, feel what remains of his physical body, his grainy consistency somewhere between sand and dust. I am holding him again, feeling him in my hands, my senses, my soul. It is not enough.

I want to feel him, be embraced by him even more closely than the coolness of the cave. I lift bits of him out of the glass and feel his weight in my hands. Now I slowly begin to rub him onto my chest, then my arms, and onto my thighs. I bring him to my face, as I have in countless loving moments, and rub him onto my cheeks, my forehead, my lips. I rub the dusty sand of him deep into my skin.

Hot tears now stream down my face as I rub harder and harder, passionately trying to experience him penetrating my skin, wanting him to find his way inside of me again. How I ache to feel him there, the physicality of him touching my skin, entering my depths.

Time slips away from my consciousness. I have no awareness of how long I am standing here bathing in my beloved.

When I finally come back to myself, I reverently place the snifter in the middle of the black walnut table. Now Justin rests in the center of the center.

Spent, I leave the cave alone carrying my clothes loosely in one hand. Justin remains in the heart of his cave, which has now become, for me, a holy sepulcher.

What is Love?

When I was a teenager, I was obsessed with the nature of love. I read about it, thought about it, wrote about it, wondered about it. Then, one of the nuns at my high school gave me a beautifully decorated bookmark with a quote by Pierre Teilhard de Chardin: "Love is the most powerful force in the universe." This made a deep impression upon me and I began to reflect on the meaning of the words from the man known as a mystic, scientist priest.

Today, as I actually feel my way into love as Teilhard de Chardin talks about it, I can feel the "Love of God," the "Universal Intelligence" that courses through my body and soul, as it does everything in creation.

When I truly love, I am allowing this powerful cosmic energy to flow through me into a room, into a child, into the grocery clerk, into my dearest friends, into my family. My experience is that the more I love and the more I allow, the more love there is at my disposal to give. It is truly inexhaustible.

This is not the small, fleeting feeling we have when we are attracted to or attached to someone. That feeling may fade or dissipate. Here, I am talking about the essence of love. God Force. It is a clear, dependable, unconditional stream of caring and compassion.

Parents who have more than one child find this truth in their daily living. However much you love one child, it does not diminish how much you love the others. It actually works the other way around: It magnifies. The more children or loved ones you have in your life, the more love there is to go around. All that is required is to become open and vulnerable allowing the love to flow through you.

"Someday, after we have mastered the winds, the waves, the tides and gravity, we shall harness for God the energies of love. Then for the second time in the history of the world, we will have discovered fire."

—Pierre Teilhard de Chardin

Love is

Love is
The most powerful force in the universe
And the essence of who we are

It is
The radiance that emanates from a rose
The sparkling mist rising from the ocean
The intelligence that courses through our bodies
The divine matrix that connects us all

As all matter is light
All light emanates from love

Love was the igniting spark
That banged the universe into existence
Love is the ceaseless creative force
Powering the ineffable expansion

Once we have touched
Once we have seen
Once we have loved
Imprinted upon each other's hearts
Pregnant with resonance
We soar together
The bonds of connection stretching into eternity

Love is

The bonds of connection stretching into eternity Love is One thing I know for certain is that I am committed to loving. Loving is what I am called to do and to be in every moment and every situation. Love is the essence of who I am. Especially when I am terrified, I am determined to hang in there and trust. I learn the lessons, embrace and share the gifts every relationship has to offer. I hold your heart gently and wholly open mine.

I trust in the guidance that brings us together and trust in the higher purpose we are to bring forth through our love for one another. The exquisite intimacy of powerful and fierce love relationships offers the ultimate crucible for growing myself and you and us.

Chapter Four

Brother Timothy and Brother Justin making blends in the Christian Brothers Winery lab

The Schism Band

As my second term at university began in early January of 1968, I was determined to make a fresh start after the drama with Norm before Christmas break. Evidently BJ was ready to begin anew as well. He wanted to engage more with the Newman Center's Catholic community and asked if I would like his help playing music for Sunday evening Mass. I accepted with enthusiasm. I was capable of leading the congregation in music by myself, but it would be even better to have a partner for musical support.

The following Sunday Brother Justin showed up with his long neck banjo to practice about an hour before Mass. We selected four songs from Ray Repp's "Hymnal for Young Christians" and rehearsed them until we felt ready.

As students and young families entered the church they were surprised to see an interesting addition: a young man in religious habit with a homemade banjo strapped over one shoulder. The percussive, syncopated sound of a banjo is a great complement to a strummed steel-string guitar—a match made in heaven, you might say. We were surprised by a spontaneous round of applause at the end of mass. Yes, it worked out well. Yes, we would do it again the following Sunday.

My friend Carolyn, who had felt too shy to play in church before, showed up with her guitar now that I was "forming a group." Shortly after that a Japanese percussionist named Shinji approached us one evening as we were putting our instruments away and asked if he could join us. Attracted to our sound and energy, more musicians came forward: another guitar, a gutbucket and a tambourine. We dubbed ourselves the Schism Band, a light-hearted reference to the "radical departure" our music represented from the traditional hymns and somber organ music of our childhoods. The epitome of a late '60s folk Mass band, we attracted crowds to the Newman Center church every Sunday evening.

The Schism Band continued long after BJ went back to the

monastery to work at the Christian Brother's vineyards and winery. We routinely filled the church more fully on Sunday evenings than it was on Sunday mornings. But it never sounded the same or had the same lively, raucous energy without him and his banjo.

The Olmos

Church was not the only place BJ and I began to regularly play music together. Along with his offer to help me at Newman Center, Brother Justin also began to invite me to dinner at the Olmo's home ... as long as I brought my guitar. I was pretty sure they all liked me, but I was certain they loved our sing-alongs.

Harold Olmo was a tall, large-framed man. Whether he was walking or standing, he leaned forward so that it felt like he loomed over you. This would have been intimidating if he were not so friendly and good-natured. His wife, Helen, just as friendly, seemed to always be in an apron and was in every way the mistress of the house. She had a natural talent for cooking and would easily adapt recipes according to her taste and what she had available. Both Olmos loved food and wine and frequently had students over for savory meals on Saturday evenings. Though they were well-fed and not particularly athletic, they were agile enough to live active lives.

Harold loved roaming around vineyards with his sidekick, Al Koyama, which kept him pretty fit. Years later, after Harold retired from the university, he planted a small vineyard by his house which he lovingly tended even after a fall and hip surgery. In fact, his desire to be out there was likely the reason he recovered so quickly and completely.

Helen loved opera and would sing along with phonograph recordings that the Olmos treated like prized possessions. Harold loved opera too, but everyone around him begged him not to sing because he was tone-deaf. He simply could not sing on key. The Olmos were Catholic and attended church every Sunday morning. Justin loved and respected the Olmos dearly and he treated them the way he did everyone he loved: with constant teasing. Of course, he nicknamed them both. Harold was "Bonzo" and Helen became "Madame Queen" or "Mrs. Got Rocks."

I loved how welcomed I felt in the Olmos' home, and the way they expressed their interest in me as a person. The conversation around the dining room table was always interesting and animated. I learned a lot about the biology of grapes and the chemistry of winemaking just listening to Harold and BJ talk. And. of course, I learned more as I sipped and sampled the many different wines that emerged from Dr. Olmo's wine cabinet.

Sometimes there were other students or family members for dinner. Sometimes it was just Helen, Harold, BJ, and me. It didn't really matter. It was a given that the evening would end with a songfest. BJ would get his banjo, I would take my guitar from its case and off we would go.

As with the first time, BJ and I would be completely focused on each other; watching each other's fingers for chord changes, watching each other's faces for wordless cues. Shall we sing another verse? Do you remember it? Ready to end now? Want to sing the harmony here? All this rich, subtle nonverbal back-and-forth conversation while we were singing our hearts out, never missing a beat.

Friends and family members would chime in on familiar choruses. Sometimes they would even sing a verse or two. "Michael row the boat ashore ... a-le-lu-ia ..."

Playing and singing like this with BJ was a profoundly intimate experience. It was like dancing a sensuous tango, constantly watching and listening for the subtlest signs. "I've got the lead ... now you ... let's harmonize here ... I'll take the high part ... now you ... now together ... "

The more connected we were, the better we sounded. The sure sign that we had reached the pinnacle of performance was that Harold could contain himself no longer, tone-deaf though he was. He would rise from his chair, disappear into the garage, then reappear with a metal leaf rake and a stick. Grinning from ear to ear, he would begin to beat on the rake in time to the music.

I have no recollection of how many evenings BJ and I spent at the Olmos' playing and harmonizing. I do know that each time we did was pure joy for us, and we could feel the magic for others in the room as well.

Spanish Lessons

Languages have never been easy for me. The words seem to go in one ear and out the other, never staying for more than a moment in my memory bank.

For this reason, I chose to satisfy my college language requirement by studying Spanish, the easiest and most familiar language for students growing up in California. I also strategically chose to start Spanish the second quarter of school, figuring I would slip in behind the crowd of go-getters. I wanted to be in class with the laggards so it would be easier to keep up.

Despite my clever plan, I struggled from the first day. It didn't help that UC Davis divided the school year into three quarters rather than two semesters. The system was structured to jam as much material into ten weeks as other universities offered in fourteen. In no time I was under water, barely above failing. So I asked for help.

Prior to his internship at The Christian Brothers wineries and distillery and the past two years at Davis, Brother Justin had taught Spanish at Christian Brothers High School in Sacramento. I asked him to tutor me in Spanish, and he graciously agreed. Soon I was joining him at the big table in Olmo's lab he used for a desk. I would read my psychology textbooks, he his biochemistry. Then we would go over the basics of Spanish together. I slowly began to catch up. I think I managed a C.

Spring break seemed to last only a moment, then we were back at it again. By mid-quarter I was expected to be facile enough to read a short novel. Again, I was struggling and close to failing. That's when BJ proposed teaching me some songs in Spanish. Maybe I could give a little concert for the class to redeem myself. With his help, I learned both older classics and a modern popular song. He had even composed extra verses for one of them.

Through the cadence of the music, I began to hear and speak the language in a new way. Spanish gradually began to feel natural and normal in my mind and on my tongue. The instructor and my fellow students all appreciated the little concert I gave. More importantly, I earned a B in the class. All thanks to BJ.

Our Song

Recently I sat in a room with 140 conference attendees, quietly waiting for the final morning session to begin. Then over the sound system I heard familiar strains of piano music. My eyes welled with tears as my mind swam in memories.

Sometime in early spring of 1968, Justin telephoned on a sunny Saturday and asked if I would like to go for a drive to Lake Berryessa. This was after we had been playing music together at the Newman Center for a while and the Spanish lessons were beginning to take hold. So I had no reservation about sharing time with my friend the winemaker monk. Plus my heart leaped at the chance to get up into the nearby hills. The flat agricultural terrain of California's central valley felt foreign and deeply unsettling to me. I had been longing for the hills that I could see on the western horizon, but with only a bicycle for transportation I was sentenced to life as a flatlander. BJ's invitation was like a parole from prison.

Lake Berryessa is a 20,000-acre reservoir nestled in the Vaca Mountain watershed, which is the source of Putah Creek. The creek was dammed at Devil's Gate in the late 1950s to provide agricultural and industrial water to Solano County. Below the dam, the creek flows through the UC Davis campus. Our journey would take us to the lake via the impressive Monticello Dam.

Approaching the hills, climbing above the valley floor, and driving along the rugged creek soothed my soul in ways that surprised and moved me. BJ parked the car at a turnout along the lake, brought out a blanket, and spread it out on a gravelly outcropping where we had a dazzling view of the brilliant blue lake.

That afternoon was the first time he spoke to me about his difficult childhood, his decision to become a Christian Brother, and the important mentors in his life. He spoke earnestly of his hopes and dreams. I don't know what opened his heart that day. Maybe it was the sunny weather, the sparkling light dancing on the lake, or just simply being away from school and studies. Whatever the impetus, BJ's sharing of his past and aspirations for the future were heart-warming.

As we prepared to leave the lake, I thanked him for sharing his past and the things that gave his life meaning. I also revealed that I had been on the path to religious orders before changing my mind and coming to UC Davis to become a teacher instead. It was wonderful to realize that we shared a strong connection with God and a deep desire to live a life of service.

It was dark when we arrived back at my dorm. Despite the chill in the air, I still felt warm from the sunny afternoon and our heartfelt conversation. I distinctly remember turning to him in the car as I was about to take my leave, taking his hand and looking into his craggy face. What I beheld was a beautiful human being who had grown up poor in a dysfunctional family yet had risen above it with a clear intention of making life better for a multitude of poor kids like himself. I saw the light inside of him in a way that was so brilliant and transparent. I wanted to express this to him, but the word that came to mind was about the most unlikely thing a girl could say to a super-masculine athletic man, especially one in a religious order. But as I searched my heart and mind for a different word, I found nothing else that captured the essence of what I saw in him, felt about him.

Swallowing hard, not wanting to be misunderstood, I thanked him for the day and then stammered my parting words: "You are beautiful."

Six years later, after we married, Joe Cocker released his biggest hit, "You Are So Beautiful." It immediately became our song. Wherever we were, when those opening strains came over the radio, Justin and I would stop, look into each other's eyes, and sing along. If place and space permitted, we would stop what we were doing and slow dance, letting the music and sentiments rekindle the flame of love and vision of beauty we saw in each other that day.

Now these memories are flooding back to me as the voice of Joe Cocker comes out of the conference speakers.

"You are so beautiful to me
You are so beautiful to me
Can't you see?
You're everything I hoped for
You're everything I need
You are so beautiful to me."

Cutting Firewood

In my fireplace the next fire is already laid and ready to light. Justin loved to build fires. The most special was the first fire of the fall, signaling the end of the long harvest season and the approaching winter. There was always a dramatic shift when evenings grew cold and the rain started. Work in the vineyard slowed to a stop whether you were ready or not.

As I gaze at the wood neatly stacked in my fireplace now, I am remembering a spring day long in the past. BJ and I had spent the day cutting and stacking firewood for the Olmos. A perfect chore for a beautiful early spring day along Putah Creek on the Olmos' farm. Every winter a few limbs would fall, and if the firewood was cut and gathered early enough, the cutting was easy and the wood was dense and strong. The work was methodical and refreshing after a week of studying; sitting, reading, absorbing, memorizing, and analyzing. We worked mostly in silence, naturally slipping into a synchronized flow like our experience playing music together.

The sun was warm and felt wonderful after the cold, wet Central Valley winter. BJ cut, I stacked, then we brought the wood in batches to the house in the back of the old white pick-up. There we stacked it neatly against the back wall, ready for the next winter.

By late afternoon we were done. We both felt hot and pleasantly tired from our effort and accomplishment. BJ said, "Let's go for a swim!" He took off his shirt and shoes and dove into spring-fresh Putah Creek. I looked down uncertainly at my dusty clothes, decided they could use a wash anyway, and dove in after him. We splashed and played like a couple of ten-year-old kids, enjoying the refreshing spring run-off.

Later on, after we dried ourselves, he gave me an old pair of shorts and a sweatshirt with cut-off arms to wear home. I can still remember the smell of his shirt, his own signature smell with a hint of Old Spice aftershave.

I had grown to enjoy the time I spent with BJ very much, and for some strange reason wearing his sweatshirt and later inhaling it aroused a deep affection and sense of connection with him. In addition to the intentionally ragged cut-off sleeves, I noticed a couple of tears and worn spots. Over the next week I repaired them, washed the sweatshirt along with the shorts and returned them to BJ when he picked me up to go to the Olmos' the following weekend. I never wore them again, but I never forgot the first intimacy of his clothes on my skin, his scent slipping into my senses.

Chapter Five

Maui Boys: Wayne Cody and Bill Haywood

Dutiful Doing

Three weeks after Justin died, Holly went with me to post-surgery follow-up appointments with my oncologist and radiologist. As soon as the radiologist walked into the room and saw Holly, he asked where my husband was. I quietly told him Justin had died three weeks earlier. He gulped his next breath.

He then recommended that I should undergo full torso radiation, top to bottom, to kill any possible remaining cancer cells and theoretically discourage subsequent tumors. Of course, this would also cause radiation scarring in every quadrant of my torso. I was flooded with questions. What were the chances this aggressive treatment would work? What were the chances it might fail? Either way, how harmful would it be to healthy tissue? How should I even weigh all these things together?

Holly watched with terrified eyes as I weighed the cost/benefit of what he was proposing and rejected all follow-up cancer treatment. I told my doctors that between the horrific surgery in the spring and my husband's sudden death in the summer, I had been through enough. I did not have the strength or the will to handle radical radiation therapy. I would choose the certainty of my body's ability to heal over the certainty of radiation damage and the uncertain chances that it might help.

With deep concern in their eyes, my doctors honored my decision and let me know they would always be available to me and wished me well. In stark contrast, my fragile health and debilitating grief was of no concern to the IRS or the estate attorneys with their mountains of paperwork.

Soon after my visit to the oncologist and radiologist, the assessors arrived to determine the value of Justin's estate. It felt like a horrible violation of our home and my heart, watching them take photographs and make notes. They were reducing the mementos of my life with Justin, the incredible travels we had shared and the art we loved, to their base resale value.

I then met with financial advisors and attorneys so they could take me through the intricacies of marital trust funding and estate tax returns. All this made my head spin. Normally very clear-headed and good with math, I found it impossible to focus and concentrate.

I wanted to run away more than ever. I should have. Being alone and diving into my grief would have been the most healing thing I could have done for myself. But instead, I dove into what everyone else was telling me I needed to do, had to do.

I should have looked at the assessors and lawyers and accountants and said, "I will be leaving for a while." They would have been shocked, but it would not have changed the outcome. Nothing was as urgent as they made it out to be. I should have told them all that I would be gone for an undetermined length of time and they would have to wait.

But instead, I stayed, struggled and suffered an unspoken, unresolved grief.

I can tell you now that grief does not resolve itself on its own. It does not drift away. It stays and festers and corrupts and causes all kinds of trouble until it is looked at square in the eyes and embraced. Grief needs to be yelled and cried; it needs to be spoken, lived and felt as deeply as you can. Acknowledged, seen, held, examined, sung, walked with, and transformed. It is only the magic of transformational alchemy whereby we can enter into a more alive, more openhearted life than we have ever experienced before. Grief's greatest gift is this—breaking our heart open in a way that nothing else can.

Instead of running away and diving into my grief, I dove into work and responsibility. I was responsible to and for everyone but myself. And because I didn't run away to grieve, my loss and grief embedded itself deeper and deeper into my psyche and my body. It took many years and hard work to dig out of the wreckage.

If you are reading this right now and realize you need to run, then do it. Cry, scream and rage at your loss. Look at what has been taken from you by disaster, sickness or death. Yell until your voice is gone. Yell until there's nothing left to yell about. Let your tears baptize the new life that will inevitably emerge out of a grief well-spent. There is no avoiding it. It is just a matter of sooner or later. And I can affirm that sooner is so much better than later for everyone, especially yourself.

Reason for Living

I don't know how it happened. I don't know when it happened. I didn't intend it. Somewhere along the 35 years of loving and being loved by Justin, he became my reason for living. It must have happened slowly, imperceptibly. I didn't notice until he was gone, when my will to live left with him.

I always felt so held by him. The power of his adoration and devotion were so solid, so palpable, it took just one glance from him in my direction for everyone in the room to know, to feel, our powerful connection. That glance said, "She's mine now and forever and I will protect her with everything I've got. I love her with all that I am. I am devoted to her completely. I am so proud of her and won't allow anyone to hurt her. It is my joy to hold her in tenderness and to share all our intimate thoughts, concerns, fears, failings, struggles, confusions, doubts, solutions, inspirations and successes."

One glance held the power of innumerable energetic bonds that tied us to one another. All the lovemaking and laughter, all the tears and trials, all the intimate conversations, all the long nights caring for sick or scared children. The sad sweet longing for one another when we were apart in the early years, and the longing every time we were apart during our marriage, whether it was because of a busy day or extended business trip.

When Justin died, I experienced tremendous physical pain and heartache from the sudden severing of these energetic bonds. I felt like I had been kicked by a mule square in my chest, the wind knocked out of me. Breathing became shallow and painful. But my chest and heart were not the only places I ached. For three years after the children were out of the house and our schedules were more relaxed, Justin and I had gotten into the rhythm of beginning every day with lovemaking. The abrupt ceasing of this sweet intimacy made my loins ache too. I felt like I had been somehow turned inside out like a banana slug that a kid had poured salt upon. There were no soothing words or salve that lessened my pain.

These powerful physical manifestations of loss took me by surprise, much like the surprise of discovering that Justin had become my reason for living.

You are gone now
You who were my joy
My light, my devotion
My reason for living
You are gone now.

I am left
Overwhelmed with longing
Reaching out
But not able to touch
How I ache to be held

I want to fly
Up to where you are
To reach out
And have you take my hand
And embrace me again.

Adrift

Bill Haywood and I are sitting on the rock wall in front of Maria Lanakila Catholic Church in Lahaina, across the street from his office at Hawaii's much-loved sunglass company, Maui Jim. Bill is one of our Hawaiian friends who had dropped everything to be with me when he heard Justin had died. He had arrived and, almost without a word, immediately walked into my kitchen with others from TS Restaurants, and started cooking. His presence, their presence, along with the wonderful food they cooked had been the most comforting gift imaginable. The fragrances of Hawaiian and Mexican cuisine filled the house for days. It was sad for us all when it was time to bid each other aloha nui loa (infinite aloha beyond all understanding) and a hui hou (we will be together again soon in this life or the Great Beyond).

Now, six months after Justin's death, I am looking into Bill's eyes and tearfully telling him I feel completely untethered, in a vortex, swirling in circles with no definition to my life, no solid ground to stand on.

Just a few months earlier my identity had been crystal clear. To the wider world, I was widely known as co-founder, co-leader and partner in Silver Oak Cellars. The title on my business card was "Madam of the Chateau," which startled people and made me giggle. In my private life, I was the wife and passionate lover of Justin Meyer and a dedicated mother of three children. I was healthy and carefree.

Now all of these descriptors, these roles that had defined my life, were suddenly and utterly meaningless.

I had made a commitment to myself years before not to be defined by my role in Silver Oak. It would have been so easy, so seductive to identify as "Mrs. Silver Oak" because Silver Oak had become such an institution in Napa Valley, the U.S., and the global wine world. When Justin and I started the winery, we were pioneers, outliers, with a renegade business model; we made wine from just one grape variety, Cabernet, not five or ten like everyone else. Not even a token drop of white wine in the middle of the 1980s white wine craze. Justin became famous for saying "The first obligation of every wine is to be red."

Because our Cabernets were so exceptional, and our way of doing business was so engaging, our model worked extraordinarily well. People literally lined up to buy our Cabernet Sauvignon the first day the new vintage was released each year. Other wineries in Napa Valley noticed what we were doing, but they grew other grape varieties or had contracts to buy those other varieties. So they kept making a range of different wines. But when a root-eating louse called phylloxera began devastating vineyards in the Napa Valley in the late 1980s, growers in the region were forced to replant thousands of acres of prime vineyard land. The vast majority of those acres were planted to just one variety— Cabernet Sauvignon—because everyone else dreamed of customers lining up for their wine. Thus Cabernet became the signature grape of Napa Valley, and Silver Oak was the face of that movement.

I could have played the role of "Madame of the Chateau" to the hilt. But as much as I enjoyed the perks now and then, I did not want to be defined or confined by that role. I felt my most important role, my greatest contribution to the world was to be a compassionate and engaged mother. Then one by one our kids went off to college. I certainly had some wistful moments as all parents of college freshmen do. But I also gained more time with Justin. There was more time and opportunity for quiet conversation and, every morning, lovemaking. I felt good, strong, capable and ready for the next adventure he and I would create together.

But who am I now? Not a wife. Not a lover. Not even a mother really, as my youngest, Holly, has turned 21. No longer Madam of the

Chateau. No longer playing a strategic, creative role in a business. Most concerning, I am not healthy. My cancer has no definitive end. It is a chronic condition, not a temporary illness that resolves itself like a summer cold.

Bill listens to all this with steady compassion. Then he helps me realize that losing so many identities might just be an opening for new ones. "Is there anything you would like to do?" he asks gently.

The answer surprises both of us: "I would like to live on a houseboat in Sausalito."

Throughout my adult life I have driven by the houseboats lining San Francisco Bay near Sausalito. I would look at them with a dreamy expression and say out loud, "I think it would be fun to live on a houseboat." If Justin were with me, he would turn sideways and look at me with mischief in his eyes. "Well, I guess you will have to live there alone then," he would say. "It doesn't sound even a little bit fun to me."

But there was no opposing opinion now. "Maybe I will do that," I say to Bill, who immediately warms to the idea. This is a waterman who surfed, swam, dove for lobster and loved his fishing boat more than most things. We sit on the rock wall talking until the school bell rings. Then he slowly rises and stretches to his full 6' 6" height and gives me a warm bear hug as his two boys come running out of their classrooms behind the church.

Bill's question marked the beginning, the first small step toward creating a new life without Justin. Not long afterwards, I found a way to buy a Sausalito houseboat. I named it "The Mermaid" and painted it like a rainbow of aqua, teal, and royal blue. This was my first radically independent impulse and the beginning of making a new life, with new identities that continue to surprise me.

Chapter Six

Brother Justin Meyer

Raymie Becomes Brother Justin

Raymie Meyer grew up in a family defined by alcohol. His intelligent but dyslexic and relatively uneducated father would come home from work at the Southern Pacific Railroad yard, drink a bottle of whiskey, and chase it down with a six-pack of beer. His mother would join him, both of them chain smoking and frequently quarreling, leaving young Raymie mostly on his own.

Like many first-born children of alcoholics, Raymie became an over-achiever and the functional head of the family. By the time he was an adolescent, his mother would send him out to the bar every Friday night to rescue what was left of the week's paycheck. Raymie would walk past the "No One Under 21 Allowed" placard and up to Big Ray's barstool where he and his cronies had spent the last few hours drinking and swapping stories. Raymie would stand there resolute with his hand out and say, "Mom sent me to get the rest of the money." Big Ray would roll his eyes in the direction of his drinking buddies then hand over most of what was left.

Raymie was a star athlete in high school. His senior year he was the quarterback on the football team, center on the basketball team, and a starting pitcher on the baseball team. Big Ray never attended a game during Raymie's four years of high school, until the last one. Raymie was the starting pitcher in his last game of his high school career, just before graduation. After begging his father to come watch him play, Raymie saw his dad show up half-way through the game. Drunk. Raymie's pitching won that game. He walked up to his dad after it was over, hoping to hear one kind word about the game and his pitching. His father's only comment was, "You let a couple guys get runs off you."

For Raymie, Garces Memorial High School in Bakersfield was a refuge of predictability, sanity, and appreciation. At school, he was appreciated for his athletic talent and leadership. He was popular with the other students and served as senior class president.

The Christian Brothers who ran Garces Memorial encouraged and mentored him. Not particularly excited about academics, Raymie always maintained at least a C average so he could play sports, which was the only thing that mattered to him. His teammates and coaches were primary. One coach, Brother Justin Sullivan, took Raymie under his wing, helping him become a better athlete and grow into his natural talent for leadership.

After graduation, a break-up with his girlfriend, and an uneventful semester at the local junior college, Raymie decided to become a Christian Brother, which would enable him to teach, coach, and mentor other lost boys like himself.

Raymie was 19 years old when he arrived at the Christian Brothers Novitiate in the western hills above the Napa Valley. From the moment he stepped onto the soil of Mont La Salle, he entered into a traditional, rigorously proscribed monastic life. The morning bell rang out at 6:00 am. Daily litanies were sung; prayers and rosary decades were recited before morning Mass. Meals were eaten in silence while listening to the reading of spiritual texts. Morning and evening classes covered the traditions of the Christian Brothers, Roman Catholic theology, and how to teach religion to future students. Dinner was followed by choir practice, and each young brother became accomplished in Gregorian chant. In those days, Latin was still the universal language of the Roman Catholic Church; religious aspirants and professed members became fluent in reciting the Mass, chants, and prayers in Latin, whether they understood what they were saying or not.

When the young novices weren't praying or studying, they were working. Raymie was nicknamed "Country" because he spoke with a Bakersfield twang. Being strong and agile, he was assigned to the rock wall crew. Raymie, Tom, and Patrick would head to the rock pile every afternoon to wrangle rocks from the hills and haul them down to the picnic area where they were building a retaining wall. The only saving grace of rock wall duty was an occasional cold beer delivered by their sympathetic novice master, Brother Boniface.

At the culmination of the first novitiate year there was a solemn initiation ceremony in which the young men renounced their birth names and took on monastic names. Raymie took the name Brother Justin, honoring his high school coach and mentor, Brother Justin Sullivan. It was a name he would carry for the rest of his life.

When the next school year started, all of the young monks-in-training migrated from Mont La Salle to St. Mary's College in Moraga where they took bachelor's degrees in the subjects they would teach in high school. The novices and professed brothers lived apart from the other students in St. Mary's Assumption Hall, and kept to a strict schedule, similar to that at Mont La Salle. They rose early, prayed, attended Mass, and headed off to class; then they prayed, studied and retired early so they could do it all over again.

Raymie's home life in Bakersfield had been fraught with unpredictability and disorder. Children of alcoholic parents don't know what they will find when they walk in the front door after a day at school or an evening with friends. Brother Justin found the monastic life offered the exact opposite: a schedule and environment that were predictable, dependable, and supportive. He thrived. For the first time in his life he earned top grades in his studies. He loved economics and graduated with an economics major and a minor in conversational Spanish.

While at St. Mary's, young Brother Justin tried to form a student brother's basketball team to play in the intramural sports program. Despite his enthusiastic arguments, the higher-ups denied the request. So Brother Justin turned to music, for which he had a natural ear. An older brother on the St Mary's faculty, who had some experience in making stringed instruments, mentored Brother Justin in making a guitar and a long neck banjo.

Brother Justin had a naturally clear, strong singing voice, and he needed only a few chords to accompany himself as a singer. The Kingston Trio was the country's most popular folk band at the time, and Brother Justin began to play along with their records. He soon got good enough to lead songfests at St. Mary's College, the monastery, and the Christian Brothers' summer camp along the Russian River in Sonoma County.

His musical talent did not go unnoticed. In his second year at St. Mary's College he was chosen to be the student brothers' choirmaster. He grabbed hold of this opportunity with gusto; some said the St. Mary's Assumption Hall choir was at its finest during Brother Justin's tenure. Somewhere deep in a closet I still have his collection of reel-to-reel tapes of a performance of sacred music composed by his beloved Giovanni Pierluigi da Palestrina.

Daily meditation and prayer in the monastery were Raymie's first introductions to introspection. Before that, his life had an immediate, external focus; work, earn money, spend it carousing with friends. Now he spent time in contemplation every day. This had a great calming and refining effect on his character. Years later I would quip, "I never would have married you if you had not spent those 15 years in the monastery."

Teaching and Coaching

Brother Justin's first teaching assignment was at Christian Brothers High School in Sacramento, a Catholic boys school with only two grade levels: freshman and sophomore. The juniors and seniors went to Bishop Armstrong High School. BJ was placed at the school with a few older, more seasoned brothers and a bevy of young brothers from his novitiate days. The older brothers lent stability and perspective to teaching and community life. One of his older brothers counseled BJ thusly: "On the first day of class, beat up the biggest kid in the class to establish your authority."

"I can't do that," replied young Brother Justin.

"You want to have trouble?"

"No."

"Then do it."

Brother Justin didn't hit anybody—at least not on the first day. With his size and strength, when the class got a little unruly all he had to do was push up the sleeves of his black robe in a way that meant business. But every now and then there was someone who needed a bit more persuasion. I remember his story about a student who sat during the prayer at the beginning of math class, then turned around to talk to someone behind him instead of facing front, ready for the day's lesson.

"I don't know what got into me," Justin related, "but I whacked that kid so hard he went flying out of his seat. I summarily sent him to sit in the back of the class. You could hear a pin drop for the rest of class that day. After about a month in the back row, that kid came to me before class and asked to return to his seat in the front where he had been. 'Why? You don't really want to learn anything.' 'Well,' the kid said, 'maybe you could hit me now and then.'"

This comic reply, which showed both a willingness to reform and a plea for attention, opened Brother Justin's heart. He and the student—who after all were not that far apart in age—later became friends.

The other subject Brother Justin taught was Spanish. He confessed to me that during his first year he was generally just one lesson ahead of some of his Latino students. That summer, he took a graduate course that made his head hurt. But by the time his second year as a Spanish teacher commenced, he was well ahead of the students. He was a fierce competitor and high achiever in any area he cared about.

Brother Justin loved living in the school community. Along with the older brothers, there were a number of young brothers like him, men he went through the novitiate with: Tom, Raymond, Morado, Camera. Everyone was on the same schedule: rise early to pray, off to school, afternoon prayers, correct homework and prepare lessons for the next day. There was a predictable ebb and flow to the work and community life. There was a common focus on education, service and the formation of young men.

Raymie's reason for joining the Brothers revolved around wanting to be a teacher. But even more than that, he wanted to coach basketball, football and baseball. This was his opportunity and he thrived. He had grown and gained confidence and leadership skills from his Garces Memorial coach, Brother Justin Sullivan. He couldn't think of a better life than teaching, coaching, and giving back in this same way.

As it turned out, his superiors had something else in mind.

At the culmination of each school year, a senior official in the Christian Brothers order, known as the provincial, would come from San Francisco to meet with each brother on the faculty of every Christian Brothers school in the western province. It was the provincial's job to assess how well each man was suited to his assignment, and to listen to any suggestions or concerns the brothers might have. Brother Justin's interview with the provincial, Brother Bertram, started out well. He was happy and well-liked by the students and other faculty. He loved teaching and coaching. All he asked for was the advanced Spanish course he took, so he could feel better prepared and more confident teaching.

Then came the surprise. Brother Bertram asked Brother Justin if he would leave teaching and go to work at the Christian Brothers winery. Mindful of his vow of obedience, and with respect for the leader of his province, young Brother Justin chose his words carefully. "Are you asking me or telling me?"

The provincial's answer was just as careful. "Because you joined the Brothers to teach, and not to make wine, I am asking you."

Now it was Justin's turn. He liked wine, but he loved teaching and wanted to continue. "If you are asking me," he told Brother Bertram, "then the answer is no."

At the end of his second year at Christian Brothers High School, the provincial came again, on the usual schedule. The interview proceeded as it had the year before. Brother Justin was doing a great job. Everyone was happy with him. Brother Bertram had just one more question, "Are you willing to transfer to the winery?"

"Are you asking me or telling me?"

"Because you joined the Brothers to teach, not make wine, I am asking you."

"If you are asking me, then the answer is no."

After Brother Justin's third year of teaching, the same scenario was set to play out again. But this time, when Brother Bertram asked if Brother Justin would transfer to the winery, Brother Justin answered with a question of his own.

"Are you going to ask me this every year?"

"You show great intelligence, determination and leadership," said the provincial, "and we are looking for a successor to lead the winery."

It wasn't coaching sports, but it was clearly a significant leadership opportunity. "I will go to the winery on one condition," Brother Justin replied. "If I don't like it, I will be able to return to teaching."

The provincial agreed, and that's how Brother Justin entered the business that made him famous: as a reluctant conscript.

Learning the Wine Business

That summer Brother Justin returned to Mont la Salle, but this time he arrived as a professed Brother and part of the winery team, which meant his life lay in a new part of the monastery. To the north at Mont la Salle was the novitiate where Brother Justin and other first-year student brothers learned the traditions, rules, and charisms of the Brothers of the Christian Schools. The south wing housed the boarding school for boys in the fifth through eighth grades, along with the Brothers who taught them. At the center was the chapel along with the living and dining quarters for the "Ancients"—the aged and retired brothers—and brothers who worked in the winery.

There in the middle of the monastery, Brother Justin joined Brother

Timothy, celebrated winemaker of The Christian Brothers Winery, and Brother Gregory, the winery's president. Brother Tim (as he was known to his intimates) was a tall, gracious gentleman who always had a smile and something nice to say. Brother Greg, on the other hand, was described by another brother as self-centered, demanding and all too frequently drunk.

Soon after he joined the winery team, Brother Justin was sent out on an educational tour that lasted a year. His assignment was to learn every job in the Christian Brothers' wineries and brandy distillery. The wineries in Napa Valley included the original small winery at Mont la Salle; a much larger industrial crushing facility in South St. Helena; and Greystone, one of Napa Valley's most famous buildings, which the Christian Brothers used as a visitor's center and for sparkling wine production. The winery and distillery in Reedley, near Fresno, was where the dessert wines and brandies were made. All in all, Christian Brothers at that time was one of the largest wine and spirits producers in the country with an annual production of a million cases a year.

Staff members were happy to have a young, eager apprentice and they shared generously. Brother Justin learned the nuances of brandy tasting and the differences between a column still and a pot still from Joe Kelly, the Kentucky distiller who ran the Reedley distillery. He walked through vineyards and learned the rudiments of winter pruning from Rollin Wilkinson. He worked on the bottling line and titrated acids in the lab. And every afternoon when he was at Mont La Salle, he tasted and made wine blends with Brother Timothy.

By the end of his foundational year, Brother Justin came to realize he loved the complexity and creativity of the wine business more than he did the repetitive experience of teaching. He was inspired by the artistry in winemaking and the remarkable resilient grapevines. He enjoyed the physical work with pumps, tanks and presses, the sights and smells, the aliveness of it all. Yes, he would stay on.

More importantly, he also learned how much he didn't know. When Brother Bertram, the provincial, came around in June, young Brother Justin asked to go to the state's top university for enology and viticulture (winemaking and grape-growing). Considering the future leadership role the Brothers had in mind for Brother Justin, the provincial granted Justin's request. That fall he enrolled as an undergrad at UC Davis.

The large, science-based, internationally minded university at Davis was a different universe compared to the small college campus in

Moraga. It was a thriving mix of kids and young adults from everywhere, including a large foreign student population. There Brother Justin donned street clothes and told everyone to call him BJ. This was not a matter of hiding his vocation; he just wanted to fit in and be a student like everyone else. Hard to do in a long black robe with a starched white collar.

Brother Timothy's Apprentice

At the end of each term and upon completion of his master's degree at UC Davis, BJ returned to Mont La Salle and the Christian Brothers Winery headquarters. He became Brother Timothy's assistant and apprentice. No one could have orchestrated a better practical winemaking education.

The Christian Brothers, also known as The Brothers of the Christian Schools, was founded by Jean-Baptiste de la Salle in the city of Reims, France in 1679. Saint Jean-Baptiste is credited with coming up with the concept of free parish schools for poor boys. Historically, only wealthy children received an education via a private family tutor. Father Jean-Baptiste found he could gather 50 or so poor boys who were about the same educational level and teach the group all at once. As the idea caught on, other young men were attracted to this work. Today there are 4,100 Christian Brothers in 560 schools worldwide.

The Christian Brothers first came to California in 1868, arriving in what is now the city of Martinez, led by Brother Justin McMahon. There they planted vineyards of premium grape varieties. By 1882 they began making sacramental wine and wine for their own consumption. They also began distilling pot-still brandy using the same method as in Cognac, France. Winemaking and brandy distillation continued during prohibition, supplying sacramental wines to Catholic and other Christian churches. The Christian Brothers Winery was moved to Mont La Salle above Napa Valley under the direction of Brother Timothy in 1935, not long after the repeal of prohibition. There the Christian Brothers produced and sold wine and brandy to the general public to support the running of their schools and universities.

By the late 1960s, Christian Brothers Winery produced about 40 different wines and brandies, which meant they were bottling one of their many products nearly every week of the year. In addition, every wine and brandy they bottled was a blend of various components. The simplest blends were made using just one grape variety, but often grown in different vineyards and in multiple years. Blending became even more complex for the wines called "Claret" and "Burgundy," because these were usually blends of different grape varieties as well as different vineyards and vintages. Not only that, but a bottle of "Claret" from one year would often contain a mix of all those variables that was not the same as the years before.

This sounds strange to modern wine connoisseurs. The explanation is that the primary goal back then was to achieve the same flavor profile every year. This is a profoundly different approach from today's fashion for showcasing the individuality of a particular grape variety, vintage or vineyard. That is why the counter in the wine laboratory was frequently filled with small bottles containing samples from many different tanks and barrels of wine. Brothers Timothy and Justin would swirl, smell, taste and spit until they came up with the perfect match for last year's bottling of each wine - even if the "recipe" turned out to be quite different.

When he wasn't in the lab creating whatever blend was required that week, Brother Justin was roaming around vineyards. With his master's degree in viticulture, he had more technical knowledge of vineyards than anyone else on the Christian Brothers team, including his superior. Knowledge combined with natural leadership ability made him a talented and highly effective vineyard manager and grape buyer for the winery. Under his leadership, Christian Brothers implemented the latest cultivation practices and produced higher-quality grapes and wine than before.

"Great wines are made in the vineyard," was a remark Justin made often. Today this is one of the most common clichés in the wine business. But not back then. Justin was among the first to view the role of a winemaker as bringing out the best in each lot of grapes that came into the winery, right down to a particular block or two within a much larger vineyard. "You can make great wine from great grapes," he would say, "but you can't make anything but mediocre wine from poor to average grapes."

Brothers Timothy and Justin became an amazing team. They both loved a crowd and were gracious hosts to wine writers and those in the wine trade. More and more, BJ was being groomed to not only be the winemaker and vineyard manager, but also the future president and face of the Christian Brothers winery. He attended the Brothers' annual harvest luncheons in New York and San Francisco. He went to a cross-country ski race to help promote a hot toddy made with Christian Brothers brandy. He hosted VIP visitors at the winery and taught a wine appreciation course at Napa Valley College. The press loved him, and his photo appeared in newspapers and the wine press. He even appeared as a mystery guest on "What's My Line?" a popular TV show at the time. If I recall correctly, the panel never guessed he was a winemaking monk.

Chapter Seven

Justin Meyer and Bonny Meyer playing music together, 1974

Folk Music

I have a three-inch thick binder full of old folk songs. Some were hand-written when I was a teenager. Many are copies made with old mimeograph machines. A precious few were typed on Christian Brothers stationery using Justin's portable typewriter from his college days. None of them have a scribed musical melody. Only about half have chords penciled in. That's the way of folk songs. If you don't know the tune or can't figure out the chords, too bad.

Many of these songs are so embedded within that I need only to glance at the title to launch into the complete song with all verses and chords intact. Others whisper at me from a great distance. I can feel the melody, but it will not rise to flow into my consciousness.

A long evening of strumming and singing defined the first time Brother Justin and I met. Strumming and singing continued on through our years together. During my time at UC Davis we took out our instruments and led a songfest deep into the night almost every time we were at the Olmos' house or a gathering somewhere. Those were the days when hootenannies were popular and people, young and old, were ready to sing traditional folk songs and those made popular by Peter, Paul and Mary, The Kingston Trio, Joan Baez, Pete Seeger and others.

Justin and I had a natural and effortless synergy when we sang. Our voices complemented each other; he a lively baritone, me a vibrant alto. Our voices always blended in an improvisational dance—we would weave in and out, alternately singing melody and harmony lines. One chord could signal the next song and a quick glance would move us into a crisp ending complete with a musical flourish.

After we had children, we played less at home but were still in demand at the little Holy Family Church in Rutherford, near our home. We led the liturgical music most Sundays, from a place up front right next to the altar. The music helped the service come alive for everyone there. When our children were toddlers, they quickly learned that they would be unsupervised as soon as we picked up our instruments. Members of the congregation would smile, and friendly hands would reach out to play with or corral our kids as needed. There was an elite group of women who commanded the back row of the church and who ultimately adopted our children on Sundays. Because they brought snacks for the children, they soon became known as the "Cracker Ladies."

As our children grew they sometimes joined us up in the sanctuary by the altar to lead the singing. Their voices were strong and clear, beautiful reflections and blends of their parents'. They later outdid us as they starred in musical theatre, looking relaxed and accomplished on stage. They never took up folk music, though. It was the music of our time, not theirs.

First Kiss

It was late on a Saturday night after another wonderful dinner at the Olmos' house. BJ and I had both enjoyed some wine that evening, and I think even a little brandy after dinner. BJ was driving me back to my dorm room, which meant taking a dirt track along the creek out to the paved county road. As always, we would chat a bit about the evening, he would drop me off, and that would be that. He was a sweet, gentle friend and a great musical partner, but he couldn't be anything more. He was a monk on a mission.

But on this particular evening, the path took a bit of a turn. About three quarters of a mile after leaving the Olmos' house BJ stopped the car on the levy and turned to me, suggesting we go down by the creek and enjoy the stars. I thought it a curious but lovely thing to do, so I joined him on a blanket he had brought from the house. We lay there for a while, looking up and enjoying the night sky through an open web of tree branches.

After the evening chill began to make us both a bit uncomfortable, we returned to the car. BJ put the blanket into the truck, shut the lid, and turned to me ... then took me in his arms and kissed me. I can still see the moonlight on his face, shining in his eyes, as he told me, hands shaking, that he was in love with me.

I searched his face and then my heart. What I found were flashes of recall: the joy and wonderful ease of playing music together, how my heart jumped when I saw him unexpectedly on campus, the warm emotions conjured up by the smell of his sweatshirt ...

I hadn't allowed these impression and emotions to enter my consciousness until that moment. But now, in an instant of insight, I realized I was in love with him too, and told him so. We kissed again and then held each other tight, leaning against the back of his car in the early April moonlight.

It was a quiet ride home, both of us feeling a crazy combination of relief, expansive affection, and trepidation. We hadn't been looking for love, but there it was, acknowledged and beautiful. And troubling. Neither of us knew what we should do with our feelings for each other, or where they would lead. For now, it was all we could do to rest in the immensity of the truth: we were in love without any way to be a couple.

In Love

After our first kiss near midnight by Putah Creek, the secret was out – but only for us. And as one kiss naturally leads to another, we spent more and more time together. We ended study hours, "chance" meetings on campus and evenings at the Olmos' house with more clandestine kisses.

That spring, BJ drove me to the town of Winters one warm night, with the windows rolled all the way down so we could smell the orange blossoms. (I still get dreamy whenever I smell orange blossoms!) We inhaled that amazing fragrance for miles. Then we stopped and kissed. He took me to Putah Creek to "watch the submarine races." And we kissed. We took walks in the arboretum. And kissed. We kissed in the enology department wine cellar as I helped him rack some of his experimental wines. We reached for each other and kissed whenever we had a moment alone together.

We continued to play music at church in our Schism Band, and BJ tutored me in Spanish at his lab table. We joined the other viticulture and enology grad students for drinks after late-night study hours. All these activities and times together took on an energetic dimension that hadn't been there before.

Our hearts skipped a beat each time we caught sight of each other. Our time together was more and more precious. I'm sure the quality of our singing and strumming together took on a certain quality of heart and meaning as well.

We managed to keep our love for each other secret from everyone, or so I thought at the time. From a more mature perspective, I'm pretty sure one of BJ's fellow graduate students, a man named Gordon, caught us kissing one night after we stole away from a study group.

At first, BJ and I both felt caught like deer in the headlights. We were excited and surprised at this unexpected, unlooked-for turn of events. We asked each other if kissing was permissible for a monk, then decided (conveniently) that because neither of us was married, we were not betraying anyone. We watched in wonder as our love, delight, and desire to be together grew. Then slowly, as spring deepened and the days got warmer, we felt the impending change of seasons coming to our relationship as well. Would we, could we, carry this growing love affair beyond the end of the university term in May? Justin would be staying on campus for the summer to write his thesis. I would return to Los Altos to two summer jobs that were waiting for me. I would be back in Davis in the fall, but he would be leaving then after completing his research and master's thesis.

We knew there was no real future for us together. But how would that "no future" arrive? Would everything fade away as naturally as it had grown into being? Given the circumstances of his professed vows, this would be a bittersweet blessing and a relief. Being in love was exquisitely beautiful, but the ever-present specter of an untenable future was torturous.

The last days of school held multiple dramas: completing term papers, taking exams, and knowing we would be going our separate ways. By the end, we were both physically and emotionally exhausted. Our good-bye was heart-wrenching.

Thus ended our first chapter together, in love and grief.

Love Letters

The first letter from BJ that summer made me flush with surprise and joy. Then I received an unexpected phone call. Then came another letter, written on what I recognized as BJ's portable typewriter in his room at the Olmos' home. Still a teenager, I wrote back in pen on binder paper.

Each letter, each call, was filled with news and longing. His letters gave me the same thrill that seeing him across campus had. But we were careful to take our time. Even once a week would have been too obvious to others. Once every two or three weeks seemed judicious. No one would notice.

(Years later I met Pat Dettman, the secretary receptionist at the Christian Brothers Mont La Salle winery. She shared with me that she knew about our romance early on because she was the first to see any mail that would come for the brothers, and it did not take long to notice the regular arrival of thick letters for Brother Justin in hand-addressed envelopes. And here we thought we were so discreet!)

Letters became our way of touching in with each other. We shared our thoughts, lives and longing through these epistles. As we kept in touch, our love grew. Uncertainty turned into hope, and hope turned into deeper and deeper longing.

That summer BJ spent long hours writing his thesis at UCD, then worked in the vineyards and winery at Christian Brothers on the weekends. I spent the summer working at Libby's cannery in Sunnyvale and at a Sears department store in Mountain View. The cannery pay was good, but the work was backbreaking. Standing on the production line putting fruit into cans doesn't look that hard, but after a few hours the constant reaching and repetitive movements were wearing. I enjoyed working as a part-timer at Sears much more. Staying busy helped keep our minds off missing each other. But then evening would arrive, and we would lie in our beds and wish we could magically teleport into each other's arms.

On a rare occasion we would talk on the phone. Here again, we had to be careful. Long distance charges added up and we didn't want to raise suspicion. So we exchanged more letters, ushering in a new phase in our relationship. This was no longer a spring fling that ended with the first rays of summer sun. Instead, it deepened with every sentence written and every phone call; bridges across the distance between us.

As I write this, I realize that this experience is part of the trajectory of every extraordinary love affair. After the delight and ease of initial attraction and affection, a Great Difficulty arises in Act II of the story. We see the path before us and feel the karmic pull and choose to step into our story despite all reasonable internal and external voices telling us otherwise. This need to take a leap, hold our breath and strive to connect beyond what is easy and safe, against all good sense, is a necessary part of the hero's journey. The way becomes clear, courage is summoned, and we journey forward committed to face the unknown.

I have often thought my life can be characterized as running from safety. This was surely that.

First Embrace

As summer and BJ's time at UCD came to a close, it was also time for the Department of Viticulture and Enology annual fall party. A park in the town of Woodland had been chosen as the location and members of the department had signed up for dishes they would bring. On the designated Saturday afternoon people loaded up baskets and tote bags with food and wine, and everyone headed off to Woodland to spend the afternoon and evening.

I had just arrived back on campus for my second year, and was invited to accompany Dr. Olmo, Helen, Paul Olmo and BJ. I was ecstatically happy to reunite with BJ, see the Olmos and attend the party. I had gotten to know many of the people in the viticulture and enology department the previous school year: professors including Vernon Singleton, Ralph Kunke, and Maynard Amarine; lab assistants Al Koyama and Billy Little; and graduate students including Gordon and Rich. I knew this would be a great occasion, and it was.

The food was fresh and delicious. We had barbequed meats and salads and "Madame Queen's" famous wild rice casserole. The wine was a focal point, as you might imagine. Most people brought a bottle or two that they wanted everyone else to try. There was plenty of wine and good cheer to go around. As it turned out, all three Olmos had a bit more wine than perhaps they should have. So Brother Justin drove us all home. The three Olmos in the back seat were not completely aware of what was going on in the front seat.

Fueled with a little wine ourselves, Justin and I sat close together, with his arm around me and my head nestled into his shoulder. When we arrived back at the Olmos' house, Harold and Helen stumbled off to bed and Paul went to his house down the levee road.

Then, BJ and I quietly went into his room. In the fullness of that night, in the fullness of our love for each other we embraced and kissed. Then he slowly lifted my dress over my head and laid it on the bed and I stood there in my little white slip. I remember standing there in the moonlight feeling beautiful and filled with the beauty and exquisite intimacy of the moment.

Then he lifted my slip over my head. Soon we were standing there naked in the moonlight in each other's arms. Neither one of us had really prepared for this moment. Neither one of us had really thought it through. The path to this moment had been long and full of laughter, trust and emotional intimacy. We trembled in each other's arms feeling the overwhelming closeness and vulnerability of standing there naked together. After a little while we made our way over to Justin's single bed and lay there in each other's arms for the longest time.

That night, passion pushed us past awkwardness and we reached the physical point of no return. As soon as he entered me fully, we both stopped moving, becoming perfectly still. Suspended there in stillness and silence, so intimately connected, we entered the expansive territory that lovers share beyond time and place. We were embraced not just by each other, but by love itself. We were awed by the power and tenderness. We had surrendered to love and felt held by God and carried into the sacred mystery.

Both virgins and totally unprepared, we would not take the risk of active intercourse. More importantly, in the forefront of our souls was the gravity of this act, clearly stepping over the boundary of Brother Justin's vow of chastity. With stolen kisses and embraces around campus, we could make a case that we remained chaste. No longer. Something had shifted. We were clearly on a new journey without knowing where we were headed.

There must have been a disturbance in the energetic field that rippled through the whole house, because we heard Harold's footsteps coming down the hall, approaching the room where we lay naked together. I burrowed my head into Justin's chest and held my breath.

Justin fired an "all's well" shot over the bow by audibly clearing his throat.

This seemed to satisfy Dr. Olmo. We heard his footsteps fading to the far end of the house. We waited until all was quiet before we began to breathe again.

Without speaking, we knew we would never again share a bed in the Olmos' home. Not because we felt guilty—our love was too powerful for that. It was because we didn't want to embarrass or disappoint Harold or Helen. Our love for them was powerful too.

And so as we took a bold, spontaneous step into a new stage of our love, we also could feel the outside world pressing in on us like never before.

The Morning After

The next morning was Sunday, the week's holiest day. Our first day as lovers would begin in church. BJ had driven me home the night before, a mostly wordless journey deep in the night. So, I arrived at Newman Center alone and waited anxiously to speak with BJ after Mass. When I saw him, my usual happiness was tempered with a cool dose of reality. He was dressed in his black robe, looking sober and deeply concerned. Rightly so. We had crossed a line. We had officially violated his vow of chastity, not to mention the official Catholic prohibition of premarital sex.

Yet no matter how I turned it around in my mind, I could not find my way to feeling guilt or regret. Except for the moment when we thought we would be discovered in bed together, I felt like I had experienced a sacred passage. We had been so filled with love and yearning for each other for so long—our reverential joining wrapped in stillness felt like the natural culmination of a force bigger than both of us. Like the life force that propels a seed to germinate and reach skyward, our coming together was just as natural, pure, and a part of life's longing for itself. It all just felt overwhelmingly beautiful, expansive and right.

Maybe the palpable sense that we had been embraced by something sacred was real for him too. But of course I wasn't the one who had taken a vow of chastity.

I waited for him outside the church after Mass. Without a word said, we made our way around the corner of the building to a spot where we could have some privacy, under a tree between the church and the rectory. I waited for him to speak.

As he did, I looked into his eyes and listened intently with my heart, searching for the smallest hint of guilt or remorse—and found none. I let out an audible sigh of relief as my whole body relaxed. Evidently, he was standing in the same field I was; knowing that love is what we are ultimately called to. In that moment I felt that surrendering to love in tender nakedness and authenticity is the highest calling and the greatest gift we can give each other and God.

BJ's reaction was a mirror image of mine. He had been searching my face to see if I was troubled. His love for me was so great that he was deeply concerned and hoped that I had not felt guilty or dishonored in any way. Seeing that was not the case, he relaxed and smiled with the deepest tenderness.

None of this resolved the larger question hanging over us. Justin was leaving Davis just as I arrived. We were lovers who would not make love again. Our passion for each other was undimmed yet blocked by everything else in our lives.

Later that afternoon Justin presented me with a stunning gift: a banjo he had made for me over the summer. It was perfectly proportioned, about half the size of the long neck five-string he had made for himself a few years before. Somehow a petite walnut and ebony banjo neck had come into his keeping. He had built the missing nut and peg head and installed Scruggs tuning pegs. Then he had added a new head, bridge and strings. The result was a beautiful refurbished antique with a wonderful sound. I was amazed, touched, and excited all at once.

BJ showed me a few chords in the key of C and within five minutes I was playing tunes I knew. The banjo sounded sweet and felt natural in my hands. It would be a perfect remembrance, a symbol of our love of music and for each other—and a way to always hold BJ in my arms.

Olmo's Lab

When BJ left the university for the winery, the large table that had been his lab desk became mine. Officially I didn't belong in Dr. Olmo's lab at all, much less with my own space. I was not his graduate student or even an undergrad viticulture student. He did once invite me to study viticulture and enology with him, but I had declined, knowing that even with a winemaking degree, a woman in those days usually wound up in a windowless laboratory—really a closet with instruments—doing chemical analysis all day. Men made the wine. Women got to help them do it.

Dr. Olmo's lab was exceptionally large and open. Besides him and me, it was populated with another grad student or two and a couple of lab techs. Short, round Billy Little did wine analysis and slight, lean Al Koyama, Harold's sidekick, was always ready to tromp through vineyards somewhere. They both befriended me and invited me to their homes for dinner, as did Helen and Harold. Professor Olmo's cluttered office was across the hall. There were so many books and papers everywhere, there was barely enough room to walk in and sit down. Notes for future books (which never got written) filled multiple filing cabinets stored in the lab. I kept my textbooks there in a bookshelf BJ had made. The lab became my home between classes and most nights, as I preferred to study there rather than a crowded dorm room or shared apartment. I enjoyed the quiet, and the study breaks with other grad students down the hall.

The professors and grad students seemed to like having me around, perhaps for the novelty: a young coed in a sea of men. They didn't seem to mind that I wasn't a vit or enology student. Besides, it didn't take long before I was able to keep up with their technical jargon and conversations about malolactic fermentation or Brettanomyces. Over time I came to know all the professors—Maynard Amerine, Ralph Kunke, Curtis Alley and Vernon Singleton, Webb, Ough, Kliewer, and Cook. I enjoyed impromptu conversations with all of them but grew to treasure Harold Olmo, in particular, as a dear friend and father figure.

One day in spring Al Koyama asked me if I would like a job helping him cross-pollinate grapes for Dr. Olmo. This offer I enthusiastically embraced. For all his gentle humility, Harold was the foremost grape geneticist in the United States and respected throughout the winegrowing world. Every spring he would determine what grape varieties he wanted to cross, or hybridize, in search of new varieties that would produce better wine in borderline growing regions such as California's hot central valley. He would do the same with table grapes, always in search of better-tasting varieties that were also resilient enough to be shipped and stored. Ruby Cabernet and Emerald Riesling are just two of more than 30 new varieties introduced to the grape and wine industry by Dr. Olmo.

With Al as my teacher, I quickly learned to use a pair of tweezers to remove the tiny petals and stamens from grape clusters that were a couple of days away from flowering. Then I would dust the exposed pistil of each baby grape and enclose the cluster in a brown paper bag. That cluster would produce an average of 80 grapes with 4 seeds each, resulting in about 320 unique genetic expressions. These seeds were planted and grown first in a greenhouse, then in an experimental vineyard plot. After the third year, grapes were harvested from the healthiest of these carefully cataloged vines and made into wine. Table grapes were likewise crossed, grown, harvested and brought in to be tasted and tested.

Dr. Olmo's downstairs production lab was much larger than the upstairs lab where I studied. For three summers I was part of a crew making 500 different wines, which we fermented in milk bottles that were tagged and set in long rows. We analyzed about as many unique table-grape varieties each year. I weighed each table grape cluster, counted the grapes, noted the color, size, shape, number of seeds, fragrance, and finally, the taste. My job on the winemaking side was primarily doing titrations to determine the acid level of the must (grape juice) before fermentation. I earned a reputation for speed and accuracy, which was important as the grapes came in fast and furious in the middle of harvest and we had hundreds of grapes to test and wines to make.

After the wines finished fermenting, they were "racked," or poured off the lees (dead yeast cells and bits of grape skin) into dark green wine bottles. The bottles were corked and stored in a cool, dark area until the moment of truth arrived. That arrived in the form of the two days a week Dr. Olmo would line up 10 wines next to the upstairs lab sink for tasting. If I was there, he would call me over and we would stand side-by-side swirling, sipping, savoring and spitting; noting color, aroma, and flavor profile using the Davis 20-point scale developed by Harold's department colleague, Maynard Amerine, in the late 1950s.

I loved being part of the viticulture and enology department. I loved the field and lab work. I loved the aliveness of the grapes and the wines we produced. I loved all of it, but I never imagined for a minute that I would end up in the wine business.

Kisses, Music, and More Kisses

Young Brother Justin, newly graduated from the university, found innumerable reasons to return. He would talk with Brother Timothy about a question or problem he wanted to solve. Soon he would be on the road to Davis to talk with his former professors ... and with me.

BJ would let me know ahead of time whenever he was heading to Davis. Sometimes, he would even arrange to stay at the Olmos' house on a Saturday night. After his official reason for visiting the university was behind him, he would swing by my dorm and pick me up. We would go to visit the Olmos or other friends. There was a local nightclub we liked to frequent—ironically named The Abbey. We would go there with PhD students Rich and Gordo to listen to the Easy Money Trio and dance to their mellow, romantic jazz tunes. I must admit to doctoring my driver's license, which was easy to do in those days, so I could go to these hang-outs with my over-21 friends. The Olmos frequently hosted enology and viticulture graduate students for dinner on weekends. We would be invited to dinner and encouraged to bring our instruments and then play music into the night. As always, we knew we were on a roll when we saw Dr. Olmo head out into the garage and return with his leaf rake, "strumming" it with wild abandon and great joy.

Wherever we went, whatever we did, the evening would end in BJ's car kissing. I'm not sure if anyone in the history of time has ever steamed up car windows so consistently and so completely as we did. Always ever-vigilant about not letting others see us exchange kisses or even come-hither glances, we spent a lot of quality time in his car.

To be completely open about it, kissing was not exactly all we did. Once the threshold of lovemaking is crossed, there is no turning back. Nor did we want to. But we were caught by our own values, by wanting to honor Brother Justin's vow to the best of our ability. We were pushed on by deep and passionate desire but held back by our decision not to follow it to its natural culmination. We were caught by not being protected by birth control which, of course, we weren't supposed to be needing anyway.

So, we would kiss and connect in the most intimate, tender ways we could, then we would back away from the brink of consummation. Like our first embrace, it felt like a sacrament, a form of communion. It arose from and was the natural expression of deep love and emotional connection. It was indescribably exquisite, yet profoundly painful.

Chapter Eight

Justin Meyer at a wine tasting at Franciscan Winery

Wanting to Die

After Justin died, I wanted to die. It's not that I had any desire to inflict violence upon myself. It's just that I was consumed by a yearning to be with him. He was in the spirit world, so that is where I wanted to be.

I had come very close to dying four months before. I was in the hospital, recovering from major surgery—though "major" may not be sufficiently descriptive in this case. After removing a large cancerous tumor, the surgeons had also lifted, examined and washed most of my internal organs before tucking them back more or less into place, disturbing and tearing my abdominal connective tissue in the process. Nothing was functioning normally, so I had tubes going in for nutrition, tubes going out for draining and elimination, tubes stuck here and there for who knows what.

Four days later my heart stopped. I have only a vague memory of someone jostling me to take an EKG in the middle of the night. Then nothing. I barely remember the next couple of days during which I did not have the strength to talk or move. Somehow, I did not feel concerned. It was disorienting to feel that everything around me had turned sidewise, but I wasn't afraid.

So when I wanted to die to be with Justin, it didn't feel dramatic. I could focus my intention, give a little energy to it, and be done.

During this dark period, someone suggested that I write a journal. I wrote down how I felt in graphic detail. I wrote about the anguish of watching Justin die and not being able to prevent it. I wrote about the ride down from the Sierras and the powerful feeling of wanting to run away into the woods. How I still wanted to be anywhere but where I was, in all this pain. I relived the most poignant moments of the memorial; Holly singing the "Our Father" prayer, Chad's composure as the M.C., the missing man formation, the lone plane heading into the sunset, the white doves circling and disappearing.

Over and over I relived in my mind the details of my cancer surgery and the days in the hospital and how horrendous it had been. The physical pain, the visceral feeling of having been horribly violated, the lingering sense that my insides were now literally out of place. Along with writing I made visual images to express these feelings. Raw, angry masses of red and purple covered the pages.

In every other rough passage I had been through as an adult, Justin had been there to support and soothe me. This time he was not just absent. He was dead.

I wrote all this in my journal and more. The images and feelings I wrote about were so dark, so scary, that I hid the journal where no one could find it. Then a few years later, I ceremonially burned it in the fireplace one night, so my children would never read it.

They were, as I was, in shock from their father's sudden death. One day he was here and life felt normal and good. The next day, it's as if the world had turned upside down. Everything was out of balance. The natural joy of living had been wrenched away.

The shock my children experienced seemed not as profound as mine, though I could see that it went deep. And over those initial months, I witnessed their shock morph slowly into a kind of terror. They watched me struggle. They monitored my pale and fragile face. They watched my memory falter and my thoughts fall into confusion, and they were scared. The once unthinkable prospect of losing a parent in the prime of life was now a near and present reality for them.

This tender tether is what kept me alive. I repeatedly decided to renew my hold on life, for them. It felt like wading through deep, energy-sucking mud as I inched forward: simultaneously being beckoned and tempted by death, and yet over and over again tearing myself away from that precipice toward life.

Grief

Grief is a profoundly deep longing for an intimate connection that has come to an abrupt end. Sometimes the end is anticipated, and grieving occurs as a series of incremental losses. Other times the end is sudden. Then the shock is primal and powerful, throwing us dangerously off-balance and adrift in what seems a meaningless world.

That is how it happened for me. One afternoon Justin was laughing and teasing his friend Ruggero, giving me a warm hug and the next minute he was gone, his lifeless body carried off by an ambulance.

I know grief well. Grief is a lover who slipped into my heart unbidden and took me over. Like a lover, it filled my days and nights with a kind of ecstatic pain that disoriented my mind and gripped my heart with an unnamable ache.

Sometimes I felt I had to keep grief at bay. If I were to get even simple things done, grief would have to wait. Other times I feared that if I fully engaged with grief I would be blown apart, the pieces impossible to put back together again.

Ultimately, I came to understand that I could not avoid grief indefinitely without paying a dear price. I found it critically important to embrace grief and allow myself to be taken over by it, for there were great treasures at the bottom of that deep, dark well.

For me, the gifts of grief took a while to become clear. They unfolded slowly but were profound. I found some of the gifts in my relationships with others, which began to shift and change. Some people and friendships drifted away, but others emerged in ways I never would have expected. I became more able to make room in my day for things that would ease the pain and help me heal.

The more I surrendered to grief, the greater became the gifts. I found that grief broke my heart open in a way that nothing else on earth could have. When I embraced grief instead of letting it torment me, I was left transformed.

Symptoms of Grief

Sleeplessness
Difficulty going to sleep
Waking up in the middle of the night and not being able to return to sleep
Overwhelming tiredness
Sleeping a lot
Depression
Crying
Inability to cry
Overwhelming desire to be alone
Isolation
Mind goes to mush

Thinking is like slogging through mud
Loss of short-term memory
Forgetting
Forgetting conversations
Forgetting appointments
Forgetting people's names
Forgetting phone numbers and addresses
Inability to make decisions
Shouldn't make decisions
Can't process information
Loss of creativity
Deep physical heartache
Impatience
Nervousness, jitteriness
Anger
Blaming
Intolerance of noise and chaos
Intolerance of others
Work becomes unimportant
Overwhelming desire to run away
Inability to do simple things like type and spell
Overeating
Under-eating
Unsettled stomach
Digestive problems
Erratic behavior
Erratic schedule
Substance use or abuse to mitigate the above
Alcohol, caffeine, sleeping pills, other drugs
Other things that numb
TV, movies, work, all forms of busyness

Grief comes in waves. Sometimes I am knocked over and tumbled, hit hard by a wall of water and plunged to the depths. Sometimes I am able to ride the peaks and troughs of the waves and even dive through them and come out the other side only to face the next wave and the next one and the one after that.

Things that Help
Getting hugs
More hugs
Laughter
Funny movies
Poignant movies
Movies that make you cry
Listening to beautiful music
Playing music
Flowers
Beautiful and serene surroundings
Nature
Walking
Simple pleasures
Yoga, Thai Chi or Chi Gong
Meditating
Masturbating
Just being quiet
Massages
Journaling
Drinking tea
Eating healthy, organic food
Hugs
The Way Out
Falling in love
Falling in love with a child
Falling in love with a pet
Falling in love with a project
Falling in love with life

Gifts of Grief
Imperative to re-prioritize
Renewed focus on what matters most
Learning who matters most
Some relationships become deeper and better than they ever would have
been
Some relationships dissolve and become unimportant or even toxic and

fall away
Gratitude for who and what I still have
Renewed sense of abundance
Renewed commitment to live life to the fullest
My heart feels broken open
I am more vulnerable
I am more passionate
I am able to love more deeply
I am more compassionate
My creativity is more available to me
My life has expanded in new directions
I have become more generous
I have become more tender
I feel closer to God

On My Own

The most significant event in my childhood was when I told my father I hated him. I don't remember why, but I was nine years old and furious about something. His response was to stop listening or talking to me. For a year.

I have vivid memories of walking up to him as he read the newspaper in his chair after work, the chair that no one else was allowed to sit in, and saying, "Hi." No response. He acted like he could neither see me nor hear me. Month after month went by. He was unrelenting. So was I. I would walk up to him and speak, knowing he would not shift his gaze or reply to me.

On the outside, my relationship with my mother was not affected by this. But she did nothing to help me either. She allowed my father to shut me out and act like I did not exist. So my relationship with her was also profoundly changed.

I did not know at that time that pretty much every child tells their parents they hate them at some point or another. Probably multiple times. I do remember that I quickly forgot why I had been angry with him, and I had the presence of mind to understand that his behavior was incredibly juvenile. In fact, to my mind, both my parents were behaving more like children than adults. They were both complicit in failing to emotionally connect with and care for me, their child.

Slowly the awareness formed in my consciousness that while I had moved past the original incident with my father, my parents had not. I was now the adult in the situation. And as the only adult in the house, I would need to look out for myself.

I went about my school life and home life doing my best to support myself physically and emotionally. I did my homework, played with friends, was active in scouts and developed my sense of self-containment and independence.

But I was still only nine years old, living in a house where the people responsible for my well-being were allied against me in an emotional cold war.

One night, in the middle of the night, my breathing began to accelerate. No matter how hard I inhaled, I felt I could not get enough oxygen. I panicked and went into my parents' room to get help. Startled out of sleep by my out-of-control hyperventilation they both responded. I saw fear in my father's eyes as he looked at me for the first time in months. He and my mother rubbed my back and comforted me until my breathing returned to normal.

My parents grew up and grew into being somewhat better parents that night. Yet I could not go back into childhood again, because I could not trust my parents to be truly mature. After I became a parent myself and reflected on this whole experience, I became even more horrified by their behavior toward me and my siblings when we were growing up. I remained wary of my parents' judgement and behavior with regard to me or my children. On the few occasions we were together, I would monitor them with vigilance. When they would criticize or belittle one of my children I would rush to protect them.

I did not judge my parents. None of us know how to be parents until we are. It is all pretty much on-the-job training and learning by trial and error. We do the best we can, given our emotional capacity, maturity and life experience. Critical to this process was what I learned about deep forgiveness from my friend Jerry Jampolsky. Forgiveness is not only the path to world peace, it has a more immediate value in my life—the path to personal peace. Forgiveness freed me to heal, replacing the old hurt and blame with compassion for my parents.

My dad's early emotional abuse was also a gift of sorts. Because of it, I grew into a strong, capable, independent teenager and adult. I was ready and happy to leave home, and capable of listening to and following my own internal compass when reckoning my way forward.

Now, it is time for a new reckoning. Justin is gone, our children are now in their twenties and are busy creating their own lives and paths forward. I am on my own again.

Chapter Nine

Bonny Smith & Brother Justin at Bryce Canyon

Sangre de Cristo

Two years after earning his master's degree, BJ felt the growing expectations laid upon him by the winery, the order, and the Christian Brothers' schools. The community at Mont La Salle did not have the singular purpose and fraternity of the teaching community in Sacramento, where he had lived previously. The winery was at the novitiate and retirement complex, where there were only two or three brothers BJ could relate to and have a full friendship with. Among "The Ancients" there were few he found to be loving, kind, and spiritually evolved. Most of the retired brothers seemed bitter and resentful after their 40 years of service. BJ didn't want to become one of these casualties.

Also, deep down, some part of him yearned to be with me and have a family. Later on, he was known to quip, "I have come to realize that celibacy is not hereditary." But how could he leave and create a life for himself, when so many had given him so much, and now were counting on him to move The Christian Brothers' wine business forward to support so many schools and deserving students?

These questions weighed on him heavily, even with his constant stream of work responsibilities. In 1970, Brother Justin asked for and received permission to spend the winter at the Christian Brothers' retreat center in the Sangre de Cristo Mountains near Santa Fe, New Mexico. The Brothers had established the center as a place of rest and renewal for Brothers in their middle years. The retreat center was far from their home monasteries, a place where they could rededicate themselves to their vocation. Brother Justin would have 100 days to meditate, pray, and renew.

At Sangre, BJ met monks from Christian Brothers schools all over the U.S. and the world. The brother who became his best buddy was a crusty old monk from De La Salle University in The Philippines. BJ and Brother Ben Ladinski would stay up late playing cards, drinking brandy and talking about everything.

BJ told Ben of his work at the winery and how much he had grown to love winemaking and caring for vineyards. He shared what it was like to live at Mont La Salle in the sometimes challenging mixed community of retired brothers, boarding school teachers and winery brothers.

Then he disclosed his love and longing for me.

BJ gave some of my letters to Ben to read, because he would find nothing incriminating there. On the contrary, I was unwavering in my encouragement to BJ to follow his calling. I could feel the depth of his struggle, and though I longed to be with him, what I wanted most was for him to know his own heart. I never wanted to influence his way forward, wherever that path may lead him and us.

In addition to letters, BJ sent me tapes. I loved receiving these spoken letters. Hearing his voice warmed my heart. There was also music. He was enamored with The Fifth Dimension's "Age of Aquarius" album, which was hugely popular at the time. He listened to those songs over and over again and shared them with me. Listening to those old tunes, even now, can easily bring tears to my eyes.

Through his letters, I followed BJ's experience there in the Sangre de Cristo Mountains. The radical shift from work-a-day life at the monastery and winery was like a deep exhale. The 100 days were broken up into thematic weeks which created structure and added interest to the program. BJ had time to meditate and reflect on his life as a monk and on what the future might hold for him. There were many trails and he frequently hiked up into the mountains. There were times when everyone was silent and times when they sang to Brother Justin's banjo or laughed at his jokes. He even procured some grape cuttings and planted a small experimental vineyard on a sunny ledge there.

After a hundred days of prayer and reflection in the mountains of New Mexico, Brother Justin came to a decision: He would stay. He would rededicate himself to the order and life as a Christian Brother. I believed we were both relieved on some level, but also had some trepidation. It was a relief to see a clear path forward. At the same time, we were both aware and afraid of this road, and all too familiar with the pain of separation. What would this new separation look like? How would we begin to walk separate paths?

Tryst in the Canyonlands

As it turns out, we did not begin separately. BJ came up with a plan. He was in pretty good shape after hiking around the Sangre de Cristo Mountains. He wanted to hike the Grand Canyon. More specifically, he wanted to hike down to the Rio Grande and back up to the rim in the same day. As long as he was driving through the southwest, he would also like to visit the region's other famous national parks, Bryce and Zion.

He asked me to join him.

I accepted immediately, excited to see him and be together with him! We then had a sober discussion about his vows and our commitment to them. We were clear that he was going to remain a Brother. But neither of us had much money, so at night we would share the same room in a motel. We would sleep in separate beds of course. We were resolute. We could do this.

I played hooky from school and flew to Salt Lake City. My heart leaped when I saw BJ's smiling face waiting for me at the arrival gate. He looked tanned and fit from his three months away from the winery routine. He drove us to the rim of the Grand Canyon that very afternoon. We made it to the canyon overlook and campground just as the sun was setting. The expansive site took my breath away! The setting sun added to the drama as the long shadows heightened the depth perception and lit up the reds and golds of the canyon walls. That sight is forever in my memory.

After cooking a simple campfire dinner, we settled into our sleeping bags, kissed, held hands and fell asleep.

Over the next few days we toured and hiked Bryce Canyon and Zion Canyon. As I look at photographs from that time, our faces shone as bright and deep as the canyons. Every moment of that trip felt blessed, beautiful, and magical.

Except for the last day.

Our last stop was a friend's cabin near South Lake Tahoe. We would spend the night there, then the next day BJ would drop me off in Davis and head home to Mont La Salle. It was March, and there was still snow on the ground around the cabin. We bought some groceries and prepared a particularly nice meal as this was our last evening together. The fire in the fireplace warmed our bodies and our hearts as the flames were reflected on our flushed faces.

Then it was time to go to bed—separately of course. We had been so successful with this arrangement so far. We had been so clear about Justin's path forward, which, by reason of my love for him was also our path forward. There was never a moment when I was not in full support. Then he asked me to come to bed with him.

In that moment, with his request hanging in the air, everything fell apart. I knew he was saying out loud what we both were aching for - and right behind it, the fear of separation welling up inside us both, the separation that would come with the dawn. Not talking about these things had kept the raw truth at bay. Now, here it was between us, forcing us to wrestle with it.

We talked, cried, and writhed in anguish half that night. Finally, we fell asleep well past midnight. Separately.

There was no romance in the air the next morning. This next phase was going to be an extremely hard one. We could be impressively idealistic a couple of thousand miles apart or hiking together through breathtaking canyons. But we were now headed back to school and winery, to routine real life. This was going to put our determination to a much stronger test.

We managed to stay apart for only a couple of months. Maybe it was three. We exchanged letters, hoping that would be enough. But our love, our yearning to be together would not be contained. He found he had reason to come to UC Davis and we fell back into what had become our routine of seeing each other when he came to the viticulture and enology department to confer with the professors there. We told each other that our love affair could not and would not continue, but we could not stop seeing each other.

The Decision

I finished my bachelor's degree in March of '71 and was accepted by San Jose State University to study for both a teaching credential and a master's degree in psychology. I intended to become a high school teacher and school psychologist. Instead of waiting until the next fall to enter graduate school, I decided to begin taking spring and summer education classes there at Davis. What began as gap-filling extension classes became early entry into the Davis Middle School Education Program. The people in the education department there talked me into continuing beyond the spring and summer and getting my primary and secondary credentials there at UC Davis.

During my student teacher days, I began dating a man named Chuck. I felt he likely wasn't the man I wanted to spend the rest of my life with, but we had glorious fun and our time together was filled with laughter. One winter's day, BJ came over to my apartment for a visit. He approached me in the usual way, smiling, ready for a romantic kiss and hug. But something fundamental had shifted in me. I knew I would be leaving Davis soon and we would be parting for good. I turned away from BJ and he left deeply troubled.

All of our other partings had been by mutual decision. This was different. I had taken a step back, reserving my physical affection for another man. If there was to be any fundamental shift between me and BJ, it was now or never.

On a Saturday, a week after my turning away, I was at the Olmos' home on their back patio covered in wisteria and grape vines. Chuck and I had come over to use a saw and hammer from the garage to construct some hands-on math learning tools for my fourth graders. We were hard at work pounding nails when Helen opened the sliding glass door to the patio. Standing just inside the door, she called me over to her. I looked into her face and immediately knew something very serious was going on.

Unbeknownst to me and Chuck, BJ had come to see the Olmos, entering their home through the garage door, as usual. He had come to talk with them, then discovered that I was there also. Now he wanted to talk with me, too. Privately. I tried to look past Helen to get a glimpse of BJ who was likely somewhere behind her in the family room. But my eyes were accustomed to the bright winter sun outside, and I could not make him out. Probably just as well, as the shock at seeing him there would have reverberated through my system in a way that would have been obvious to Chuck.

The geometry boards and my students now forgotten, I wondered what had brought BJ to the Olmos'. What kind of conversation I would be walking into?

I told Helen I would come inside in a few minutes. Then I turned and walked back to Chuck. He knew right away something was up by the look of consternation on my face. I told him that BJ had unexpectedly shown up, and had something serious he wanted to talk with me about. It would likely take a while, so I suggested he head back to campus. I would catch a ride later with BJ or the Olmos. Chuck's face immediately clouded up like a storm front had suddenly rolled in. He knew enough about my love for BJ to realize that the unfolding events probably portended nothing good for him.

He was silent as we walked together to his motorcycle. I tried to reassure him as I gave him an affectionate hug and kiss, though I don't think my words and actions did much good. I stood and watched him ride down the gravel driveway, out to the frontage road and out of sight. Slowly I turned and retraced my steps back to the patio, then through the sliding glass door into the Olmos' dimly lit family room.

Helen had disappeared. BJ was standing there alone. I looked up into his face and saw that it barely concealed intense emotion. His eyes, however, were brilliant and clear; a deep Pacific blue. Looking down at me, Brother Justin slowly and deliberately spoke words I had never expected to hear.

He had decided to leave the Christian Brothers.

There was a long silence between us as the immensity of what this meant sank in. I searched his face to see if he really meant it, if he was sure. I found assurance there, the kind of knowing that comes from long and deep contemplation. Then with trembling hands and moist eyes, he took my hands in his, looked deeply into my eyes and asked me if I would marry him.

Without a moment's hesitation, I said yes and hugged his neck with tears of joy streaming down my face. Both of us trembled with suddenly unbound emotion. When we released our embrace, it was to kiss—for the first time not caring who might see. Then we laughed out loud as joy overtook us. Hearing our laughter, Helen and Harold walked in and hugged us both. The somber mood within the house evaporated and was replaced by joyful celebration.

Betrothed

The seven months from "The Decision" to our wedding was a time of preparing, working, playing and deep contemplation.

We decided to marry in my home parish. St. Williams was a beautiful church with a friendly pastor. We visited with him a couple of times. He assessed our seriousness and we talked about the ceremony and the music. The church organist would play the wedding march. After that, my fellow folk group members would lead the music. I would not pick up a guitar during the ceremony, but I would join the musicians in a couple of songs at the reception. The reception would be at my family home. My mother and I had toured a few event venues, but in the end, I felt so much more comfortable at home. My father decided he would borrow a carpet of artificial grass from one of the local mortuaries if they didn't have a funeral that day. The tentativeness of this made me quite nervous.

My parents had mixed reactions to our engagement and upcoming marriage. Since the first moment my mother suspected there was a romantic connection between BJ and me, she had expressed her deep concerns and stalwart disapproval. "He is so much older than you are— 11 years! You will be happier with someone closer to your age. He is from Bakersfield and is so rough around the edges. He swears!"

In short, Justin was not the kind of refined gentleman she had in mind for me. My dad took me aside and expressed some deep concern about Justin's interest in sex. He had chosen a celibate life and my dad was afraid Justin likely had little or no desire for lovemaking. He wondered aloud if my own yearnings and sexual passions would be satisfied as a former monk's wife. Without going into details, I assured him I had no concerns when it came to Justin's sexual desire or romantic passion.

Now that we were betrothed, Justin and I had serious concerns of our own that were quite a bit deeper and different than my parents'. Justin talked with his cousin Dick, who was concerned about our age difference for a different reason: "She is young and beautiful and energetic, I am not sure I can keep up with her."

I expressed and discussed my concerns directly with Justin. One of the things I emphasized was that we were both very strong individuals. We were beautifully matched in that I could push hard against him and he would hold steady, giving me a deep sense of safety. The opposite was equally true, I held fast as he pushed against me. I had always felt uncomfortable with young men I dated who deferred to me. "Whatever you want" was not what I wanted to hear. I knew I needed to be with a man who could meet me, match me, and stand strong. Now, I wondered out loud if this dynamic would lead to problems and challenges down the road. If our strength ever turned into a contest of wills, it would make for a mighty fierce battle.

I was also concerned about Justin's drinking. After five years in college, I had witnessed fellow students over-drinking and over-dosing to the point of oblivion. Justin never got that drunk, but he was a hearty and enthusiastic consumer. Hearty drinking in and of itself was not concerning to me. But I understood the difference between enjoying and using. And I had noticed that Justin used alcohol to liberate and soften himself emotionally. Wine helped him be more vulnerable with me, and more relaxed and playful in social situations. He had been toughened up by his upbringing. Fifteen years of meditation, self-reflection, and prayer had softened and opened Justin's heart. The emotional armor he wore was thinner than when he was in his teens. But he still felt like he needed to fortify his courage with a little extra wine or glass of brandy.

We discussed these things openly, agreeing that we would find our way through living together honestly. We also made plans. Justin left the Brothers with nearly nothing of value, beyond an old car, a few pieces of clothing, and $5,000. What he had in abundance was knowledge and experience. There were people who valued his vineyard and winemaking expertise, and Justin had quickly begun consulting for them. So it made sense for us to settle in Napa Valley, where he knew so many people in the wine industry. There was a real community in the valley that he felt a part of.

During this time, we spent just about every weekend together. I was living with my parents and working at a Los Altos antique auto repair shop as a bookkeeper and babysitter to the owner's two-year-old. Justin was living in a little farmworkers shack in Rutherford on highway 29. His friend, Bernie Skoda, had bought the property and was developing a vineyard around the house.

Every other weekend I would drive to be with Justin. Every other weekend he would come down to Los Altos to be with me.

Sex? Oh yes.

For the first time in the five years of our relationship, we had no-holding-back sex. I began taking birth control pills and we embraced each other with wild passion and freedom. When Justin visited me, he would be assigned to the childhood bedroom of my older brother, Ron, who had moved out and married a couple of years before. My room was a few steps down the hall. Justin would come and go as quietly as he could manage, doing his best to not disturb the slumber of my younger brother and sister, both home from college for the summer.

Justin accepted the gift of a couple of twin beds for his little house on the highway. Because we were only betrothed, not married, we thought two beds showed the proper decorum to any visitors who might happen by. When nightfall came, we would move the beds together, make love and sleep in each other's arms.

The wine business was relatively small in those days. I knew of only 15 or 20 wineries in Napa Valley in 1972. Everyone knew Justin. Word about him leaving the Brothers spread quickly through the vintner grapevine. Some had seen me with BJ at a wine industry barbecue or technical conference when BJ and I played music together. Our friend and prominent viticulturist, Bob Steinhauer, tells a story about Justin and me during that period, when he was delivering a last load of grapes to the winery at Beaulieu Vineyards towards the end of the 1971 harvest. In the story, Bob is standing on the crush pad next to famed enologist, André Tchelistcheff, watching gondolas of grapes being dumped, de-stemmed and crushed. Bob sees Rollin Wilkinson and another guy dressed in a ragged sweatshirt and tennis shoes held together with athletic tape. They begin offering glasses of wine to everyone on the crush pad. Clearly, Rollin and this ragged fellow had already begun to celebrate the end of crush. He tells a couple of racy, off-color jokes, then he and Rollin are off to the next winery to spread good cheer.

Bob, a good Presbyterian, asks André, "Who is that guy?"

"That's Brother Justin," comes the reply.

"What?!"

Bob's image of a Christian Brother was someone who spent most of his time in church, dressed in black, and spoke in respectful, tones—not like this straggly-dressed hooligan passing out drinks.

The following summer, the wine industry's big annual viticulture and enology conference was held at the Hotel del Coronado in San Diego. Justin and I had just become engaged by then. We attended the conference with the Olmos as our official chaperones. Every night Justin and I were at the Friez & Friez hospitality suite for the late-night party and songfest. Justin and I had brought our instruments, and we played and people sang till the wee hours of the morning. At some point, Bob came by, looked through the doorway at the room filled with people singing, and saw the two of us in the center of it all.

He turned to the guy next to him and said, "Who is that?"

"That's Brother Justin."

"I know that," Bob said. "I mean who is that playing guitar with him?"

"Oh, that's his girlfriend."

"What?!" Bob had reconfigured his idea of monks enough to include Justin as a wild and woolly winemaker, but not yet enough to allow for girlfriends.

Justin and I thought we were putting on a good, proper face to the outside world. We found out later that the neighborhood farmers and the wine community in general talked about my weekend comings and goings during our engagement. Everyone looked closely to see if my little red sports car was parked outside Justin's house as they passed by. They particularly noted if it was there real early on Saturday or Sunday mornings. We were way more exposed and in the public eye than we realized. And apparently, we were hot news.

Yes ... And

Every couple knows that as soon as the bride-to-be says yes there is a lot of work to be done. In our case, there was a lot more than happy wedding planning.

Justin had been a Christian Brother for 15 years by then. There were hundreds of men and thousands of students who he was representing and supporting through his work at the winery. He needed to tell them all he was leaving the Brothers of the Christian Schools. He also needed to write letters and be officially released from his vows by the Pope.

Being a religious monk is a strong and very public identity, especially in BJ's case. It took tremendous courage to tell the members of his Christian Brothers community he was leaving. First, he shared his decision with Brothers he was closest to, the Brothers he lived and worked with, and then the greater Christian Brothers province. Some of the Brothers told him they felt betrayed and turned away from him. As hard as this was, the resentful Brothers tended to be the grouchy old men Justin didn't want to turn into. Other Brothers, like Timothy, remained strong supportive friends through his transition and beyond.

Justin left the Brothers in March of 1972. More than anything, he had wanted to remain at the Christian Brothers Winery to lead the business forward in the way Brother Bertram and everyone close to him had envisioned. This is what he had trained for at Davis and under

Brother Timothy's mentoring. The Christian Brothers, however, would not let him stay. He was 33 and had had the privilege of leading a staff of much older and more experienced men, by virtue of the fact that he was a Brother—a representative of the order that owned the winery. Having a non-religious winery president was not part of the Brothers' plan, nor could they imagine it as a new possibility

Justin was deeply wounded and disheartened by this. He had studied diligently at Davis so that he could lead the winery and distillery forward, creating more revenue and opportunity for the Christian Brothers schools and students. In the end, that short-sighted policy led to the eventual demise of the Christian Brothers winery and distillery; for they had turned away the only person who had the education, training and leadership ability to lead their business into a successful future.

In the early 1970s, the California wine industry, led by Napa Valley, had begun to change rapidly and dramatically. By 1980, a decade of change had put everything in place for a "boom" in consumption of California wine. Sadly, Christian Brothers winery missed the transition. After BJ left, the company slowly declined until it was sold to a spirits company, Heublein, in 1989. The history of wineries purchased by liquor companies in the U.S. is a sad one, and Christian Brothers was one of the first to go down that road. What pained Justin so much was that he knew this would not have happened if he had been in charge. Over the ensuing years, he offered business advice to the Brothers running the winery, but they would not or could not listen. His willing and wise counsel fell on ears not able to hear.

There were moments when Justin doubted himself, doubted he was doing the right thing. There were moments when he felt lost as the layers of relationships and roles he held were peeled back and taken away. He was no longer the cellar master's apprentice, no longer in charge of all Christian Brothers vineyards, no longer winery president-to-be, no longer important or meaningful to wine writers, customers, agents, restaurateurs, and distributors. He no longer had access to the tools of his trade. No pruning shears, no refractometer, no tractor, no vineyard, no crusher, no fermentation tanks, no barrels. In so many ways he was stripped naked of his identity, purpose, roles, and everything he had accomplished in his adult life.

All of a sudden, he was a 30-something with no job and almost no money. He was excited about starting his life with me, whom he loved deeply, but he had no clear idea how he was going to support us. His consulting business seemed promising, but there were precious few people pursuing that business model in 1972. The Christian Brothers winery community had also been the center of his social life. The people who worked at the various winery facilities were his friends, as were the presidents and winemakers of other Napa Valley wineries. Now he was suddenly without a basis of relationship for most of them. No official status, no ownership status.

Then Louis P. Martini called.

Mr. Martini's father had started growing wine grapes in Napa Valley and Sonoma County almost 40 years earlier. He would subsequently become a living legend, but at that time he represented one of the few local wine families with enough land and production to hire people outside the family to management positions.

Louis knew and respected Justin for his leadership, knowledge, and drive. They met, and he offered Justin a job. Justin deeply appreciated the offer, but he turned it down. He correctly understood that when you work for a family business, you can go only so far in the company before you bump into the family who will occupy the top leadership positions by birthright. He knew he would become frustrated without the authority to make critical decisions.

Justin met with Bill Jaeger, the managing partner at Freemark Abbey, a winery that had been making wine since the late 1800s. Bill encouraged him to take his time to consider what he wanted most. Justin thought about that. Turns out there was something he wanted.

The most valuable possession Justin carried with him to the little house on Highway 29 was a dream. It began with an experiment he had run at UC Davis involving aging Cabernet Sauvignon for different lengths of time in barrel and bottle. He expanded this experiment at Christian Brothers where he had the luxury of longer periods of time and more barrels. He became convinced that both barrel aging and bottle aging made a huge difference in the flavor and drinkability of Cabernet Sauvignon. Time allowed the natural, plentiful tannins in Cabernet to slowly bond with each other, forming longer molecules that would glide over and stimulate the taste buds rather than clogging and overwhelming them. This translated into a smoother, velvety- tasting experience.

Justin also recognized that American consumers generally drink a bottle of wine soon after they purchase it. This may sound normal and obvious, but back then the classic French model for Cabernet Sauvignon ruled the wine world. Under that model, producers sold their Cabernets a year or two after they made it, and then the buyers had to keep it for five to ten years—or more—so those tannin molecules could link up and mature into a silky, wonderful wine. Justin, raised in a working-class family, understood that most people did not have a wine cellar. If they drank Cabernet that was still young, they would miss out on most of what a great Cab could offer.

Then there was winegrowing, which preceded any issues of making or selling. Although he had never been to Europe, Justin knew that centuries of experience had taught the French and Italians that certain grape varieties produce better wine in certain areas. These wine regions or appellations would be given official names, and regulations would dictate which grapes could be planted there. That's why Cabernet Sauvignon is grown in Bordeaux, Pinot Noir is grown in Burgundy, Syrah is grown in Chateauneuf-du-Pape and Sangiovese in Chianti.

From his grape-buying expeditions and tasting various lots of Cabernet with Brother Timothy, Justin knew that California Cabernet Sauvignon was at its best when grown in the Napa and Alexander Valleys. He went so far as to assert that Cabernet is the only variety that should be grown and vinted in these two areas of northern California.

Justin may have left the Brothers and lost his position at the winery, but he did not lose his knowledge or convictions. He dreamed of building a winery that made only Cabernet Sauvignon from Napa Valley and Alexander Valley. He would age it long enough and carefully enough at the winery, so that it was already a beautiful, elegant, and luscious experience when people purchased it.

This was a radical dream, particularly for a young couple with no financial resources. Aging multiple vintages of wine is expensive, entailing what businesspeople call "excess inventory costs." Yet we talked about our dream winery with great excitement and purpose. We were two strong-minded people who loved to work hard and collaborate, and who knew anything was possible!

In the meantime, Justin was focused on making some money for us to live on, which was how he became a consultant. Fortunately, the timing was perfect. Many people were interested in establishing vineyards and wineries in new areas. When they called winery principals in the Napa Valley for advice, they were referred to Justin as someone who had expertise in both grape-growing and winemaking. Justin began to travel frequently to the Central Coast; Santa Inez, San Louis Obispo,

Temecula, and Santa Maria working for clients. He would identify promising vineyard sites and suggest grape varieties that would do well there. In a couple of instances, he got the chance to design wineries based on his understanding of efficient, high-quality wine production. Justin loved this work: meeting new people, seeing possibilities in new areas, and using all of his skills to help starry-eyed entrepreneurs establish new vineyards and wine production facilities.

I remember accompanying him on one of these trips, when he was working for Newhall Land and Farming. We spent a night under the stars in sleeping bags on Pismo Beach. Unaware that the camp site-parking lot was popular with folks harvesting clams, we were awakened pre-dawn as clam diggers walked past us to take advantage of a particularly low tide. We quickly rallied, jumped into our jeans and walked the beach with them watching for signs of life bubbling up from under the hard sand at the water's edge. It was thrilling to see a quick and skillful shovel maneuver score a large Pismo clam.

Throughout this time, I compassionately listened to Justin's struggles and shared his small successes; a connection here, a vineyard consulting job there. I was glad I never once encouraged him to leave his religious order, the Christian Brothers. I certainly had responded to his offers of friendship and affection but had never tried to seduce him away. As a result, I felt clean, without any sense of guilt or sense of being complicit in his decision. That was the good part. The challenging part was seeing him struggle and wondering how and when we would found our winery.

Chapter Ten

Justin Meyer pruning Bonny's Vineyard

Prayer for a Challenge

I really don't know what possessed me. But I remember the searing emotion and intention of it. I was alone in the house and filled with powerful spiritual fervor.

I had been attending Holy Cross Catholic High School for probably three years by then. I had learned to play the guitar by watching older girls play songs around the campfire and following their chord changes. I used that skill to learn the guitar accompaniment to songs from the "Hymnal for Young Christians" by Ray Repp and began leading our student body in liturgical folk music for our monthly school Masses. I had been inspired by the devotion, faith, love, and wisdom of some of my teachers who were Sisters of the Holy Cross. I had been filled with messages of how important it was to aspire to be Christ on earth; to be willing to spread love and care as well as be willing to suffer as He did on the cross for the good of all. In quiet meditation, I sought and experienced moments of pure joy and powerful connection with God.

It was probably all these things put together that moved me. I remember standing in a dimly lit hallway, my will and spirit reaching out to God and asking Him for the ultimate life challenge. Somehow, I knew I was up to the task, able to take on an unimaginable challenge that would hone my heart and spirit.

A couple of years later, I fell in love with Brother Justin: an impossible relationship. What followed were years of exquisite joy and deep anguish. Then, miraculously, we found our way as a couple, we flourished, we created Silver Oak and grew a family together. We also grew in love and passion for each other as every year went by. We would look into each other's eyes on every anniversary with wonder, knowing we were more in love than we had been the year before. Then, just as life was slowing down and becoming sweeter, Justin died.

I learned a long time ago that the human capacities for joy and sorrow are mirror images of one another. The epic love I felt for Justin was matched by epic grief; grief I both felt and ran from, fearing it would kill me or blow me apart. Because I was determined to stand my ground and rise in joy, it did neither.

My prayer has been answered. Nothing but the fierce crucible of committed relationship could have honed and burnished my heart and spirit like this.

The Hardest Thing

Being in love with Justin while he was a Christian Brother was by far the hardest thing I have ever done in my life. I was filled with ecstatic anticipation when I knew I was going to see him. Jubilant when we were together. Always discreet, doing my best to hide my love for him when we were in the company of others. Miserable after we parted, not knowing when the next time would be. Always, always, always holding and accepting that we could not be together as a couple.

He had taken vows. He had chosen a life of service for himself. Others had made a life around him; believed in him, depended upon him to keep his promises to them. No matter how deep and sacred we felt our love for one another was, we would never be able to fully consummate it. It would never come to full fruition in the form of a life and a family together. We would never have the children I longed to have with him.

During my time at UC Davis I dated other young men. I held strong intention to find someone else. Couldn't I fall in love with someone who was actually available? Someone near my age, no strings attached? Someone bright, happy and free? Please?

I would spend time getting to know these young men, laughing and enjoying time with them. I even received more than one marriage proposal. But in the end, I had to honestly tell them all that I was in love with someone else. Then I would walk home alone.

I don't know how I knew this, but I was absolutely certain that if I failed to have the courage to live my truth, I would pay dearly for the rest of my life. I could never bring myself to be less than absolutely impeccable with the men I dated by saying yes, when I secretly longed to be with someone else – even if that someone else and I were not free to be together. That would be a lie that would forever weigh on my soul. From time to time during those five years, Brother Justin and I would decide to stop. We would agree to not see each other again. Ever. We would kiss and cry and kiss some more. Then walk away in opposite directions with tears streaming down our faces.

There would be silence after that and many more tears, solitary tears. During those times of deep melancholy, I would take solace in my guitar, singing and playing songs of love lost.

Then at some point, for some reason, I would get a letter or a shaky phone call. Elated and scared I would respond. Then we would begin seeing each other again. He would, again, find an excuse to visit the university.

Those were the hardest times of my life; whether we were in or out of our impossible relationship. It didn't matter which.

The hardest times, until the day he died.

Chapter Eleven

Bonny & Justin Meyer on their wedding day, September 16, 1972

Deal with Ray Duncan

In mid-June of 1972, Justin received an offer that was better than anything he could have imagined, from a man he had met only a couple of times before.

Ray Duncan had experienced great success in the oil and gas business in Colorado. He was first attracted to the Napa Valley by his childhood friend, Jack Novak, who in early 1972 had purchased one of Napa Valley's heritage properties, the vineyard and winery in St. Helena known as Spottswoode Estate. The beauty of the countryside and Jack's boyish enthusiasm convinced Ray he should partner with Jack in some vineyard land, which included the Spottswoode vineyard and a hundred-acre parcel in the Alexander Valley to the north. While the Alexander Valley property was mostly hay, prunes and pears, it did have a block of young Cabernet Sauvignon vines. In homage to their friendship, Jack and Ray named their partnership Los Amigos Vineyards.

Ray came back to Napa from Colorado later that spring and spent time talking with Louis P. Martini, Robert Mondavi, and Brother Justin who was then managing all of the Christian Brothers vineyards. Little did he know he was talking to three future giants of the industry. To Ray, they were just hard-working men like himself, who happened to be unusually generous with their time and knowledge. It was the way in those days. A new fellow in town? Let's help him.

But they struggled to answer some of Ray's questions, particularly about which land had potential for vineyards. He would ask, "Why is there a vineyard on this piece of ground and not that piece over there?" More often than not, the response was, "I don't know." Viticulture was still a young science then. Ray decided he wanted better answers than that, so he sent his Colorado-based landman, Tom Connelly, to California to create what was probably the first map of land ownership in Napa Valley. He created a graphic rendering of public information garnered from Napa County tax records.

Ray and Tom took this map to their "technical team" of Louis, Robert, and BJ. They were particularly interested in purchasing land on the valley's broad, fertile floor, and ultimately focused their attention on the Keig Dairy ranch in Oakville, with its 500 acres of pasture, a silo, and some milking and hay barns. It was a large, beautiful, centrally located piece of ground that could be turned into a vineyard without too much difficulty. His vintner team agreed. Ray took an option on purchasing the property, contingent on financing. (Ever after Ray would quip, "Don't come to the Napa Valley in the springtime or you will buy more land than you had planned on!")

Ray quickly lined up financing from Connecticut Mutual, but it came with a requirement: Ray had to hire a professional vineyard manager to oversee the conversion of the pastureland to vineyard. Ray asked Brother Justin, who was still at Christian Brothers, if the Brothers would develop and manage the vineyard for him. BJ informed him that the Christian Brothers didn't custom farm for other parties, particularly not at that moment when they were already developing a couple of hundred acres of new vineyard land for their own winery. BJ was deep into this project, so he had his hands full.

Ray kept looking, but there were few experienced vineyard managers anywhere in California in those days, and like BJ they all had good jobs with growing companies. As Ray's option to purchase the Keig property came closer to expiring, Tom began calling all the people he had met in the valley, asking for any leads to a vineyard manager experienced enough to convince the bank to finance the sale.

There was no internet in those days, and people in the wine business were not sitting by a phone during the day. So the process moved slowly through the late spring of 1972. As it happened, that worked out to Ray's benefit. One day, Tom was on the phone to a valley vintner and heard some surprising news: Brother Justin had recently left Christian Brothers and was working as a consultant. Ray flew out from Denver the following day and arranged to have dinner with Justin that evening. The ancient farmworker house Justin was living in had no insulation and was hotter than Hades in June. So the two men ate their dinner outside. Over steaks barbecued on a portable hibachi, Ray asked if Justin would turn some Oakville pastureland into a vineyard for him. He was greeted with something south of enthusiasm. Justin was enjoying consulting and finding vineyards for people new to wine: he loved the challenge of intense research, then the completion of project reports and recommendations. He liked the people he was meeting and liked being his own boss. He could work hard then take a few days off before the next project began. At that moment, he was working on a significant project for Newhall Land and Farming, which had acquired a couple of thousand acres in the Santa Maria area.

Then Ray began to describe the Keig property. The south parcel was contiguous with the Napa River, and the north parcel bordered Conn Creek. That parcel included a ranch manager's house Justin could live in.

Now that got Justin's attention: a real house deep in the valley instead of a critter-infested hot box on the highway. But then Justin started talking about his dream of a winery where he would make great Cabernets. Ray began to see a potential problem here; he didn't want to hire someone to develop and run his vineyard if that person's heart was in the wine cellar instead. Ray asked Brother Timothy's protégé if he actually knew how to make wine. Met with a definitive yes, Ray suggested a 50/50 partnership in a winery based on the Keig property.

Done.

Silver Oak Cellars was conceived that evening in June at a rustic redwood picnic table by Highway 29 as the occasional car rolled by.

Just a couple of weeks later, over the fourth of July weekend, I helped Justin move his few possessions to the Keig ranch manager's house. Barbed wire fencing separated the house from dairy cattle still grazing in the fields. As we sat in the small breakfast nook in the kitchen, we communed with the dairy cows just 10 feet away, gazing at us as they peacefully and methodically chewed their cud. It was a simple house built on piled rocks around the 1880s, with a bit of grass in the front yard. No family had ever lived in this farmworker house long enough to plant a garden. But it was solid. A modern block foundation had been added to augment the original piled rocks. Justin and I were very excited. We would have a real house, shaded by two ancient old oaks, to raise a family in!

More important than this, we could pursue our dream of a Cabernet-only winery right away. Instead of boot-strapping it with our very limited resources, we would have Ray's financial strength and business experience to start out on solid footing.

When I look back and think about these two men, Justin at age 33 and Ray at 41, I am impressed by their boldness and the confidence that they could make big things happen. There were some nervous moments, especially in the beginning, but they had no fear. When I would express trepidation, Justin would just chuckle and say, "If it all goes to hell we can always go down to the cellar and drink some good wine!"

Before Ray left for his hotel that momentous night, he asked about the new winery going up across the highway. Justin laughed. It was called Franciscan, and it was sure to fail because it was a project put together by a bunch of San Francisco businessmen with no wine experience. He was right, Franciscan did go bankrupt – otwice in three years. What Justin didn't know that night was that he and I would be the ones to resurrect it for good.

Humble Beginnings

We were married in mid-September and honeymooned on the shores of Electra Lake in the mountains above Durango, Colorado. Ray Duncan had a family cabin there which he generously offered us for our first week together. We hiked during the day and fished late afternoons into the early evening when the lake was flat and the insects were out playing on the water's surface, enticing rainbow and brown trout to rise. I had never fished before but grew to enjoy it, and proudly caught my fair share of fish which we savored for dinner each night or breakfast the next morning. We explored the cowboy town of Durango and rode the narrow-gauge railroad to Silverton the day the first snowflakes of the season fell. It was a magical and memorable interlude between single life and marriage, away from all responsibilities.

Los Amigos Vineyard in the Alexander Valley, the property Ray had purchased with boyhood friend Jack Novak, had a few acres of producing Cabernet Sauvignon vines. The Keig Ranch had a small Zinfandel vineyard on it that Christian Brothers had some interest in. So Justin arranged for Brother Timothy to take the Zinfandel grapes in exchange for letting us use the Christian Brothers winery to crush our first vintage of Silver Oak Cabernet Sauvignon. This was all accomplished seamlessly given Justin's close relationship with Brother Tim and the cellar crew there. On cue, Dane Petersen, the Los Amigos vineyard manager, let Justin know the Cabernet had reached optimum maturity by late September. As we were flying back from Colorado, Dane delivered just over 18 tons of Alexander Valley Cabernet to

Christian Brothers winery as planned. Thus, the first vintage of Silver Oak was crushed the same week we were married.

Sometimes I'm asked how we managed to get Silver Oak off the ground and I begin by saying, "When we were married, the sum total of our fortune was a dog and a car. Justin had the dog and I had the car." The real truth, is that in addition to Sam, Justin's Golden Retriever, and my sporty little red Capri, we both had good university educations, some solid work experience, and, with Ray, a supportive financial partner who provided the all-important collateral for bank loans and lines of credit along the way. But that came into play later.

The day after Justin and Ray's handshake agreement to found a winery, Ray gave Justin a tour of the 500-acre dairy property that Justin would convert to a vineyard. In addition to the loamy valley floor soils and location, Justin took special note of the solid cement barn that for all intents and purposes felt like a wine cellar to him.

So it began. Just after we moved Justin into the house over the July fourth weekend, he immediately began designing the vineyard layout with its irrigation and frost protection systems. By that fall, the whole property was planted to new vines except for the four-acre pasture of clover in front of our house. That field was left, at least for a time, as a playground for the horse Justin had promised me as a wedding gift. Following vinification, our first young Cabernet was aged in new American oak barrels in the cool cement barn once used to store milk.

Justin loved going over to his precious milk barn winery to check on the barrels and top them up as the wine very slowly evaporated through the wood of the barrels. Occasionally he would transfer, or "rack," wine from one barrel to another. I was delighted to be there with him and serve as his original "cellar rat," a wine industry term for workers who follow the winemaker's instructions in the cellar, whether it's moving barrels, pulling hoses, or running pumps.

I had made hundreds of experimental wines in Dr. Olmo's lab, but I was unfamiliar with cellar equipment at first. That changed in a hurry. Justin and I regularly topped the barrels to leave no room for oxygen; otherwise the dreaded acetobacter, a bacterium that turns alcohol into acid, could turn our fresh young wine into vinegar. Working together, we quickly and easily found ourselves moving in sync, beautifully echoing the way we made music together, each anticipating the other's next move as we went from barrel to barrel. It was a new kind of rhythm for me, but I caught on quickly. And I loved being in the cellar with him.

The dim light, the aromas of the wine mixed with the scents of oak and Justin; Old Spice and vineyard grit. I know he loved having me there too; partners in this grand new adventure together. From time to time he would look at me and smile, then surprise me with a squirt from the hose, or steal a passing kiss.

Tico Taco

Justin asked me what I would like for a wedding present. He would tell friends later that he was hoping I would say, "You!" Instead my reply was, "A horse!"

I learned to ride when I was a girl scout. Our whole troop took riding lessons at nearby Pink Horse Ranch. We rode English style and I learned a proper trot, canter, and how to jump over small gates. When our lessons were over, I continued to go to the ranch to ride. I would clean out stalls in exchange for a couple of hours of riding privileges.

I continued to ride horses at UC Davis, taking lessons in Western style and enjoying the fine horses they kept there on campus. Naturally, I begged my father for a horse when I was a teenager, but was never successful. Now that I would be living in the country with Justin, I figured there would be room to keep one.

My wonderful, patient, and loving husband-to-be Justin said yes. He didn't even hesitate, despite the fact that he had had a horse as a kid and knew better than I did how much work and trouble it could be to keep one at home. Soon after we were married, he set to work building a corral in front of the ranch house then made sure the four-acre clover field in front was well fenced and secure. He surprised me with a beautiful leather and suede saddle for my birthday soon thereafter.

In the spring, we visited Stewart Dairy to look at a three-year-old half Arabian, half Quarter Horse Justin had scouted out. He was a beautiful roan with a white blaze, white socks and the sweet, friendly disposition Arabs are known for—spiced with a mischievous sense of humor. He would follow me around the clover pasture, tracking me more like a dog than a horse. If he sensed his rider did not know how to take charge, he would kick up his heels and give them the run-around. On a sunny day, he would lie down in the clover and I would lie beside him, resting my head on his neck or belly. He was that kind of horse. I named him Tico Taco.

Maui, First Time with Mom

In the winter of 1973, my mother called and invited me to join her and her best friend, Barbara, on a Hawaiian vacation. Without hesitation, I declined. Justin and I had been married for only four months and I didn't want to even entertain the idea of leaving him to go on a vacation, much less to a romantic destination like Hawaii. A couple of weeks later I casually mentioned my mother's invitation to him. His response was also immediate: "Go! Go to the islands. I never want to go there because the beaches are too crowded, and I don't like crowds. This is your chance. Go!"

So, I packed my bikini and a couple of pairs of shorts and joined Barbara, my mom, and a random group of other tourists on an organized vacation tour that included Maui and Kauai. We arrived, received plumeria leis, and boarded the bus headed to the Royal Lahaina Resort. The hotel had just added a distinctive high-rise building to its traditional garden bungalows. But we happily talked the front desk into giving us an "inferior" bungalow accommodation nestled among the orchids, hibiscus, and ginger.

To say I was surprised and delighted with all the sights, sounds, and experiences of the Hawaiian Islands would be an understatement. The moment I began to descend onto the tarmac I was enveloped in fragrant, warm, moist air. To this day, the warm smell of plumeria carried on the breeze is my "welcome back home" when I return. The Royal Lahaina had an open-air dining room with birds flying freely in and out. Those birds and their cousins woke me up just before dawn every morning with a loud cacophony of twitters, squawks, and calls.

One afternoon I rented a mask and snorkel and had the time of my life floating on the surface looking down. I was fascinated by the wave patterns in the sand and the occasional school of translucent fish, which blended in amazingly well with water and ocean floor. (I was unaware that just 300 yards down the beach there was a verdant reef, home to a rainbow array of Butterfly Fish, Moorish Idols and the Hawaiian state fish: Humuhumunukunukuapua'a.) I got the worst sunburn of my life that day on my back and the backs of my legs, lulled into complacency by the cool water and losing all sense of time.

My mother and Barbara had been to Maui before and knew the ropes. They knew all the restaurants that would send a car for us. One memorable evening we ate at Pineapple Hill. An old plantation owners' home, it was a large Hawaiian-style house with lush gardens and gregarious parrots that greeted diners at the front door. That evening, I had turtle soup garnished with fino sherry. It was delicious and so memorable I can still taste it in my imagination. Turtle soup, of course, has been banned from menus everywhere for some years now. But I am happy I had it once upon a time when sea turtles were plentiful, and I could enjoy it in naïve bliss.

My most memorable experience on Maui was aboard a sunset sailing trip. The afternoon was perfect, the mai tais and puu puus abundant and delicious, and the trade winds brisk. I spent just about the entire time on the trampoline suspended between the twin hulls of our catamaran, dressed in my bathing suit. The ocean spray that came up through the webbing was fun and refreshing. As we cruised along, I took plenty of photographs of the coastline. In '73 there were only two hotels on Kaanapali Beach: the Sheraton and the Royal Lahaina. Everywhere else, sugar cane fields descended to the sand. I wanted Justin to see the farmland and uncrowded beaches.

When I returned home I shared all these sights, sounds, and experiences with him. I told him that the resorts were filled with old people celebrating their 25th anniversaries huddled in the shade of palm trees around the pool. No one was in the ocean! I considered this such a waste, because with all the water sports and the great weather, Hawaii was ideal for young people. We should not wait until we are too old and decrepit to enjoy it. I showed Justin my photographs of the Kaanapali shoreline and exclaimed, "See, it is all agriculture! You would love it!"

Magical Maui

Five years later Justin and I got our chance to go to the islands together. The instigator was a man named Wayne Cody, better known as "The Mate," whom we knew from Napa Valley. The Mate had found his way to Napa from his native New Zealand via southern California. When he first arrived to surf the southern California beaches, he found a job at a surf shop owned by Jack Novak, Ray Duncan's partner in Los Amigos Vineyards. Because he was strong and willing, The Mate was invited to move north with the Novak family to help restore the Spottswoode

Estate in St. Helena. The Mate put his surfboard in storage and moved into the estate's carriage house. For two years Jack and The Mate spent their days restoring the historic main house, now the Novak family home. When the restoration was complete, he worked for the family as a nanny to the five Novak children: every day an adventure. At some point, The Mate's sister, Jill, came from New Zealand to help with the children.

The Mate and his surfer friend, Graham, turned their energy and some rudimentary construction knowledge to building vineyard irrigation pump houses and doing other odd jobs in the vineyard for Justin and Dane Petersen, our vineyard manager. When Justin and I bought a Sunfish to sail in the vineyard reservoir, The Mate and Graham excitedly helped me rig the sail and launch it on its maiden voyage. Catching the afternoon breezes, sailing back and forth in the middle of the vineyard, delighted all of us. (People driving by on Oakville Cross Road would wonder and shake their head when they saw the red, white and blue sail going back and forth in a sea of vines.) There are other legendary stories about The Mate leading a vineyard planting crew to a higher degree of performance ... and being chased through the vineyard by our Rhode Island Red rooster, Tommy.

But eventually, ocean waves began to call. One afternoon in late fall, The Mate came into the vineyard office and announced that he was going to Maui for the winter to surf. He would be back in the spring, he said.

He did not return. Instead, he called to say he had gotten a job as a wine sommelier at the Maui Surf Hotel. He really didn't know much more than the average person about wine, but no one there could tell. He had arrived from Napa Valley, right? Later he got a construction job, laying the wood floor in Kimo's Restaurant on Front Street. When the construction was completed, he became a waiter there. His New Zealander buddy Graham and sister Jill joined him on Maui shortly thereafter. Graham started working as a real estate broker and Jill signed on as a salesperson in the Hobie Shop next door to Kimo's.

Within a year or two, Graham had sold a beautiful rambling house to John McVie of the rock band Fleetwood Mac, then at the height of its fame. John was on the road recording and performing with the band most of the time, so he needed a caretaker for his new island home. Graham proposed a perfect solution: The Mate, who immediately moved in.

That's when we got the call. The Mate said, "Come to Maui! I am living in John McVie's house and he is never here. I am in this huge house all by myself and there is plenty of room for you to stay. Come to Maui and I will pick you up at the airport!"

So we came. We landed. We looked for The Mate. We called. No answer. We waited. Finally, we rented a car and headed to Lahaina town. We drove very slowly down Front Street, which in those days was a very sleepy street in midafternoon. We spotted the sign for Kimo's. "I think that's the name of the restaurant where The Mate works," I said. We parked and went in.

There was a group of young local guys hunched over the bar nursing their drinks and swapping stories.

Justin asked, "Anybody here know where I can find Wayne Cody?"

"Who, The Mate? You can't," was the response.

"What do you mean, we can't?"

"He is in Los Angeles at the Grammy Awards!"

And so, he was. John McVie had invited The Mate to the Grammys at the last minute and he had hopped on a plane. He totally forgot we were coming.

"We're supposed to stay at his house," we said,

"Wayne's sister Jill cleans the house, and she has a key." "How do we find Jill?"

"She works at the Hobie Shop next door."

Luckily for us, Wayne's sister Jill was at the shop that day and said she would meet us at the house with the key when she got off work.

She not only let us in, she organized a big dinner party that night. We bought groceries and cooked, and Jill brought a group of friends who were working in restaurants and tourist shops. It was a memorable night. I can still picture us, about 15 people crowded around the dining room table laughing and having a great time in John McVie's spectacular Maui home.

While we were partying, Fleetwood Mac won the 1978 Album of the Year award for their "Rumours" album—still my all-time favorite Fleetwood Mac album. A couple of days later, The Mate arrived back in Maui ... with John and his girlfriend Julie.

Surprise!

We immediately prepared to pack and find another place to stay, but John graciously insisted we continue to stay in his home. He and Julie stayed in the master suite at the north end of the house while Wayne,

Justin and I stayed in the "kids wing" on the south side. Every morning we invited John and Julie to dinner later that day, and every afternoon when we returned from the beach, they declined. We watched whales breach and spout, we snorkeled, heard whale songs and saw reef fish of every shape and color. We explored and we socialized with Wayne, Jill, Graham, and their friends.

We enjoyed getting to know John and Julie and the other members of the band who came to Maui to celebrate their well-earned Grammy success and accolades. We shared our wine, John shared his home, Justin cooked. Everyone had a marvelous time. John invited us to come back again and stay. We did.

Another important connection occurred during our initial trip to Maui. We met the owners and managers of Kimo's Restaurant where The Mate was working. Rob Thibaut and Sandy Saxten liked our Silver Oak wines and we struck up a business relationship and friendship that has lasted a lifetime. TS Restaurants began with Kimo's in Lahaina, and expanded to include other restaurants on Maui, Kauai and Waikiki as well as Del Mar, Malibu, La Jolla and Lake Tahoe in California. They take pride in saying all TS Restaurants have two things in common: Silver Oak and Hula Pie.

Those connections with The Mate, John McVie, and the folks from TS Restaurants, along with the magic of Maui, kept us coming back almost every other year. Justin would conduct wine tastings for the TS staff and other restaurateurs. Sometimes we would come by ourselves, sometimes we would bring our kids.

Coming to Maui is bittersweet now. I come alone.

Magus Maui

I am the ocean
Waves cracking like pistol shot
Erupting through blow holes
Womb of Life
Caressing the shoreline

I am the trade winds
Whipping water into frothy peaks
The devastating hurricane
The tropical breeze
Whispering ancient Island wisdom

I am the morning mynahs
The cooing doves
Gentle laughter, talking story
Slack key riffs
And intricate whale song

I am the warm Island sun
Rainbows playing on coral reefs
Kissing flowers, radiating mana
Relentless, burning, beating down
Soft dawn and evening glow

I am the regal orchid
The red banana blossoms
Fragrant plumeria
And the exquisite tuberose
Reminding you of heaven's scent

I am pineapple rain
Sudden downpours
Flash floods
Water falling through lava fingers
Filling black lava hands

I am mystic Haleakala
The pali in the rain
Sacred Black Rock
Pele's molten tresses
Turned to stone

I am the rising mauka moon
Smiling above the West Mountains
Hanging in the midnight sky
Waves shimmering silver/gold
Melting into the horizon

I am Magus Maui
Wherever I walk
The sun, moon, ocean, and fragrant wind
The lava, laughter, and rain pour forth
From my Aloha heart

Chapter Twelve

Justin, Chad, Holly, Bonny, and Matt Meyer in front of Silver Oak Cellars

Family & Winery

Our family life and winery life evolved and unfolded together. When Silver Oak's first grapes were crushed the same week we were married, it set the tone for the next thirty years. Our love affair, winery, and family life continued to be inextricably intertwined.

By mid-1975, the 500 acres of grapes Justin had planted in the fall of 1972 were ready to offer up their first commercial crop—about the same time I was ready to give birth to our first child. We had readied a place in our house for the new baby, but unfortunately, we were not able to do the same for the grapes. There were too many new vineyards in the Napa Valley, all starting to produce at the same time. To everyone's surprise, the price and demand for valley fruit unexpectedly plummeted. There were no wineries eager to buy 500 acres of untested Cabernet grapes from a former pasture. And we were just weeks from harvest. Ray Duncan was in dire need of a winery to purchase and process his grapes. So we bought one.

It was Franciscan, the winery across the street from Justin's first little vineyard house. As Justin had predicted, its out-of-town owners had mismanaged it. They sold it to a Canadian company that also failed with it. In just a three-year period Franciscan had gone from working winery to double bankruptcy. With Justin's support and urging, Ray appeared before the bankruptcy judge with a cashier's check from a bank and bought Franciscan on the spot. Our first-born son, Chad, was born the same week we took over ownership.

Franciscan struggled to sell wine for the oldest reason of all: much of it wasn't very good. Justin and I would change all that. We took possession of the facility in mid-August. Justin led the effort to get the cellar ready for crush. I was in charge of getting the tasting room open and making the winery and the grounds look inviting after years of neglect. I was up on a ladder painting the interior columns in the tasting room when I noticed I kept having what felt like curiously strong

Chadwick, Justin, and Matthew Meyer outside the original Silver Oak Cellars milking barn cellar

Justin Meyer and daughter Holly picking grapes in Bonny's Vineyard

menstrual cramps. By early the next morning I realized those cramps were labor pains. Chad was born at noon.

It was love at first sight for me and Justin with our newborn son, and I spent a couple of quiet days in the hospital healing from the birth and learning how to nurse him. But the winery could not wait. A few days later I was back at Franciscan, directing painters and landscapers with Chad on my chest in a baby carrier. Our goal was to open the tasting room by October 1st and we had just four weeks to get everything done.

One of the challenges was clearing out the failed winery's inventory. The bottled wine had been bank collateral, and the lender took possession in the bankruptcy. (It's not uncommon for a winery business, a facility, and wine inventory to have the same name but separate financial status.) Knowing that the bank didn't really want to deal with the bottled wine, we offered to take it on as a project. We would give the bank 50 cents a bottle—probably more than they could get in a liquidation sale—and we would sell the wine for $1 a bottle and keep the rest. The bank readily agreed. Now we had to sell a lot of wine fast. Some of the wines were good and some of them weren't. We figured if we gave everyone a chance to taste the wines, customers could decide for themselves if they liked it and wanted to take a few bottles or boxes home.

We still needed to get people to stop at a winery that had no reputation for anything worth stopping for. So we hired a company to fly a replica of a hot air balloon with a sign attached that read; "Wine Sale." Our hearts sank opening morning when we arrived and found that the event company had traded out our classy hot air balloon for something that looked like a miniature yellow dirigible. So now we had a yellow blimp flying over our winery! It did get people's attention though ... probably because it was too ugly to miss. There was a photo of this mini dirigible balloon on the front page of the local newspaper, the St. Helena Star. We ended up getting a lot of flak from the wine community for flying something so tacky over our winery. Vintners were trying to bring a bit more dignity and professionalism to the Napa Valley wine scene and here we were looking like the grand opening of a gas station. They were probably asking each other, "What were those crazy kids thinking?"

Meanwhile, we were wondering something else: would anyone show up for our sale? Then we opened the doors ... and were inundated. With baby Chad in my front carrier, I worked the cash register and helped people with their wine purchases while others poured samples for eager customers. Our dollar-a-bottle sale became famous and continued through the winter until all the Franciscan wine was gone. That sale helped us keep the lights on for the first number of months.

After the sale, which was all-hands-on-deck, Justin and I settled into our respective roles based on our talents. Justin naturally was master of the cellar and in charge of general management. I was in charge of the tasting room, which meant organizing the flow and setting a welcoming tone of friendliness. I also was in charge of the building exterior and interior and creating a new visual identity for Franciscan, including wine labels, business logo, and stationery design.

It was particularly ironic that the original Franciscan label featured an image of a Franciscan monk. Given that no monks were ever involved in the enterprise, Justin, as a former monk, was of course adamant that any reference to, or suggestion of, the Franciscan religious order had to go. Most Napa Valley wine labels in the mid-70s featured fine line drawings of the winery. That would do, as our new winery was distinctive and lent itself to this type of representation. I hired an artist and together we redesigned the labels for bottles and cases, the letterhead, and all the other business collateral. The result was well integrated into every aspect of our marketing and, more importantly, a more honest representation of who we were.

I would bring Chad to the winery so I could nurse him during the day. There he became known as the "chairman of the board" as he was often asleep in his straw basket on top of the boardroom table. I was at Franciscan three or four days a week to work in the tasting room and on design tasks. When Chad was less than a year old, I realized I was expecting again; it was perhaps not the best idea to be constantly lifting cases of wine onto the counter or into customers' cars. So, I transitioned out of the tasting room and began keeping accounts and organizing winery events.

Our son Matt arrived on New Year's Eve, which made our celebration even sweeter. We had two children, a working winery, and a producing vineyard. Now we just had to keep up with it all.

This next stage was a blur. Justin worked hard perfecting the wines and forging deals with distributors all over the country. I juggled my work responsibilities, two babies, babysitters, play groups, and social events. We both were deep into growing vines, a winery, and our family.

Franciscan Winery

Within five short years, Justin, working like crazy and leveraging his Christian Brothers' distributor contacts, took Franciscan from bankruptcy to national distribution in all 50 states with a roster of delicious, well-made wines. What started as a hodgepodge of odd varieties and generic gallon jugs of Chablis and Burgundy was transformed into a strong line-up of popular well-made varietal wines.

We knew promoting Franciscan was important, but we didn't have a budget for advertising. Justin came up with the idea of writing a monthly wine education column which we made available free of charge to newspapers all over the country. His column offered general wine knowledge that helped consumers feel more comfortable tasting and talking about wine. It also supported brand recognition for us by simply including "Franciscan Vineyards" under his name at the bottom. This brilliant idea helped create more confident wine drinkers, it helped our distributors sell more wine in general, and that helped us sell more Franciscan. Everybody came out ahead.

By 1980 the facility was attractive and welcoming. The bushes and trees that we so hurriedly planted just before our opening in October of 1975 had filled out. With a maturing landscape, gracious tasting room and friendly, knowledgeable staff, Franciscan was humming as never before.

The late 70s and early 80s were a time of great opportunity and expansion in the Napa Valley. Eighteen wineries were founded in the Napa Valley in 1972, Silver Oak among them. All became widely known and influential. The "Class of '72," as they are sometimes called, heralded a new era in the wine industry. The winemakers and grape growers, like Justin, had learned their craft in the halls of UC Davis and Fresno State, so their wines were technically superior to those grown and made by folks who did it the way grandfather did. There was a strong movement away from gallon jugs of mixed red and white grapes toward wines of superior quality made mainly from one variety and from a single vintage year. Then came the so-called "Judgment of Paris" in 1976, when a Chateau Montelena Chardonnay and a Stags Leap Cabernet from Napa Valley topped much more famous French counterparts in a blind tasting held in Paris, with French judges. This told the world that Napa Valley wines were to be taken seriously and could clearly hold their own with wines from famous French producers. The Europeans took notice. In California, they saw a combination of promising wines and available land, coupled with a favorable exchange rate. Soon long-established European wine companies were coming to Napa Valley looking to purchase fledgling wineries.

An established brandy and fruit juice producer from Germany, Michael Eckes, noticed our success and paid particular attention. He approached Justin about buying Franciscan. Justin told him that Franciscan was not for sale. Ultimately, Michael and his team made us an offer that was too good to refuse, and we sold Franciscan to the Eckes family in early 1980. As part of the deal, Justin agreed to stay on for two years to run Franciscan while the new owners got up to speed. We journeyed to Germany as a family to tour Michael's various production facilities in May that year. During the course of that month-long tour, symptoms I now recognized as morning sickness returned, heralding yet another little miracle for me and Justin.

With the sale of Franciscan, Justin and I had enough money to remodel the 1880's farmworker house we lived in. We had already purchased it from Ray Duncan four years earlier, and we had been thinking and dreaming about fixing it up ever since. We hired Ray Rector, an architect who, in the late 1960s had transformed the old Groezinger Winery, a beautiful brick building that served as the architectural focal point of the town of Yountville. The result was known as Vintage 1870, an open-architecture facility that preserved the character of the original stone and brick building while giving it new life with contemporary shops, restaurants and offices. I felt he was the perfect person to help us renovate our old farmhouse.

Then I saw his first design sketches, and my heart sank.

I realized that I wanted a house unlike the ones I had grown up in, that I lived in now, and that everyone else I knew was living in. These houses all had separate living rooms and dining rooms that people didn't use all that often. They had small kitchens that felt crowded like ours did when our children joined me or Justin there —which was pretty much whenever they could. So, I had the idea of incorporating our living, dining, and kitchen functions in one big room. Today everyone calls this a "great room." We didn't have a name for it in the 1970s because almost nobody actually had one. Fortunately, Ray Rector understood. Together we designed a large, rustic great room with a kitchen in one corner, a large dining table across from it, a music corner (of course!), and a fireplace in the final corner. We decked the open-beam pyramid ceiling with old-growth redwood staves salvaged from wine tanks from an old abandoned winery.

The day after we left for Germany to visit the Eckes, the entry and kitchen of our farmhouse home were demolished. We returned a month later to live in the "pool house"—a former carport that The Mate had helped us convert into guest quarters.

Because we were on a tight budget, I was the contractor of record for our major home remodel. Every morning I conferred with our builder to answer questions and make on-the-fly decisions. Then I would drop off our two boys at the babysitter and head to work above Groezinger's wine shop at Vintage 1870 in the little office I had rented there to manage Silver Oak.

Building projects always proceed slower than you think. We were planning to use the completed great room for our annual Christmas caroling party because Justin and I couldn't think of a better way to christen our new living space. As delays accumulated, we picked out a 25-foot Christmas tree that would touch the high rafters. I bought some cheap red balls and baby's breath since I knew we didn't have enough ornaments to decorate such a large tree. We organized the wine and the song sheets. We were ready for anything!

Without warning, my water broke on the newly finished tile floor the morning we moved back into the main house. Because Holly was my third child, I stayed only one night at the hospital— and that at the hospital's insistence. Two days later we hosted our first Christmas caroling party in our house with the huge Christmas tree in the center of the new great room.

I sat on the sofa surrounded by around 70 friends and their families, holding two-day-old Holly in my arms. She was dressed in a tiny Santa Claus suit. Justin was behind me in the center of our new room joyously leading the singing with a celebratory glass of Silver Oak in his hand. Our artist friend, Diane Peterson, had brought her French-Canadian parents to the party. Her father sat across from me singing, sipping brandy and sweetly weeping with the joy of it all.

Silver Oak Early Years

Justin oversaw the hundred-acre Los Amigos property in Alexander Valley as it was converted from some prunes, pears and vines to a beautiful Cabernet Sauvignon vineyard. The 1972, 1973 and 1974 Silver Oak Cabernet grapes all came exclusively from that vineyard and were all crushed and vinted at Christian Brothers. Silver Oak enthusiasts will remember that the appellation on those early labels was listed as "North Coast." Wine regulations require wineries to state the name of the place that the grapes come from on every bottle. These districts are called "appellations," Napa Valley is the most famous appellation in California, as it was then. We were sure that no one in the mid-70s would know where the Alexander Valley was. The "North Coast" appellation technically includes anywhere in Napa, Sonoma, and Mendocino counties. It had been featured in a popular ad for the Italian Swiss Colony winery and therefore sounded familiar to wine-drinkers. After Silver Oak became well known, of course, a lot more people recognized Alexander Valley as a respected winegrowing region. We used the appellation proudly from the 1975 vintage on.

Following vinification, the first young wines were all aged in new American oak barrels in the former milk storage barn near our home in Oakville. By the 1974 vintage, we needed more room, so we insulated the adjacent milking barn and the 1974 vintage rested there. Justin never missed a chance to visit both buildings to check the barrels. He would walk in the door and stop for a moment to inhale the wonderfully familiar cellar aroma of oak mixed with Cabernet. Then he would walk around the barrel racks, knocking on each barrel head listening for any hint of a hollow sound and looking carefully for leaks. Justin not only had a beautifully intimate relationship with me, he also had an intimate relationship with each barrel of wine. He would tune in and listen. Satisfied all was well, he would walk back out into the sunshine and exhale.

There is a photograph of a motley group of vineyard employees and friends in front of the milk storage barn in the summer of 1975. It was a banner day as we were bottling the inaugural 1972 vintage of Silver Oak with hand-operated equipment, me very pregnant with Chad. Later on, Chad and his younger brother Matt helped out at our dairy barn cellar once they were big enough to hold a hose. There is a photo of Matt when he was about three rinsing a barrel and inadvertently getting a face-full of water when he missed the bung hole of the barrel and the spray bounced right back at him.

When we bought Franciscan in August 1975, Silver Oak Cabernets were made, aged, and bottled at Franciscan along with the Franciscan wines. Silver Oak's general business and sales were also handled by Franciscan personnel, with the wines often sold alongside each other to wine shops and restaurants.

In addition to the vinification, aging, bottling, and sales of our Silver Oak wines, various departments within Franciscan had taken on bits and pieces of running the business end of Silver Oak. With the sale of Franciscan, it was important to gather and consolidate everything under the Silver Oak name: California and out-of-state sales, marketing, bookkeeping, licensing, compliance—in short, everything but the farming and winemaking. With Justin committed to manage Franciscan, I took over managing Silver Oak.

It sounds so simple to write this now. But at the time, women did not run winery businesses. Yes, they were partners in marriage and, therefore, in a community property state, financial partners in wineries with their husbands. But the men ran things. Justin and I didn't think this way. We equally shared our dreams and plans and how to get things done. For example, he had joined my band at the Newman Center, not the other way around. I had joined him in Dr. Olmo's lab and the cellar as we topped barrels. Our history was one of collaborating out of pleasure and success, not of focusing on who was leading what. When we went into the wine business we didn't worry about our genders, we worried about the long list of tasks we had ahead of us each day.

Working in an office at Vintage 1870 was wonderful. I was initially attracted by the convenience of the copy machine and receptionist I shared with other tenants. Then I met the tenants and realized how lucky I was. Across the hall was Pam Hunter, who had just launched her wine-focused PR company; around the corner was Jay Corley, a fellow vintner who was in the early stages of creating Monticello Vineyards winery. I came to enjoy spontaneous hallway conversations with Pam and Jay as we shared the trials and tribulations of business development and facility design.

I learned how to sell wine from Tom Gosh in Los Angeles and Larry Maguire in the Bay Area. In those days women simply didn't go into the back rooms of wine shops and restaurant kitchens. It was a man's world.

I ignored the warnings about leering wine shopkeepers and the Playboy centerfolds thumbtacked to their office walls. I showed up, pregnant with Holly, eager to support and expand Silver Oak wine sales. At first, I was a little nervous entering these cluttered male sanctuaries, but I soon realized that the wine shop owners and wine buyers enjoyed talking first-hand with a winery owner. They generally enjoyed learning about our wines, hearing my stories and the latest news from the Napa Valley. There was only one other woman I know of who plied this all-male territory in the mid-1970s: Janet Trefethen, whose family owned Trefethen Vineyards. We must have done our job well because within a couple of decades, there were as many women in wine sales as men. Distributors realized that the fairer sex were naturals when it came to representing fine wines.

I sold Silver Oak wines directly in California, which meant we did not use a middleman or distributor. At first, we had a few dozen direct accounts with restaurants and wine shops around the state. Soon there were hundreds. All of them needed a personal visit or a phone call on a regular basis. After about a year on my own, I hired a part-time bookkeeper and another salesperson to help carry the load, because national sales were also growing, which meant managing different distributors for each state. I vividly remember nursing Holly while on the phone with a particularly difficult distributor in New York, who was trying to pull one over on me. I had a business and a family to protect. He did not succeed.

Once we sold Franciscan, our minds turned to the next big project: creating our own winery in Oakville. Crushing our wine at other wineries was not convenient, and our two former dairy barns on the old Keig property could not hold all the barrels we needed. We were renting cellar space all over the valley. Our vision of cellaring our Cabernet Sauvignons until they were really ready to drink, not at the earliest opportunity, meant we needed more and more cellar space. We needed a real winery with a large cellar where Justin could focus on perfecting each vintage he made.

From 1980, the year we sold Franciscan and Holly was born, until 1982, Justin and I designed and built the Silver Oak Cellars winery in Oakville on the site of the original dairy, incorporating the milking and milk storage barns where we had stored our first barrels and hand-bottled our first Silver Oak vintage. We wanted to always be connected to our roots, our humble beginning. After a positive collaborative experience with architect Ray Rector on our house, I partnered with him again to design our winery.

At first, he sketched a building reminiscent of a Napa Valley barn. This made sense given the dairy site and the barns that remained on the property. But for Justin and me, it wasn't quite right. We began to talk about and visit the wineries we loved. Silver Oak was made in an elegant style, and we wanted a facility that reflected this esthetic. Together we drove all over the valley looking at other wineries for inspiration. We ultimately realized we were most inspired by historic Greystone, the Christian Brothers tasting room and champagne cellars where Justin used to work. So, instead of a barn, we built a more classic, split-faced block winery with high dormer windows to let light into the cellar. When the winery was completed, Justin, Ray Rector, and I were surprised and very pleased that Silver Oak won an architectural award for the most beautiful commercial facility constructed in Napa County that year. I'm not sure anyone noted that the leader of the design process was a woman.

We moved into our new winery just prior to the 1982 crush, and held two huge open house celebrations to welcome the Napa Valley winemaking community and our friends. Silver Oak Cellars had a real home for the first time since it had been founded ten years earlier.

A few choice employees migrated with us from Franciscan to Silver Oak. As Justin and the early staff arrived and took on tasks, my responsibilities narrowed and focused. The exterior and interior design of our new winery was finished. I turned to refining our Silver Oak labeling and packaging designs and to overseeing sales, marketing and messaging.

This focus was not only at the heart of what I enjoyed the most, but it was also project-based and worked well as I juggled working and caring for our growing family. The children were now 2, 6, and 7, and I enjoyed being actively involved with them at home and in their schools.

The next two decades were a beautiful blend of growing Silver Oak and nurturing children. I worked at the winery primarily during school hours so I could be home with the children for homework and after-school activities. When I had to work into the late afternoon or early evening, they would be at the winery; drawing pictures for the staff, playing in the barrel racks and later helping in the tasting room. The winery was definitely their home away from home.

The kids joined 4-H and raised sheep, chickens, and rabbits. I became the Rutherford 4-H leader for a time. Our small barn and corrals held a menagerie that at various time included all the above animals plus horses, a Shetland pony, Hereford cows, wild pigs, Labradors Retrievers and cats. Justin and I were deep into making great wines and raising great children.

When the boys were teenagers, they went to Europe to stay with a host family and backpack through a half-dozen countries. Holly followed suit a few years later. They learned and matured so much from these experiences. By the time they left for college, we were confident they could handle whatever experiences presented themselves with a perspective and wisdom born from grounded independence and autonomy.

The Alexander Valley Winery Ghost

It is easy for me to remember the Silver Oak milestones. Without intending to, we naturally fell into a rhythm of ten-year leaps. Our first crush for Silver Oak was in 1972. We built the Oakville winery in 1982, and our Alexander Valley winery was acquired in 1992. Not quite ten years later, we sold our 50% of Silver Oak to the Duncan Family, which owned the other 50%.

Our first three vintages, 1972, 1973, and 1974 were labeled North Coast and from the Alexander Valley. As our young vineyards began to produce commercial-quality fruit, Justin first thought of blending our Alexander Valley wines with our Napa Valley Cabernets. The idea was that there would be just one wine, labeled North Coast, that would be the quintessential perfect marriage of the best barrels from each vineyard from each year. But by the 1976 vintage, he decided that the Napa and Alexander Valley wines were unique enough they should each stand on their own thus: we created Silver Oak Napa and Silver Oak Alexander. Then in 1979 we decided to produce a third wine, made only from the four acres in front of our house, Bonny's Vineyard, as that small block of vines had proved itself to be remarkable and distinctive in its own right. There were moments later when we regretted this decision. Not that there weren't unique and definitive differences between the wines from these different locations. We just felt that producing one spectacular wine each year would have been simpler, and given Justin full latitude to blend the best of the best in the cellar for each vintage.

Our Alexander Valley grapes were initially crushed at Christian Brothers and vinted there in accordance with Justin's specifications. When we bought Franciscan out of bankruptcy in 1975, Alexander Valley was crushed, cellared, blended and bottled there. We moved into our Oakville facility in time for the 1982 harvest and Alexander Valley grapes were delivered, crushed, fermented, aged and bottled there. With each vintage, the demand for our wines grew. Because we aged our wines four or five years before they were released, we did our best to anticipate and expand our crushing, fermenting, and aging cellars way ahead to meet our projected sales.

By 1992, the popularity of both our Alexander Valley and Napa Valley wines had grown beyond the production capacity of the Oakville winery. Anticipating this, Justin had been in an on-going conversation with the Lyeth family, whose winery in Alexander Valley had been struggling to find its way following founder Chip Lyeth's sudden death some four years before. Justin eventually reached an agreement with the family and its financial partners that enabled us to acquire the facility. With a sense of relief, we took ownership of this beautiful winery between Geyserville and Asti in the late fall of 1992. Though it had very modest fermentation and cellar areas, it had a beautiful central courtyard, and three spacious en suite second-floor guest rooms accessed from a spacious and elegant salon and library with high ceilings and vineyard views. All this was serviced by a well-appointed kitchen.

As soon as the winery deal was consummated, the cellar was prepared to receive our Alexander Valley grapes and I took on furnishing the offices, tasting room, and guest rooms. I wanted to create comfortable overnight spaces for our family, the Duncans, and the occasional wine trade visitor. This project offered me the opportunity for a lot of creative expression. In one odd-shaped bedroom where the bed faced a large blank wall, I commissioned a trompe l'oeil artist to paint a vineyard scene as if one were looking out a window there into the vineyards beyond. It turned out just as I had imagined and made the room come alive.

But before I could attend to all these details, there was the matter of the winery ghost.

We had heard from the winery manager, Tony, that there had been several reports of employees and guests experiencing strange, startling and annoying phenomena. The telephones rang at odd hours with no one on the other end, the security gate performed erratically, and there were even some sightings of mysterious apparitions in the upper salon and guest rooms. All this made ghostbusting the first order of business. We didn't want our staff or visitors to be scared by spirits.

I checked in with Margaret. She was the first person to move into the office to man the phones and attend to any tasting room visitors who might come by. Yes, she had heard the stories and the telephones were indeed a little freaky. The cleaning lady said "something or someone" would rattle the shutters when she was cleaning upstairs. I asked Margaret if she thought I should call in a priest to bless the winery. She said she was not quite ready for that, so I decided to take it on myself.

The next weekend I talked our sons Matt and Chad, along with MG and Jim, a couple of their teen friends from school, into going to the winery with me for an overnight. There was no furniture there yet, so we had a sleeping bag slumber party. We arrived with plenty of food and snacks and a Ouija Board. That evening the boys and I took turns with the Ouija Board, asking questions. At first, it seemed like great fun to them ... until we began to get coherent answers! Then their eyes widened and their joking around was punctuated by nervous laughter. Yes, there was a spirit. Yes, his name was Charlie. Yes, he had lived on the property before the winery was built and had been disoriented by all the activity there.

I had come to understand that generally spirits haunt places until they have been acknowledged. I hoped our Ouija session with Charlie would be all that was needed. Nevertheless, I think we all slept with one eye open that night.

On Monday morning, I gave Margaret a rundown of the information the kids and I had gotten on Saturday night. She confirmed that the reports she had heard involved sightings of a crusty old seaman wandering about. His name was Captain Brunelli. The week that followed proved to be quieter, but there were still problems with the phones. I returned a couple of weeks later to take an inventory of all the things that were needed to properly set up the office and tasting room areas and to spend a couple of nights at the winery. The first night, my phone went off in the middle of the night. I really hate being awakened like that as I always have a hard time getting back to sleep. So, I mentally spoke with Charlie. "We are here to make wine and entertain visitors. I need my sleep and it is important that we are able to do our work without interference. I acknowledge your presence. You may stay as long as you think you need to, but please do not bother us again."

I slipped back into sleep without receiving any signal or answer from Charlie. If he was listening, though, it seems he got the message. None of us saw or heard from him again.

Chapter Thirteen

The King of Cabernet by Gina Gigli
Photo by Rick Bolen

Ruggero and Gina Gigli

I met Ruggero and Gina Gigli in 1981 at the Orange County Fair Commercial Wine Competition. For this event, one of the largest in the industry at the time, wineries submitted their wines for blind tasting by industry professionals – winemakers, winesellers, and sommeliers. The wines that best exemplified their categories received medals. It was my fifth year as a judge in the competition—and I was still the only woman. At the time, there were only a couple of woman winemakers in the industry and most winery wives rarely ventured into the cellar. Because I had tasted so many wines with Harold Olmo and participated in university blind tastings that tested my palate, I had the chops to discern the difference between the technically sound, the good, and the great.

The Orange County competition, founded by Brant Horton and led by Jerry Mead in 1977, had a bold mission: to judge every California wine that was sold in Orange County. And if a wine was sold there, it was usually sold throughout Southern California. Wineries were invited to enter their wines voluntarily, but if they didn't, the competition would purchase them from a local retailer. Thus this judging represented an exhaustive survey. By 1981 there were 1130 entries, representing more than 100 wineries.

For two days we judges tasted and ranked flight after flight of wines ranging from awful to amazing. Then came the Summer Wine Extravaganza, a giant walk-around tasting that was open to the public. Representatives from wineries all over the state stood behind tables and poured wines for anyone with a ticket, whether they were connoisseurs or just curious. I poured Silver Oak Cabernet, which attracted a fair number of the thousand tasters who attended

Holly was six months old and I was nursing her, so wherever I went, she went. She slept and played quietly in a woven bassinet basket while I was judging for the wine competition. During the big public tasting, I held her in one arm and poured our Cabernet with the other.

One time-honored tradition of large public tastings is that those behind the tables cover each other from time to time, so that we can get off our feet or go around the room to taste other wines. Needing to take a restroom break, I left my neighboring vintner in charge of the Silver Oak table and slowly cruised around the room with Holly onboard, tasting a few wines as I went. When I spotted a table displaying wine-related etchings, I made a beeline toward it. Silver Oak was in the early stages of building the Oakville winery, and this art would look wonderful in the tasting room and upstairs mezzanine.

As I admired the etchings, I fell into conversation with the person behind the table, a stocky fellow with a round face topped by an unruly shock of greying hair. He wore his shirt open at the neck, revealing a gold necklace and grey chest hair, and spoke with a pronounced Italian accent. He introduced himself as Ruggero Gigli and explained that the artist, his wife Gina, was away for only a few moments. I was immediately drawn in by his friendliness and authenticity, so when I told him about the new winery I also admitted that I had no budget for art due to construction costs. Instead, I proposed that the Giglis might like to display some etchings in the winery as a way to promote their art in Napa Valley.

Ruggero said he would discuss this idea with Gina, and that reminded me why I had been walking past their booth in the first place. I asked Ruggero if he would hold Holly for a few moments while I took a restroom break. He was a bit surprised but seemed happy to hold a contented baby, and I headed down the hall.

When I got back, I met Gina who presented quite a contrast with her husband: she was tall, slender and American. I later found out her given name was Jane but Ruggero, like Justin, had a habit of renaming people he loved. Gina was a name he could pronounce more naturally; it also sounded more musical and, well, more Italian. After talking some more about the art and featuring it at Silver Oak, I took a business card and returned with Holly to my table.

Years later I heard about the conversation between Ruggero and Gina when she returned to the table after her break. Naturally she was surprised to see him holding a baby.

"Ruggero, where did you get the baby?"

"A woman gave her to me."

"A woman gave you her baby?!"

"To hold."

"Who is the woman?"

"Ah, I don't know."

"You don't know?"

"No, but she seemed very nice. And she needed to go to the bathroom."

"You don't know her name?"

"No, but she will be back for the baby!"

That was the unusual beginning of a lifelong friendship. A couple of months before Holly turned two, the winery was completed. The Giglis brought 30 etchings and some posters that we offered for sale in our tasting room. We held a couple of open houses for our fellow vintners and friends to show off the art once it was decorating the walls. Sometime later, the Giglis moved to St. Helena and became regular visitors to our home. I don't remember Ruggero ever knocking on our front door. He generally walked right in and announced his presence by loudly wondering where he could get a glass of wine.

"Justino! I am thirsty! Is there any wine in this house?"

Full glass in hand, Ruggero would then head straight for the kitchen. He would grab a dish towel and tuck it into the back pocket of his jeans: a clear signal that he was ready to cook. When Justin and I entertained, we loved cooking together, moving in the kitchen in concert with each other in much the same way as we played music and worked together. But when Ruggero was around, he and Justin would take over the kitchen, constantly teasing each other, all the while creating a delicious meal. Gina and I would play with the children and catch up on news and life.

Ruggero and Gina were perfect examples of the people Justin and I were drawn to most: open, friendly, fun-loving, and authentically down-to-earth. In the first year of our marriage, we received invitations from the beautiful people of Napa Valley. After a couple of cocktail parties at the elegant homes of the "in crowd," we decided we would rather hang out with farmers and salt-of-the-earth folks. Like the Giglis, they were unpretentious, hard-working, generous, and able to laugh at themselves. Most importantly, they could handle Justin's wicked sense of humor and dish it right back.

When the Giglis moved from St. Helena to Markleeville, on the east side of the Sierras, we didn't see them as often. But a few times a year they would drive down from the mountains to buy wine for Villa Gigli, the restaurant they created in the art studio next to their house. Their

Jeep would be loaded with Pedroncelli Zinfandel, but there was always room for a few cases of Silver Oak, at a special price.

Ruggero and Gina always stayed overnight in our home when they were making these wine runs, so there was always good food, great wine and lots of laughter when we saw them. When Holly spent two of her teenage summers helping Ruggero and Gina in the restaurant, Gina taught her the basics of etching. Little wonder Holly became an artist and graphic designer herself.

Villa Gigli was a destination restaurant for locals and for visitors who came to the mountains to hike in the summer, ski in the winter, or soak at nearby Grover Hot Springs. It became wildly popular partly for the authentic Italian food, and partly for the genuinely Italian host and chef. Ruggero's tiny kitchen was open to the dining room and outdoor deck, and from there, while minding multiple pots, pans, and the oven, he would give full voice to the arias from his favorite Italian operas.

Father's Day

Gina was a master of intaglio etching, a mostly forgotten art. Over the years, Ruggero became a master printer using the traditional Italian press he had imported from Italy and handmade Magniani cotton paper from his hometown of Pescia, northwest of Florence. Their images were of the Sierras, where they lived, and grapes, vineyards and wine, which they loved.

The last intaglio etching that Gina made, and the most complex that Ruggero ever printed, was called "King of Cabernet." It depicted Justin as a playing card king, holding a glass of wine with the Silver Oak Cellars logo on it. There were 18 separate plates, which together created a beautiful embossed pattern that augmented the image itself. Even for a printer as experienced as Ruggero, this was a challenging piece of work, so he made fewer than a dozen copies.

Justin and I were deeply moved by the artistry and love behind "King of Cabernet." But it never hung in the winery. Justin was too humble to present himself as the king of Cabernet Sauvignon winemakers—even though, in the eyes of many, he was.

Gina stopped producing etchings after that, warned by her doctor that etching zinc with nitric acid and ferric chloride created fumes that were hazardous to her health. She had begun to exhibit some Parkinson's-like symptoms, so it was better to be safe than sorry. After that, Gina turned to making fanciful Venetian-style masks and colorful silk banners. She was a tireless creator and was always working on one project or another on the large art table that Ruggero had built for her. It was a sad day when I got Ruggero's phone call that she had died. Her ability to function had diminished over the years, but Ruggero's devotion had not. He had cared for her tirelessly, never quite believing she would not, could not, get better ... until her body finally gave out one afternoon.

Ruggero has his own print of "King of Cabernet" hanging next to his pasta machine. He fingers the gold necklace his mother gave him when he prays every day for his mother, for his friend Justino, and for Gina.

Twenty years after Gina and Ruggero produced the prints, I acquired the last three and gave them to my sons and daughter for Father's Day. Their eyes grew wide with recognition and remembrance, as my heart grew heavy with a familiar weight.

God bless Justin. God bless Gina. Angels both.

Chapter Fourteen

Bonny & Justin Meyer and the Bonny's Vineyard Sign

Bonny's Vineyard

Initially, in front of our humble house was a luscious four-acre field of clover the dairy cattle used to love. This became the personal pasture for my wedding horse, Tico Taco, during the first three years we lived there. Every other bit of pasture was converted quickly and efficiently into vineyard. But not Tico's pasture. We saved that for later.

An Arabian-Quarter Horse mix, Tico Taco had the personality of an Arabian. He would follow me around the pasture like a dog and was comfortable with me lying down next to him, my head on his belly, when he took a mid-afternoon nap. He was always happy to go out for an adventure and would happily run over when I called him. Unless, of course, he had escaped to go visit the neighbor's horses. Then I would patiently get the coffee can I used to scoop sweet grain, fill it partway, and give it a good shake. A sucker for sweets, Tico would run flat out in my direction and skid to a stop right in front of me to get a mouthful. His sweet tooth made him easy to catch when he was out galivanting.

In the early 1970s there were not so many vineyards or grand homes in Napa Valley as there are now. That meant that fences and estate gates were also few in number, so Tico and I were free to wander in every direction without restriction. It was a wonderful time and place for a young woman on a young horse.

One day I rode Tico Taco down to Oakville and across Highway 29. There was hardly any traffic down the middle of the valley on that sleepy afternoon. We continued to head west toward the UC Davis experimental station on Oakville Grade. There, tucked into an opening between valley oaks was a sweet vineyard bordered by a stand of eucalyptus on one side and Lincoln Creek on the other. Marking the entrance was a beautiful hand-painted sign that said "Martha's Vineyard." Not wanting to trespass or disturb the owner, Tico and I just stood there and took it all in for a long while. Then we turned around and headed east, back towards the Vaca Mountains and home.

Later that evening I told Justin about my lovely ride west of the highway, and how I came across Martha's Vineyard. Without really thinking about it, I mused out loud, "Wouldn't it be nice to have a vineyard named after you?" He agreed and that was the end of it.

A couple of years later, Tico's clover pasture was ripped and prepared for planting as a vineyard. Because this plot of land was relatively small and directly in front of the house, I volunteered to plant, cultivate, and prune this new vineyard. It would be my personal project.

That was in 1975, the same year we bought Franciscan and Chad was born. I learned how to drive a tractor, and to sucker and prune grapevines, but with everything else that was going on I had little time to spend in the vineyard. True to form, Justin teased me about neglecting my vineyard duties. He did this as he gazed at me, smiling eyes full of pride, while I nursed our firstborn.

The grapes from the front-yard vineyard were harvested, fermented and barreled separately from the other lots of grapes that came into Silver Oak. That was one of Justin's cornerstones as a winemaker: bring out the individual character of each place that produced grapes for your wine. Even though most of these individual lots went into the same wine, Justin was like a composer who knew every note in his compositions. The fact that they all became part of one piece did not mean they had lost their individuality. It meant they had contributed something unique to a complex, multifaceted whole.

In the case of my little vineyard, Justin noted that the wine had a depth of character and distinctive spicy flavor that he considered extraordinary. My merry response was, "Of course! Just like me!"

By the 1979 harvest, Justin had a more serious response: he decided that the wine from the former clover pasture was too special to blend into Silver Oak's Napa Valley Cabernet Sauvignon. Instead he would make what vintners call a "vineyard designate": a wine that comes from a single vineyard and bears the name of that vineyard on the label. Thus "Bonny's Vineyard" changed from family joke to an official viticultural place name.

The Christmas season before the first Bonny's Vineyard wine was released, Justin secretly found an artisan who carved wood signs and commissioned one. On Christmas morning, after all the gifts under the tree were unwrapped, our young children grabbed me by the hands and insistently pulled me down our driveway. Justin followed behind with a big grin on his face. As we turned the corner and came to the edge of our property, there was a brand-new redwood sign elegantly carved with "Bonny's Vineyard." As soon as I saw it, I ran for Justin and hugged him with tears in my eyes while the children danced and jumped around us.

Not long after our first release of Bonny's Vineyard Cabernet, it became the second "cult wine" from California. (The first came from that little plot of vines that originally inspired me: Martha's Vineyard.) I have never liked the term "cult wine," though I admit it is descriptive in the sense that people become so attached to a so-called cult wine that they must have it at any cost. Wineries usually welcome the windfall from such bottlings, because they are so profitable—and have a halo effect on the other wines from the same producer.

We didn't see it quite that way. The Bonny's Vineyard wine, or "Bonny's" as it is now affectionately known among wine enthusiasts, is limited in production by its source: a tiny, four-acre vineyard. There simply wasn't enough to go around to keep our Silver Oak customers happy. Most wineries get around this problem by raising the price of the wine until the number of people willing to pay it matches the amount of wine available. This is why individual bottles of wine can cost more than a thousand dollars. But cranking the price up to the sky was not our style. Our philosophy was to make great wine affordable for people, not precious.

Ultimately, we decided to stop making Bonny's Vineyard. We did this against the advice of almost everyone. The last Silver Oak Bonny's was 1991. After that, we again blended the fruit from the vineyard into our Napa Cabernet. But people remember. Every now and then when I meet someone from outside the valley and tell them my name, they will ask, "Are you the Bonny?"

A month after Justin's death Bonny's Vineyard rose again. The grapes were harvested, fermented, barreled and bottled by our son Matt, under the label of our current winery, Meyer Family Cellars. We turned this 2002 vintage into a special memorial bottling and gave it to friends and neighbors. I remember proudly handing a bottle to every member of Justin's male gastronomic club, the GONADS, at a Christmas party in 2007. Each vintage of Bonny's Vineyard is made by Matt and his wife, Karen, who is also an enologist, in the same way that Justin made these wines decades ago. Those who remember the earlier wines are now swooning again over the familiar dark cherry, cassis, chocolate and peppery nuances. They say the Bonny's Vineyard Cabernet has a depth

of character and distinctive spicy flavor that is extraordinary.
Of course!

Winery Kids

Our family grew as our winery grew. From the first days at Franciscan, when I carried Chad around in a corduroy baby front pack while I made landscaping decisions and sold wine, all the way through their university years, the children were in and around the winery.

In those early days, I did everything having to do with design; beginning with the critical landscape planting and tasting room esthetics and flow, then migrating to label re-design, which led to a business system re-design, case design, and marketing materials. I worked in the tasting room myself, setting the tone and culture of friendliness, generosity and professionalism for everyone else who served our customers. Later I migrated to the office and worked as a bookkeeper when pregnancy didn't mix so well with wrangling cases of wine.

Meanwhile, Justin was in the cellar, making better and better wines from the vineyards he had planted. As the vines matured, so did the wines. He loved having our children in the office when I was there. He would pop in, happy from tending his wines in the cellar, and delight in making our boys giggle, such as by putting them up on his broad shoulders for a walk around the winery. They also eagerly sat on Justin's knee while he drove the tractor in front of our house.

When we sold Franciscan five years after bringing it back to life, the boys, now three and four years old, came with us to Germany where we toured the Rheingau and Mosel wine regions. The boys were more interested in the soccer ball we bought than tromping through steeply sloped vineyards and dank, dark underground cellars. Nevertheless, Germany made an impression; Chad sang a song in German about Rudesheim and wore a pair of lederhosen for years after that. Matt, for his part, never outgrew his love of liverwurst for breakfast.

With the change in ownership, I established the administrative office for Silver Oak above Groezinger's, a wine shop in the Vintage 1870 complex in Yountville. That was when I began taking the boys to spend time with a woman from our church who had set up her home as a place where little ones could spend the day in creative play. Holly, who was born a few months after our time in Germany, kept office hours with me until she was weaned and too animated for me to get any work done.

Things shifted again when we moved into our new Silver Oak winery and the boys began to attend school. A few select employees migrated from Franciscan to Silver Oak which meant instead of managing everything, I could again specialize in marketing, design, and other project-based tasks. I always wanted to be home when the children were home, because as much as I loved the winery my family came first. There were plenty of times when I was not able to finish the day's tasks before school was out. On those days I still picked up the children, but then we went back to the winery instead of heading home. They would race up the stairs, raid the candy jar, grab a fistful of markers and copy paper, and turn the office into an art studio.

Soon after we moved into the new winery in 1982, we continued a tradition that had begun at Franciscan—monthly blind tastings. In the center of the tasting room was a large redwood table around which 16 people could sit with an array of lettered glasses in front of them. A volunteer would uncork eight different wines, remove the foil capsules at the top of the bottle, and put each bottle in a brown paper bag. This prevented tasters from identifying a wine by its packaging. Another taster would mix up the bottles then label them anonymously, with letters of the alphabet. The wines would then be poured into glasses bearing the appropriate letter of the alphabet, and the wines would be tasted and discussed.

One of the eight was always a Silver Oak. The other seven were Cabernet Sauvignons from other producers that we considered benchmarks for high quality or particular characteristics we were interested in. After inhaling, swirling and sipping the wines, each taster ranked the eight wines according to his or her own reactions. Then we would add up the results, come to a collective ranking, and unwrap the wines. That moment always sparked surprise and animated conversation.

We followed the tasting with dinner, which added a strong social dimension to the professional one. Attendance grew as our staff and our friendships grew. We added more and more tables, even opening the doors to the cellar as we outgrew the tasting room.

Others saw our children at these tasting dinners and began to bring their own. The range of their play and activities grew as they grew. Holly started out playing with the basket of rolled-up Gigli wine posters in the tasting room where we tasted and ate. Older children headed up to the mezzanine with typewriters, paper and pens, or toys they had brought. As they got taller and stronger, they began to push each other around on pallet jacks and play hide-and-seek in the barrel racks. Then they started climbing the barrel racks. Then ... goodness knows what. It's a miracle there were never any falls or broken bones.

Holly is certain, however, that she suffers from claustrophobia after being trapped in the winery's dumbwaiter. It was my idea to install it, so we could easily get plates, cutlery, wine glasses, food and wine up to the boardroom on the third floor, which doubled as our VIP tasting room. The dumbwaiter was basically a wooden box with a removable shelf in the middle and a latching door that opened outward into the room. The box was raised and lowered with a looped rope. Pull on the right side to send the box and its contents up. Pull on the left side to send the box down.

Our children discovered that they could remove the shelf, climb into the box, and haul themselves up or down between floors. Better yet, they could give each other rides. This was never the intended use of the dumbwaiter, so there was no doorknob on the inside. Once the door was closed, someone on the outside had to open it. Otherwise the rider remained in the pitch-black dumbwaiter with no way out. This happened to Holly more than once, and it stayed with her.

Even more than their dumbwaiter rides, the children loved racing down the vineyard avenues on three-wheel all-terrain vehicles, or ATVs. I think Chad was seven when he first learned to drive our balloon-tired ATV. Matt would hop on behind him and they would take a slow tour of the vineyard around the house. Of course, as they grew, they went faster and faster until they were racing flat out, their hair and the dust flowing behind them.

After our neighbors, the Groths, bought the property next door, our boys gave rides to Suzanne and Andrew Groth. The next thing we knew, the Groths bought two new three-wheelers. Now there was a pack of juvenile motorists raising dust through the vineyard. Our children knew that their riding privileges depended on safe conduct, so they always came home dusty but in one piece—except for the time Matt ran off the creek levee into the raspberry bushes with his little sister behind him. It was only when Chad, Matt, and Holly were in their thirties that the stories began to come out of ATVs tipping over and young bodies flying through the air.

They did their share of flying in airplanes as well. They all went with us to the annual conferences of the American Society for Enology and Viticulture (ASEV). Most winery families did the same and the children got to know each other, with the older ones minding the younger ones. Holly still has a sweet spot in her heart for the Hotel Del Coronado in San Diego, home of the ASEV conference for many years. Justin also took a child with him on promotional trips now and then to meet our distributors and consumers.

As the winery and the children matured, my work continued to become more specialized. For example, I was happy to delegate the job of visiting accounts and selling wine so I could focus on our strategies for increasing sales and fine-tuning our pricing and distribution. I also continued to direct development of everything involving our logo, labels, packaging and marketing materials. This was an important part of my personal strategy. I wanted the flexibility to work hard for Silver Oak, be involved with the children's school, and be home when they got there. It wasn't always easy, but Justin loved having me at the winery and home when they were home. He also encouraged our children to be creative and think entrepreneurially.

Their "Silver Oak Chips" business was a great example. Oak barrels are an important element in aging and refining red wine in California, because of the complex chemical interaction that takes place between the wine and the wood. Rather than retire barrels that had been exposed to wine for a couple of vintages, we would shave the inside of our oak barrels to expose a fresh surface. This gave each barrel a second life.

Justin, a BBQ enthusiast and never one to waste anything, brought some of these cabernet-infused shavings home and threw them on top of his charcoal fires, where they definitely gave a little cabernet character to the grilled meat. He then set the kids up in business. He invested in hundreds of sealable plastic bags, I designed labels, and Chad, Matt, and Holly spent after-school time bagging and labeling the barrel shavings. These were now elevated to the status of "Silver Oak Chips," and were sold in the tasting room for a dollar apiece, cash only. The tasting room staff kept a cigar box below the tasting bar for that precious revenue. I have no recollection how they spent their Silver Oak Chip money, but I do know it kept the children occupied and taught them that with a little imagination and a fancy label you can make money from something that would otherwise be thrown out into the vineyard.

As the kids got older, they began to gravitate towards their personal passions at the winery. Chad, gregarious and engaging, liked giving tours. By the time he was ten years old, he would help the tasting staff in this way after school and on Saturdays. Chad has a phenomenal memory for details and a ready sense of humor, so visitors were informed and delighted to have him as their tour guide. Matt was more naturally quiet and preferred to spend his time in the garden. As a 4-H member, he won top awards at the Napa County Fair three years in a row for his pumpkins and vegetables. So as he got older and could help in the winery, he gravitated to working in the vineyard and the cellar. In his teen years he ran vineyard crews composed of other youngsters from his high school. Holly loved to bake and became famous for her warm, just-out-of-the-oven chocolate chip cookies that she would deliver to the delight of the winery staff.

Any of our children would do whatever needed to be done, when there was a time or labor crunch. For example, we kept them home from school one day each fall to harvest Bonny's Vineyard. This apparently appalled the principals of their schools. We were not aiming to do anything subversive. We just felt it was important for our children to experience and understand such a fundamental aspect of their family's business.

The dinner table was another primary venue for education and edification. Justin would frequently invite neighbors or a winery visitor, such as a Silver Oak customer or a distributor whose company he enjoyed. The children got used to listening in on wine and business conversations around the dinner table. And they were always welcome to have a little of what we were drinking.

They actually seemed to enjoy the tart taste of wine as babies, but that changed quickly with the beginning of their toddler years. Then somewhere around adolescence, they enjoyed sipping wine again, this time with discernment and appreciation. They didn't drink wine often, but they would partake of a wine that others were raving about, or one that was rare or unique.

When they went to college, they had little interest in "going out drinking" with their classmates. What they wanted was a nice wine to accompany a nice meal. We helped make the nice meal more likely by giving them a list of restaurants that served Silver Oak near their universities. They could take a friend out to dinner once a month, paid for by the winery, as long as they personally thanked the wine steward or owner for carrying our wine. Just as when they were children, they were excellent ambassadors for Silver Oak, and for the Meyer family.

Vintner Reunion

Todd Anderson came to Napa Valley as a man in his mid-twenties with a dream of an agrarian life. He sought out Justin because of his admiration for Silver Oak wines. Justin offered to help Todd, as did other vintners, notably Joe Heitz and Robert Mondavi. Justin gave Todd one of the most precious gifts imaginable; pieces of Cabernet Sauvignon vines—"budwood"—from Bonny's Vineyard, which could be used to create a genetically matched new vineyard. With that precious scion stock, Todd created a new vineyard. He won rave reviews and awards for his first commercial vintage, in 1987, and that launched him on a successful life in the wine business.

Todd recently came to visit, with flowers and a rare bottle of his 1987 Conn Valley Vineyards Cabernet, graced with his signature. We talked for hours, mostly about the valley in the 1980s when the culture of helping each other was as commonplace as the cultivation of vines.

I told him about my first visit to Napa Valley in 1968. The Napa Valley Wine Tech Group was having a summer BBQ and Brother Justin invited me to come along and bring my guitar. The group was small, but there were names that even I, a girl of 18, knew by reputation; Luis Martini, Jim Nichelini, Jack Davies.

My father had worked his whole life at Ford Motor Company. The recurrent and unrelenting dictum from on high was that Chevrolet was the archenemy. The industry was rife with secrets, industrial espionage, and fierce competition. Never would a Ford man be caught dead befriending someone from General Motors. Now here I was in the Napa Valley, and these winery owners were not only talking with one another but eating, drinking and laughing together. It blew my mind. And it didn't just change my ideas about how people in the same industry could interact with one another. It also changed my assumptions about the presumably staid character of men who founded and led famous companies. Jim Nichelini played a mean Italian squeezebox, Luis Martini had a great voice and loved to sing, and Jack Davies was a gifted percussionist who carried a perfectly polished, matched set of silver spoons in his breast pocket for those moments when the wine was flowing and the music was right.

Over time I discovered that there was a strong, resilient culture within the Napa Valley based on one fundamental agreement: if we all help each other make technically good wine, then more of us can make exceptional wine, and that will put Napa Valley on the map to everyone's benefit. And that's just what happened.

In the early 1960s, Napa Valley primarily produced generic wine that did not refer to grape variety or vineyard location. In the 1970s we were still bottling gallon jugs bearing European appellation names such as "Burgundy" and "Chablis"—meaningless labels for wine made in California. But steadily the industry embraced a new U.S. labeling system for premium wines, which included a vintage date and the name of the grape variety that made up the majority of the wine in the bottle. The passion and determination to make fine wines rose year after year, and with it more sharing of information, technology, processes and techniques. If a disaster occured at a winery during harvest, other wineries didn't gloat; they made space in their facilities or loaned critical equipment, so the affected winery would not miss their only chance of the year to crush and ferment their wine. The entire upward movement of the valley's reputation was fueled by this extraordinary culture of generosity and collaboration.

Every time a newcomer arrived with hopes and dreams of making great wine, every time a new vineyard or winery began to take shape, neighbors showed up to offer help. Equipment was loaned: a forklift, a cultivator, a hand corker. Technical advice was shared; which root stock to plant, which grape variety to graft onto it, complementary lab analysis, how best to filter a cloudy wine without stripping out its flavors and character. Grape cuttings were shared, like Justin did with Todd. It all added up to better and better Napa Valley wines. The quintessential affirmation for me was when Justin and I were visiting a remote island in the Caribbean. Someone asked us in pidgin English where we were from. Our answer, "Napa Valley," immediately sparked recognition that we came from a place with great wine. The plan had worked! Napa Valley and great wine were synonymous even on a tiny island thousands of miles away.

Chapter Fifteen

Bonny & Justin Meyer

The Romance of the Forbidden

"The Sound of Music." "The Thorn Birds." What attracts us to these romantic stories? Is it the romance of the forbidden? Are we attracted to the love matches at the heart of these stories because they weren't supposed to happen? Or is it the story of innocence rewarded with a wondrous love affair? And what makes these romances so strong, enduring, and epic?

These are all great questions, but there is another question that has puzzled me even more. Why aren't most romances strong, enduring, and epic?

It's possible that the love affair between me and Justin was so enduring because we never intended it. Instead of pursuing romance, instead of fostering it, nourishing it, or even simply being attracted to romance for romance's sake, we did our best to avoid it. We actively turned away from each other multiple times.

My relationship with Justin began with sharing music. Not exactly "meeting cute" as the romantic leads do in movies. It's hard to think of anything more wholesome than singing folks songs together after dinner for the enjoyment of mild-mannered university people living in a farmhouse. There was no flirting. There was no giddy girl-chat with friends, recounting every moment of every encounter with him. There was no tricky navigating or tortuous buildup to our first kiss. Definitely no planning for sex or what might come after it.

More often than not, it seems, people these days engage in sex before they engage in really knowing each other. Initial chemistry and the superficial aspects of romance take precedence over taking time to grow a solid relationship. So maybe being caught in a forbidden romance allows room for the slow simmer of lasting connection.

I don't necessarily recommend it. I do recommend being interested, playful, patient and kind. Come together when the spirit moves and enjoy the feeling of shared world-views and experiences. Do not rush into relationship or even be attracted to it. Allow the tender fibers of connection to grow organically without being tugged and driven by desire and premature action.

I don't honestly know if this is a surefire recipe for an epic love story, but it is the recipe for beautiful and enduring friendships that can germinate, develop, mature and last a lifetime.

The Mystery of Love

There are mysteries at work in the universe that we will never work out. How and why we fall deeply in love with another is one of those mysteries. There is no explaining it. No preventing it. And no cure for it. Loving just is. The only choice we have is what we do with it. How we express our love as friend or lover, beloved or partner. Even then, none of this really matters. What matters is that we love. The depth of our compassion and commitment to one another defines us as human beings. That we love with deep passion and a pure heart is our highest calling.

Expecting nothing and receiving everything.

I suspect that although the anatomy of great love affairs is exquisitely simple, they are rare because they take extraordinary courage. My friend Jerry Jampolsky famously titled his best-selling book, "Love is Letting Go of Fear." In "Passionate Marriage," Dr. David Schnarch says, "Loving is not for the faint of heart ... a profoundly good marriage means the vulnerability of having more to lose." He goes on, "The end result of loving a cherished long-term partner is grief few of us are prepared to handle." Passionate marriages are at times daunting in the living of them, and the consequences of our partners' death are even more daunting. The ultimate act of love is to say, "Honey, you go first. I will handle all the hard stuff that is to come."

I actually said this to Justin not long before his sudden, unexpected death. Had I known how devastating the grief was going to be, I think I might have pulled back from the brink of this cliff. But then again, I eventually learned how to fly.

"The risk of love is loss and the price of loss is grief, but the pain of grief is only a shadow when compared with the pain of never risking love." —Hilary Zunin

Commitment

From the first strums of his banjo, then the quiet talk over a Coke at a Dairy Queen, I felt safe with BJ. He must have felt safe with me too, because ours was an open-hearted, expansive, dynamic relationship filled with surprise and playfulness held within the powerful container of commitment.

Commitment came easily for me and BJ. Certainly, we were not a "committed couple" during our first five years of knowing each other. We struggled mightily with being in love—and wanting not to be. I did my best to get to know and date other men. Justin did his best to dedicate himself to his vows, to the winery, his community and the Christian Brothers order. But because we felt so beyond-a-doubt safe with each other, we easily and naturally committed to being vulnerable, open-hearted, and emotionally intimate; always striving to be honest, speak our truth, share our feelings and the stories of our lives. Abundantly nourished by this, our love and relationship continually deepened.

A friend once asked why I stayed true to BJ in my heart during those difficult years, when I was certain we would never be together as a couple. The answer is, I never had a thought of "staying true" to someone I was "waiting for." What I saw and experienced was a man with the strength of character to be a profoundly intimate, honest and cherished friend to me despite the great differences in our years, backgrounds, and intended futures. With every year of knowing BJ it became harder to settle for anything less.

Just because we seemed to naturally and effortlessly share ourselves and love deeply, that didn't mean we never overstepped a boundary or that we were always a perfect partner. We certainly gave each other opportunities to practice forgiveness. Fortunately, we both had a high value for that famously Christian virtue. So we did not take each other's errors and omissions personally, or put heavy consequences on them. This prevented an enormous amount of strife. Never holding a grudge or anger for long meant we lived a joyful, fun, peaceful existence with each other. We somehow knew that resentment would kill our relationship and that forgiveness renewed it. Or maybe we just thought resentment took way too much effort, and lovin' was more fun than begrudgin'.

As Justin and I came to know each other better and better over the years, our love for each other deepened as a natural consequence. Over time little annoyances became endearments. An example of this is Justin's snoring. He was often described as "larger than life," and this certainly applied to his snoring. It was epic. When Justin went on a hunting or fishing trip with the guys, no one wanted to sleep in the same room with him. Even alone, doors closed, they could all hear him down the hall as his snores rattled the windows and walls. Me? I loved his snoring. Yes, I was awakened now and then. But to me, Justin's snoring meant that the man I love was sleeping right there next to me. To this day, I volunteer to room with the snorer in the group when I am at a conference center. The sound of snoring holds an abiding sense of comfort for me.

After we were married, each anniversary found us in bed, looking softly into each other's eyes and saying with great surprise, "I didn't think it was possible, but I love you more than I did last year!"

Commitment as defined by Steven Carter in "Getting to Commitment" is making a well-intentioned promise to be responsible, monogamous, and hard-working in a relationship, and following through on that promise. This definition makes the idea of commitment approachable and realistic. But I'm not sure it goes far enough for me. There was always a fierceness in my commitment and dedication to my relationship with Justin. An all-out, going-for-it attitude—more of a whole-hearted shout than a vow.

The Holy Longing
Johann Wolfgang von Goethe

Tell a wise person, or else keep silent,
For those who do not understand will mock it right away.
I praise what is truly alive,
What longs to be burned to death.

In the calm water of the love-nights,
Where you were begotten, where you have begotten,
A strange feeling comes over you
When you see the silent candle burning.

Now you are no longer caught
In the obsession with darkness,
And a desire for higher love-making
Sweeps you upward.

Distance does not make you falter,
Now, arriving in magic, flying,
And, finally, insane for the light,
You are the butterfly and you are gone.

And so long as you haven't experienced this:
To die and so to grow,
You are only a troubled guest
On the dark earth.

What Justin and I so often did, and what I continue to long for most, is this: to stand on the rim of a volcano caldera and dive into the molten lava. "To die and so to grow." Justin and I each died a hundred small ego deaths in our love affair together. Over time, we became more and more purified by the alchemical fire of our relationship. Without commitment, we would have run in fear from the inner struggle and pain that is the fire of transformation.

He was certainly exposed to temptation to be unfaithful. Justin traveled innumerable times across the country to visit distributors and host wine events. In the eyes of many, he was a celebrity. Men admired his confidence and accomplishments, and they loved his jokes and eloquence as a public speaker. Women were attracted to his powerful presence and charisma. Everyone loved his sensual, luscious wines. When business was done for the day, or for the evening, occasionally a woman wanted to take Justin home for something more. He always said "No, thank you" and told me about these experiences as soon as he returned home. He felt the invitations were a compliment of sorts but knew he would deeply regret any misstep forever. That long-abiding disturbance would overshadow any momentary thrill.

I, too, was tempted now and then. One gentleman, lean and agile and about my age, repeatedly invited me to lunch. I was attracted to his sensitivity, our mutual interests, and his youth. I never accepted. I didn't want to even point a toe in that direction. Justin and I talked about him and my attraction. It was a hard and difficult conversation, and we became closer because of it.

As I think about commitment now, I realize our commitment was to being fiercely honorable, honest, and trustworthy, keeping our hearts open no matter what. It was not so much a commitment to another person as it was a commitment to a way of being. That, mixed with our love for each other, meant we were always exquisitely safe in each other's arms. There was no limit to how far our love could and would expand.

People have asked me why I have not remarried or found another partner since Justin's death. I think it comes down to how I felt way back in the beginning. I will not settle for anything less than this: a strong man with impeccable character who I deeply admire, and who is fiercely committed to loving and living all out. A man who has conquered his fear of death and is willing to dive into the caldera with me so our love, and we, can rise like phoenixes.

I dated a man a few years back who was very charming. But as we became closer, his fear of intimate relationship would periodically get triggered and I would find myself repeatedly running up against his armor. Intimacy would cease. Our relationship could not grow, nor could we grow personally.

He was certainly capable of loving, because loving is a basic human capacity and basic need which we all possess. The essence of our being is love and even in the direst of circumstances, it just leaks out. We can't help ourselves. Perhaps he has been so wounded by life, he is afraid to keep his heart open. After hitting my head (and heart) against the armor that protected his vulnerability, I realized it was futile. Hide and seek is not a game I want to play.

I much prefer being alone than to be with someone who is not strong enough to be in authentic relationship with me. Besides, I am still engaged in a passionate love affair. In the quiet moments, I feel Justin's abiding love and presence. And sometimes, when he comes to me in dreams or deep meditations, I feel a lot more than that.

Chapter Sixteen

May 2018 photo of the Gonads plus my son, Chad on the far left:
Chad Meyer, Carl Doumani, Bob Trinchero, Mike Chelini, Bo
Barrett, Koerner Rombauer, Tim Crull, Stu Smith, Pat Kuleto, Stan
Teaderman, Bill Bacigalupi, KR Rombauer
Photo by Wildly Simple Productions

Driving a Tractor, Smoking a Cigar

Justin had a dream of making the best Cabernet Sauvignon in the world. He wouldn't necessarily say it that way. Humility was one of his strong suits. So rather than aspiring to be "the best" he would say "one of the best," leaving room for the other great Cabernets out there in the world. Nevertheless, that was his single-point vision.

He was a master at pulling it off. He had a depth of knowledge and knowhow that few others ever came close to, thanks to his years with Brother Timothy at Christian Brothers. He knew how to run a press, a pump, and a cellar full of fermentation tanks at harvest time. He knew how to taste the nuances in a glass of young wine and determine both its potential and what would complement it best. Then he could go search the cellar or the bulk wine market for some small lot of wine with the missing flavor component, the one that would add just the right complexity or finish.

His charisma as a leader inspired those around him. Like Tom Sawyer, he could talk the other kids into whitewashing that entire fence, even if they had to sacrifice something precious.

Before UC Davis, Justin's BA in Economics from St. Mary's gave him a big-picture business sense. He knew that every distributor, glass salesman, and equipment dealer was a business partner. His insistence on integrity in business, as in his wines, enabled him to create business partnerships that lasted beyond his own lifetime.

All these qualities made Justin strive for and achieve greatness. But when everything was in order and no one needed him, when the phone was silent and the office was empty, he would slip out from behind his desk. Going down the stairs, he would take a hard right toward the winery to avoid being spotted by anyone in the tasting room. At last he would duck into the cellar to check on a fermentation or listen intently while he tapped on some barrels. If everything seemed in order, he would grab a hose and give the cellar a general rinse, for good measure.

There were times I would wonder: Are all men this happy with a hose in their hand?

If he had an hour or two before dark, he would head to the vineyard. In mid-winter, he had a pair of pruning shears in his hand, making a careful and calculated decision about the placement and number of buds to leave for the coming year's crop. Come spring, he would hop on a tractor, head turned back looking at the disc trailing behind, turning young green grasses under so the soil could absorb more warmth in case of a spring frost. In mid-summer, he would walk the vinerows, tenderly touching the growing edges of canes, tucking a shoot here and there or removing a sucker that someone else had missed. Watching him from the house, it looked like a conversation, not a man strolling past grapevines. The vines were talking to Justin, telling him what they needed, and he understood. All this while puffing on a cigar gripped firmly between his teeth. This was Justin at his happiest—in the cellar, on a tractor, touching vines, smoking a Partagas.

G.O.N.A.D.S.

Seven Napa Valley vintners came together in 1944 to collectively solve wine business problems and promote their wines. During the war years, they faced shortages of wine bottles, laborers, and railcars. These winery owners recognized that they could accomplish their goals much better together than they could separately. Thus began a tradition that brought Napa Valley vintners together once a month for lunch to share the latest industry news and address challenges collaboratively. By long tradition, when vintners gather they eat heartily and bring bottles of wine to share—or show off. So while the Napa Valley Vintners originally came together to help each other with shared business challenges, from the beginning they referred to themselves as an "eating and drinking society."

Justin took on the leadership of the Vintners in 1982. The organization had grown considerably during the previous decade, and that year the membership numbered 52 wineries. (It includes more than 550 winery members today.) It was apparent to Justin that without a paid staff, management of the organization was taking too much of his time and would only get worse for his successor. So, during his tenure as chairman of the board he led the effort to hire the first executive director. With more organization and more capability, the organization became aware of, and involved in, broader issues affecting the valley, including political ones.

This was a natural evolution, but it didn't sit well with Carl Doumani, a fellow vintner and one of Justin's best friends. He called Justin to inform him that he was quitting the Vintners.

Justin fell back in his chair like he had taken a blow to the chest. He was surprised, he was taken aback, and, as the Vintners' new chairman, he felt a little hurt. So he asked Carl why.

"The Vintners started out as an eating and drinking society," Carl reminded Justin. "They got some stuff done, but camaraderie was the first order of business. Now it has gotten too serious for my taste. It's a damned political organization, for Pete's sake. Next thing you know, we will have infighting and lawsuits."

Justin told me about his conversation with Carl later that day, and I could tell it bothered him. He couldn't quit the Vintners, but he couldn't really argue with Carl's point, either. It took him a couple of months, but finally he came up with a way forward: a new vintners' eating and drinking society that would never get too big or too political.

Carl agreed immediately. He and Justin put their heads together and came up with the rough outline:

- No president and no formal organization
- Only 12 members, by invitation only
- Any member can veto a proposed new member
- Monthly meetings for lunch, hosted by one of the members

They didn't have to specify that the organization would be all male; that went without saying.

Then came the big question: Who are the vintners we know who would make up the best possible eating and drinking society according to these principles? They came up with a list of six other winery owners and invited them to a formation lunch. Together, those eight chose the remaining four. The group was officially established. They lacked only one thing: a name.

Early one afternoon soon afterward, I glanced into Justin's office and saw him intently poring over a massive Unabridged Webster's Dictionary. Intrigued, I walked in to ask why. It turned out that Justin was doing his naming in reverse: starting with a catchy acronym, then figuring out the words for the acronym's letters. The acronym? GONADS.

I laughed out loud, but Justin's face was screwed up in concentration. He had gotten as far as the letter "N," so he had a ways to go. "What about 'nonsensical'?" he asked.

I laughed again. "Is that really a word?"

When I popped my head back in later that day, Justin had an acronym figured out and was ready to try it out on me.

"Okay. How about Gastronomic Order for Nonsensical And Dissipatory Segregation. What do you think?"

What could I say? It was a perfect match for this rowdy group of guys plus it was a quintessential example of one of Justin's strongest and most abiding character traits: irreverence.

Justin hosted the first official GONADS lunch on the lawn in front of our new Silver Oak winery, in the shade of a newly planted valley oak. A few years later, Carl hosted the first off-site lunch in Zihuatanejo, Mexico, and invited the members' wives. He did a fabulous job finding a collection of bungalows on or near the beach for us to stay in. Spending days together in Zihuatanejo partying on the beach really solidified the group.

For a while, we GONAD wives even considered starting our own group—The Trollops. But it didn't last. Our schedules weren't as flexible or as child-free as our husbands'. We did join the men each year for an annual Christmas dinner. We have also taken other trips together over the years. The GONADS have been meeting for lunch for going on 40 years now. Nothing like good food, good wine, and good friends.

Too Many Glasses of Wine

We walked into the house late, each carrying a sleeping son. Our family belonged to a babysitting co-op and one of those families had put our boys to sleep in their sleeping bags a couple of hours before. They slept through the transfer from the babysitting house to the car and into our house, but they stirred as we put them in their bunkbeds: four-year-old Matt on the bottom, five-year-old Chad on top.

This was one of those nights when Justin had freely enjoyed his wine over dinner, finished mine, and then topped off the evening with a large glass of brandy. I knew the pattern and commandeered the keys to drive us home. Now Justin was impatient for sleep. As the boys stirred awake, he harshly demanded that they lie back down and firmly pushed them down onto their mattresses. Surprise and fear flashed across their innocent, instantly troubled faces. Terrified, they laid still and we went to bed. But that wasn't the end of it.

The next morning Justin heard heated words from me about the night before and all that had transpired. He had awakened groggy without memory of the details and was remorseful. He felt especially bad about having scared the boys, and that put him on his best behavior for half a year. Gradually he began to indulge in more alcohol and behaved in ways I didn't like. We had another talk. Remorse. Reform. Repeat.

When Holly was about four and the boys were in elementary school, Justin would come home after working late at the winery, finish off a bottle of wine, have a snifter of brandy and go off to bed while I helped with homework and tuck-ins. Something inside of me knew things were getting out of control and I didn't want "Talk, Remorse, Reform, Repeat" to be the pattern of our lives.

So I looked into Alcoholics Anonymous. After reading a number of books, I was convinced Justin was an alcoholic. I also understood enough from the books, and from my years with Justin, to know that the only person who could effectively and authentically identify him as such was Justin himself. But I was not sure how that would come about. So my first course of action was to attend Al-anon meetings.

"My name is Bonny, and my husband is an alcoholic." It felt so strange to be there side-by-side with mothers and daughters, husbands and sons, and other wives; all there because loved ones were out of control with alcohol. I listened and learned. What captured my attention most keenly were stories of wives worrying into the night about the whereabouts of their husbands. Is he safe? Or has he fallen down drunk, lying on a sidewalk somewhere? Has he been in a car crash? Should I call the hospital? Should I leave the children and go out looking for him? Time after time, night after night they would be in agony over their husband's whereabouts and safety.

These stories took hold of me and would not let go.

I knew I was not going to become one of those women. I was not going to subject myself or the children to this agony of waiting and worrying. Despite the fierceness and depth of love I had for Justin, I was not going to live that life. Better to take the children and leave; choosing a life of clarity and purpose instead of becoming imprisoned within a never-ending heart-wrenching drama. My mind was clear and my decision was made. I chose the day I would tell Justin and prepared myself emotionally for that moment.

That conversation never happened.

Before the chosen day arrived, Justin shifted. He must have felt the energetic shift in me. As my mind cleared and my resolve grew, so did his. He realized he needed to moderate his behavior, so he did. The brandy bottle was put away for special occasions. He limited himself to two or three glasses of wine with dinner—not moderate by some standards but typical of vintners. He participated more in after-school activities and homework, and helped tuck in the kids. Never again did Justin drink to the extent that he had. He wasn't perfect, he wasn't exactly sober, but he managed himself so he could be lovingly present with me and our children.

There are experienced members of AA who will say that Justin's shift was impossible, or a cover-up: once an alcoholic, always an alcoholic. Drinkers keep drinking until someone intervenes. I don't know what to say in response, except that this is not how it happened for Justin and me. Apparently, the power of our connection effected a clearer communication than any verbal conversation we could have mustered. And I imagine the power of our love for one another fueled Justin's determination to balance his enjoyment of alcohol with discretion through the ensuing two decades.

Flirting Forever

Mid-afternoon, just before I leave to pick up the kids from after-school activities, I would pick up the phone and call the winery. "Can I speak to Justin please?" He would come on the line. "Hey baby, whatcha' doin' later tonight?"

I felt playful and slightly naughty to be having these deliciously personal conversations with my handsome lover while he was sitting at his desk, in his office, at work. I pictured him turning to look out the window as he lets his imagination run.

He would play along—sometimes by playing it cool. "Hmmm, I

don't know ... What do you have in mind?"

"How about a little game of hide and seek? Or maybe I could give you a little kiss on the neck?"

It would continue like this for a couple of minutes. Then we would hang up; both warm with affection, delight and anticipation.

Other times the radio would be on during dinner, (there always seemed to be music playing in our house) and our favorite song would come on: "You Are So Beautiful." Justin and I would look across the table at each other with softened gaze, rise together and begin to dance around the room in a sweet embrace to the delight of our children.

Other times we would be cooking or washing dishes in the kitchen and surprise one another with a kiss on the back of the neck or a flirtatious caress or squeeze. This usually led to passionate kisses with soapy hands. More subtle were the knowing glances, the widening of eyes, the lifting of an eyebrow, the come-hither looks. Every now and then it was clear that others who were in the office or at a wine event noticed our flirting, because I could see a warm smile of recognition light up their faces out of the corner of my eye.

We so loved dancing around the dining room table in each other's arms. I knew my kiss or inviting glance would always be returned with interest. Justin's love was abiding and all-encompassing, like a comfortable, welcoming room where I could put my feet up and relax. I was always at home in his heart. Our children felt comfortable and safe too, watching us flirt, kiss and dance. They could feel that all was right with the world.

So many ways to say, "I love you," "I see you," "I appreciate you," "I want you."

Uh-oh, time to pick up the children.

"Sorry babe, I gotta go."

"Then I'll see ya later?"

"Oh yeah. I'll be waiting for you..."

Chapter Seventeen

Mary Kay Bigelow and Bonny Meyer

Grief Comes Again

I've spent the past three days in grief. Again.

It has been years since Justin died. I no longer grieve his physical presence, but I grieve the absence of the profound connection that we knew together. I hold foundational knowledge about creating and nurturing intimate relationship. I feel powerful in my capacity to completely give myself to another. Although all these things are true, and this is what I deeply desire, there is no other person standing in front of me now. So, I am grieving the emptiness, the absence of profound, life-affirming and life-giving relationship. I am grieving the loving and beloved Other.

So again, grief comes and I lie in my bed and cry. Strength and self-reliance give way to fragility and allowing. Tenderly my heart softens and opens. Another crucible, another transformation.

Others around me are mystified and uncomfortable. Grief is unfamiliar and nearly forbidden territory in our society. Not so everywhere, however. I read that in traditional tribes from the Lake Atitlan region of Guatemala, grieving people are expected to completely fall apart, cry, fuss, get drunk, forget to take a bath, rave, and abandon all responsibilities. They are given total freedom and room to grieve for as long as it seems necessary to do so. During this time, the whole village looks after them, cares for them, feeds them, washes their clothes, tends their children and crops. There is great wisdom in this, and great compassion. The person in grief is able to allow the energies and emotions of grief to take over, to run through them completely until it is done. Over with. Then slowly, gently, they wash their face and begin to re-engage in village life once more.

What a blessing this would be! To be allowed and encouraged to totally let go, instead of everyone around me wishing I would smile and get over it and get back to normal as quickly and politely as possible.

If they only knew how lost and bereft, I feel.

Or maybe they know, because they saw the way Justin and I looked at each other. They saw the flirting, the look, the tease, the tenderness. They felt the depth and breadth of our love, and now they are afraid. They are afraid I will be broken by this loss.

Sometimes I am afraid too.

Lifeline

When drowning in grief people often need a lifeline. Mary Kay was mine.

It was enough that she and I had known each other since high school and that she had a naturally compassionate heart. But, in addition to these beautiful qualities, she was a trained grief counselor and knew exactly what to do with all of us in those first few days and weeks after Justin died. She knew that the most important thing she could do was to gently listen and then listen some more. I watched her as she quietly made her rounds from person to person checking in and engaging in comforting and meaningful conversations with my family and many friends who had come for the memorial. It was helpful that she had met many of them before, and now she could be a warm, open, familiar presence.

Mary Kay helped us understand that the crazy mix of emotions we were feeling was normal. It is normal to feel brain-dead. It is normal to feel guilty about something you hadn't gotten around to apologizing for. It is normal to feel angry at the person who died— and then feel guilty about feeling angry. It is normal to obsess over the details of our loss. It is normal to feel aimless, wandering about like a zombie. It is normal to feel completely apathetic. It is normal to care deeply and rage about something trivial.

"Don't worry, you're normal," she would repeat.

Her reassurance was so helpful to me as I was feeling all of these things and more. The most confusing was my rage. Over and over I yelled to Justin in my mind: I can't believe you left me! I knew I was supposed to feel bad for Justin whose life was suddenly cut short. But instead I felt pissed off. And guilty about feeling it!

After everyone left—the well-wishers, the friends, the extended Meyer family, the TS Restaurant managers who had taken over my kitchen and cooked for everyone, my married sons and daughters-in-law—Mary Kay was still there. She looked at me and said, "Call me anytime of the day or night, and I will answer the phone and be there for you." I did and she was.

I don't honestly recall how many times I called her at 2:00 or 3:00 in the morning. But there were plenty. Whenever I called, Mary Kay always answered in a calm, reassuring voice and listened me through those I can't go on, there's a hole in my heart, I want to die times during those first months after Justin died. Our middle-of-the-night talks were the most poignant and intimate of all our times together. So often I would tell myself, "I shouldn't call; Mary Kay has to get up and go to work in the morning." Amazingly enough, she remembers these calls as treasured gifts. Instead of feeling annoyed at being awakened in the middle of the night, she says she felt a kind of sacredness, like she was in "God Time." She told me that these were some of the most exquisite, intimate moments of her life too.

When I was hurting the most, full of heartache and longing, the nights seemed to stretch on forever. It was so hard to sleep alone after years and years of holding Justin's hand as we fell asleep, listening to Justin's breathing beside me. Waking up to an embrace and quiet talks about the day ahead. I gathered extra pillows from around the house and held on to them, cried into them, tried to pretend they were him. It took a long time for the aching and restlessness to dissipate, but finally they did.

Mary Kay was my lifeline, holding me steady so I wouldn't sink beneath the waves of grief and drown.

Breathwork Journey

I walk into the large, dimly lit meeting room in San Francisco's grand old Palace Hotel to see thick exercise mats on the floor radiating out in concentric circles from the center. I have arrived at an afternoon of discovery sponsored by the Institute of Noetic Sciences, a research non-profit I have donated to over the years. This invitation represents both an expression of gratitude as well as one of the Institute's many efforts to foster community within the inner circle of the organization.

We will be participating in an afternoon of Holotropic Breathwork®, a method developed by research psychiatrist, Stan Grof known as a pioneer of non-ordinary states of consciousness. I have heard of Holotropic Breathwork but have no idea what to expect. Apparently, most of the others in the room are at least somewhat acquainted with the process and settle in quickly. I, on the other hand, feel a bit disoriented and nervous. I find a woman whom I had met the previous day, Lynn from Chicago, and ask her to be my partner. Like me, she is new to this experience, and I feel comfortable with her because she is down-to-earth and practical, yet open, like me, to something completely new and different.

Together we listen to the instructions and decide that Lynn will go first. This means she will lie down on a pad on the floor and I will sit by her side as a calming presence if she needs one. The instructions are simple, and the rapid-breathing technique sounds easy. We are told that the experiencer (Lynn) will enter a non-ordinary state of consciousness by breathing deeply at an elevated pace while listening to a carefully curated musical set that initially facilitates physical release, then emotional release, and finally, integration and awakening. This three-hour process is designed to allow the breather to experience a range of physical sensations and psychological states. Ideally, in this flow of unusual experience, the breather can have visions or find energy that aids in healing emotional traumas, or perhaps receive answers to spiritual questions.

Okay ... This is going to be interesting.

The lights go down even lower and the music begins. Lynn seems to be a natural at the breathing process. She gets up to speed easily and is able to maintain the pace without apparent effort. I watch her face for any sign of distress. A couple of mats over, in the corner of the room, there is a woman who appears and sounds like she is giving birth. I am relieved that Lynn does not seem to be going through anything quite so dramatic. After about two and a half hours, the music slows and eventually comes to a stop. The lights come up. People slowly stir, sit up, and look around. I help Lynn walk to the restroom as she is still a little shaky and walks like she has not quite awakened fully from a dream. She shares a bit about her inner journey, saying she has received some valuable ideas about how her work can evolve in the future.

I feel comforted by her seemingly effortless success with the process and am ready to experience it for myself. I don't have a particular question or healing goal, so my intention is simply to be fully aware and open to the process.

As I begin to breathe I can feel how the rhythm of the music supports me. This is easier than I thought. In short order, I am envisioning beautiful landscapes ... flying over these landscapes carried by the sounds that fill the room and my consciousness. I have only a general recollection of the first hour or two except that it felt three-dimensional and wonderfully uplifting. There was nothing that was particularly striking, memorable, or impactful.

Then it happens. Justin is here.

He is not just here, he is kissing me passionately. I am instinctively returning his embrace. It feels as if we are consuming each other. In some distant part of my consciousness, this is impossible, it's not what they said would happen. But my experience of Justin is far more powerful than any doubt or hesitation. I feel hot tears streaming down my face. My heart opens wider and wider. It's both impossible and inescapable, like the beginning of our love for each other. The music is reaching a crescendo. Now Justin and I are rising together, united as one being, ascending so high that there is no longer any sense of earth below. My heart is bursting with joy and my awareness is completely filled with us, nothing but us.

The music peaks and then shifts. A slower, calmer melody begins, slowing the collective pace, changing the vibration of the entire room. I feel a sense of descent. Then I begin to separate back into myself. A primal scream of refusal rips through me. With every ounce of my will, every cell of my ravaged body, and all the pure intention of my elevated spirit, I attempt to climb again to regain the extraordinary state that Justin could share with me. I am sweating and crying out, desperate and determined to keep our spirits connected.

But I cannot. Try as I may, I am unable to fight my way back to my beloved. Tears of joy turn to sobbing anguish and loss. Of all the experiences of spirit connection I have had since Justin has died, this is by far the most profound. And so is the sense of loss I now feel.

Eyes still closed, I can sense Lynn suffused with concern as I convulse and cry out in grief. It takes me a long time to quiet and come back to everyday consciousness after the music ends. I have no words for Lynn about what I have just experienced. We agree to meet for lunch the next day. I stumble out of the room, avoiding all eye contact, still in a daze.

The next day I am sitting across a table from Lynn in the hotel's airy, elegant Garden Court, telling her of Justin, the great love of my life; how he came to me during my breath work journey, and how I lost him again. How I met him as a teenager and could not have him … fell in love but denied its expression … tested the limits of chastity but stepped back … encouraged him to keep his vows while agonizing at what that meant … stepped deeper into our love only to back away yet again … finally built a beautiful life together only to watch him die at its apex … time and time again, in a never-ending cycle of ecstasy and agony, finding him and losing him again … a cycle that even death, it seems, has not brought to an end.

He Was Grieving Over the Death of His Best Friend

From the depths of old internet offerings comes an incredible gem of a story. Someone has posted the following heartfelt plea online: "My friend just died. I don't know what to do."

Here is the anonymous reply:

"I'm old. What that means is that I've survived (so far) and a lot of people I've known and loved did not.

I've lost friends, best friends, acquaintances, co-workers, grandparents, mom, relatives, teachers, mentors, students, neighbors, and a host of other folks. I have no children, and I can't imagine the pain it must be to lose a child. But here's my two cents …"

I wish I could say you get used to people dying. But I never did. I don't want to. It tears a hole through me whenever somebody I love dies, no matter the circumstances. But I don't want it to "not matter." I don't want it to be something that just passes. My scars are a testament to the love and the relationship that I had for and with that person. And if the scar is deep, so was the love. So be it.

Scars are a testament to life. Scars are a testament that I can love deeply and live deeply and be cut, or even gouged, and that I can heal and continue to live and continue to love. And the scar tissue is stronger than the original flesh ever was. Scars are a testament to life. Scars are only ugly to people who can't see.

As for grief, you'll find it comes in waves.

When the ship is first wrecked, you're drowning, with wreckage all around you. Everything floating around you reminds you of the beauty and the magnificence of the ship that was and is no more. And all you can do is float. You find some piece of the wreckage and you hang on for a while. Maybe it's some physical thing. Maybe it's a happy memory or a photograph. Maybe it's a person who is also floating. For a while, all you can do is float. Stay alive. In the beginning, the waves are 100 feet tall and crash over you without mercy. They come 10 seconds apart and don't even give you time to catch your breath. All you can do is hang on and float. After a while, maybe weeks, maybe months, you'll find the waves are still 100 feet tall, but they come further apart. When they come, they still crash all over you and wipe you out. But in between, you can breathe, you can function. You never know what's going to trigger the grief. It might be a song, a picture, a street intersection, the smell of a cup of coffee. It can be just about anything ... and the wave comes crashing. But in between waves, there is life.

Somewhere down the line, and it's different for everybody, you find that the waves are only 80 feet tall. Or 50 feet tall. And while they still come, they come further apart. You can see them coming. An anniversary, a birthday, or Christmas, or landing at O'Hare. You can see it coming, for the most part, and you prepare yourself. And when it washes over you, you know that somehow you will, again, come out the other side. Soaking wet, sputtering, still hanging on to some tiny piece of the wreckage, but you'll come out.

Take it from an old guy. The waves never stop coming, and somehow you don't really want them to. But you learn that you'll survive them. And other waves will come. And you'll survive them too.

If you're lucky, you'll have lots of scars from lots of loves. And lots of shipwrecks." —Anonymous

Chapter Eighteen

Justin & Bonny Meyer in front of Silver Oak Cellars
Photo by Wine Spectator

Setting Limits

We released our third Silver Oak vintage, the 1974 North Coast Cabernet, in 1979, in line with Justin's philosophy that consumers should buy the wine when it was sufficiently aged, not years before that. And then something amazing happened. Robert Lawrence Balzar, wine editor of the Los Angeles Times and the most influential wine critic in the country, declared it his 1979 Wine of the Year.

We had made about 4,000 cases of the 1974 Cabernet. With Balzar's critical rave plus a gold medal at the Los Angeles County Fair, we were sold out before the next vintage was released. The Wine of the Year accolades for the 1974 did not quite carry over to our 1975 and 1976 wines, because those vintages were drought years and got a bit of a bad rap in the wine press.

This taught me, early on, why most wine producers have a love/hate relationship with the wine critics in newspapers, magazines, and websites. If the critics love a vintage, we vintners are all in hog heaven. If they pan a vintage—which means they think every wine from that year is substandard—then wine producers are left selling that wine into the wind, against the current, up the hill, pick your metaphor. What makes it even more frustrating is that the wine, our wine, may be great, but it is very difficult get the distributors to trust us over influential wine critics.

This is exactly what happened with our 1975 and 1976 wines. Despite the weather challenges, Justin had managed to bring out the best in these wines with carefully calculated viticultural practices, winemaking and blending decisions.

So he had done his job. Now it was my job to convince our wine purveyors that the Silver Oak bottlings were not "typical" 1975 and 1976 wines. They were the best of those vintages and anyone who sold them would find that their customers were quite pleased. I got on the phone, wrote letters, talked with some of our Franciscan distributors and opened new markets. In other words, I did whatever I had to do, to sell out both vintages shortly before the next Cabernet was released. It took a lot of tenacity, but I got it done.

From our 1977 vintage on, we were on a roll. By then, I had a solid lineup of distributors and had hired another salesperson to help me with Silver Oak's wine shop and restaurant accounts in California. Then I turned to the sales staff at Franciscan: which distributers and retailers should I approach, and which ones should I avoid? This gave me good "intel" but I was still on my own to create the right strategies and messaging in our various sales channels.

Sometime after we moved into our new Silver Oak winery, a limousine drove into the winery parking lot. The occupant was a Silver Oak enthusiast from Texas. He stepped out of the limo, walked into the tasting room and saw our glass-enclosed "wine library"—a collection of older vintages that we held back for research, special events, and major anniversaries.

The man from Texas took one look at the library and decided he had to have it.

All of it.

In an industry with much lower profit margins than most people realize, deciding to not sell a bottle of wine is an act of faith. You must believe that you have made a wine worth keeping, at the winery's expense, so that people can experience it in a more evolved, advanced state of development sometime in the future. That wine can never be made again, so it's truly unique, a treasure beyond price. That's why we featured our library behind glass, so people could see it and understand that we were taking that leap of faith with every vintage—our wine was that good, that worthy of holding onto.

The gentleman from Texas told the tasting room person he wanted to buy everything we had in the library on display. Then he turned to his girlfriend and said, "Go to the car and get some money, Honey." The tasting room person ran up the stairs to ask me and Justin what she should do. Our philosophy was to make outstanding wines more affordable for people, not exclusive treasures for the well-to-do. But we had not really worked out how this would apply in all cases. Now we had a test case that would require us to make a decision, with a huge potential profit hanging in the balance.

It didn't take long.

Justin and I looked out his office window curious to see the limo parked in front, then walked slowly down the stairs together. As always, we didn't need to speak to be in sync: we both knew we needed a good story about why we were going to turn down a huge sum of money for a product we intended to sell someday to someone ... Just not this person, on this day. By the time we got to the bottom of the stairs, our "library policy" was ready for its first performance.

We first expressed our gratitude and appreciation for the man's willingness to purchase the entire contents of our wine library. Then we explained our philosophy of bringing great wine to ordinary people, and that this extended to our library wines. Well-aged wine was a rare experience for most people, and we wanted them to have that opportunity. Hardly any other winery anywhere operated this way, so we had to hold fast to our intention, which was to hang on to our library wines so that lots of people could have an opportunity to buy a bottle or two.

It sounded so convincing, the rich gentleman from Texas went along. We sold him some rare large-format bottles from 1974 and other vintages, plus a couple of cases of our current vintage. He and Honey left mostly satisfied. We knew in our hearts that we had taken the right approach, but I must say I can still remember that fat stack of hundred-dollar bills in Honey's hand. It would have been sweet to have a payday like that.

After this encounter, Justin and I knew we would have to come up with a wine library policy, one that our staff could execute without running up the stairs in excited alarm. That is when I began to work in earnest on our wine allocation plan for our tasting room. I had been allocating wine to distributors and California accounts for years by then, based on a rough estimate of what they had purchased the year before and a frank and open conversation and negotiation as to whether we had the wine and they had the capacity to increase that number by a small percentage year over year. Everything was calculated so that we would run out of wine about a month or two before the next vintage was released. That way, everyone was ready for the next vintage, and hopefully, our wines did not have to be pulled off restaurant wine lists for lack of inventory.

The next step, demonstrated by Mr. Texas, was to apply this same thinking and planning to our tasting room, which now was seeing many visitors each day. I did some basic estimates of tasting room sales and numbers of visitors per year. At the beginning of each vintage, visitors could buy a case of the Alexander Valley Cabernet, six bottles per person of the Napa Valley Cab, and one bottle per person of the Bonny's Vineyard.

Sometimes we found we would have to reduce the per-person allotment as we got closer and to the end of a sales cycle. Some library wines were re-released periodically: one bottle per customer until gone. Some enthusiasts would bring four friends so they could buy more than a one- customer allocation. That was okay. We admired their determination and creativity—and their love of our wine!

The goal of all this was a system that gave people equal access to our wines regardless of their ability to buy large quantities or physically get to the winery before other people. Soon thereafter, our wines were allocated across the board; to our distributors, our retailers and restaurateurs, and our tasting room visitors. Even with this system, we began to run out before the next vintage was released. The combination of Justin's single-minded devotion to Cabernet Sauvignon and his relentless efforts to make a world-class Cabernet year after year meant that Silver Oak became the benchmark for Napa and Alexander Valleys and put us in a position we never anticipated: the world consistently wanted more wine than we could make.

Release Day

Every now and then, people ask me, with wide-eyed wonder and admiration: how did we create Silver Oak release day? The truth is we didn't—our customers did.

By the time we were in our fifth or sixth vintage, our wine was allocated. This caused our most keenly interested customers to call the winery: When would our next Cabernet become available to them? Justin or I would get on the phone with them and make sure their personal allocation of our wine was set to arrive at their local retail shop. Then four customers in Arizona decided they were too eager to wait for the wine to get to their state, city, and local wine shop. They flew to Napa in a private plane and came to the winery on the first day that the latest vintage was released for sale. We were amazed and amused that anyone would go to such trouble for our wine. We had never heard of anyone doing this in Napa Valley or anywhere else. So we happily sold them each a case of wine and they walked out the door happy as could be.

That year we received so many phone inquiries about our release dates that I began to write and distribute a newsletter that included this information. On the first day of the next release, in 1985 or so, we got a call from the tasting room staff as they were getting ready to open up later that morning. Apparently, there was a line of people waiting outside the door.

This was a strange occurrence for a summer day in our sleepy rural valley, so Justin hurried over to the winery and asked the people how he could help them. They replied that they were there to purchase their case of wine the minute it was released. It was long before opening time for the tasting room, so Justin said, "Come on in and I'll make you some coffee." Then he called me. I ran to the Oakville Grocery to get pastries for these early-morning customers.

That was the beginning of what became a huge phenomenon: Silver Oak fans eagerly waiting at the door on the day we released our newest vintage.

A year later, knowing that fans would be flocking to the winery, we got the bright idea to release and sell some library wines: a few bottles from older vintages along with some large-format bottles (magnums, double-magnums, five- and six-liter bottles), alongside the regular release. That primed the pump even more. The next year, people arrived the night before release day and slept in our parking lot. They either slept in line by the door or created an agreement among themselves as to their place in line. All this so they could make sure that they got their favorite six-liter bottle for a special occasion or for a friend or loved one.

Now it was not enough to provide some coffee and donuts. We started serving cheeses, thin-sliced prime rib and vegetables at lunchtime. Around 1990 we decided there was so much demand for our wines that we could continue to release our Alexander Valley wine in August and move the release date for our Napa Cabernet six months later. This evened out our cash flow and reduced the crowd size somewhat. But even February's winter weather did not deter the early arrivers. So we began erecting tents so people would not have to stand in the rain.

By the 1993 August release, at Justin's suggestion, we ordered hundreds of his favorite ice cream bars (Heath Bar Crunch) to hand out as an afternoon treat. It ended up being cool and overcast so the ice cream bars were not as popular as anticipated. We ended up eating those ice cream bars at home and the winery for months which delighted

Justin and the kids.

So it went, year after year. More customers, some arriving earlier and earlier the evening before. We needed so much food that we hired caterers. Bit by bit the winery grew and the crowd grew. Trying to make it easier for those who camped by the door overnight, we hired someone to be there all night to hand out numbers so people could secure a position in line and then sleep in a real bed at a nearby hotel instead of in their car in our parking lot. We opened earlier, and typically would run out of the large-format bottles in the first hour. Those who came early were so happy when they got a particular older vintage or six-liter bottle.

Often, they stayed for the day, or they would go to other wineries then come back and party with us until we closed.

On release days there were too many people for our tasting room staff to handle, so we recruited customers and friends to help out. I designed a new release day shirt every year for our staff and volunteers to wear, so customers could easily tell who to go to for help or to answer questions. Our volunteers got a shirt, a name tag, a bottle of the release wine and an assignment. Some poured wine, some passed food, others welcomed folks and handed out wine glasses. The shirts became treasured event mementos.

Gradually we added other activities. We had the folks from A&K Cooperage come and demonstrate how they make barrels, and when the barrel was finished, every visitor was welcome to sign it. We had a photographer come to take photographs of customers, giving them a visual keepsake of their visit on release day. As the crowds grew, we rented more tents and the event became bigger and bigger until we had to add parking attendants and arrange for the California Highway Patrol to assign officers to direct traffic on the main road.

Silver Oak release day became kind of a legend in the valley and other wineries began to plan events on the same day to take advantage of the extra crowds. The Groths gave us an early painting of a glass of Silver Oak by Thomas Arvid. I loved this painting, which we hung up in our dining room. Over the next year or two, I saw more Thomas Arvid wine paintings in local galleries and noticed that Silver Oak was a frequent subject. I got his phone number and invited him to a release day to demonstrate how he paints his photorealistic masterpieces. He was delighted to come and I think sold a couple of paintings, including the one he created that day at our event. He received such a warm response, he continues to attend every Silver Oak release day.

Beginning with our first release day or two, customers began asking Justin and me to sign bottles for themselves or a friend's special occasions. We ended up signing bottles all day long. People would stand in line and we would sign our names to their treasured purchases. Although a bit exhausting, Justin and I enjoyed the opportunity to visit with our friends and customers one by one over the course of the day, to hear their stories, and celebrate with them. Most of the inscriptions began with "Happy Anniversary," "Happy Birthday," or "Congratulations," so we were virtual participants in countless celebrations around the country.

Toward the end of our time at Silver Oak, we had an average of 3,000 to 4,000 people visit on release day. It was truly a major celebratory event. When release day was over all the staff and the huge group of volunteers would have a barbeque and swim party at our house in summer, or music and dinner at the winery in the winter. That was yet another celebration, a time for everyone to celebrate the new wine, all the great people who had come to enjoy it with us, and our sales success. Usually, the people in charge of keeping tabs of the sales receipts would work an extra hour or two so that they could get the total and let us know how much wine we sold on that day. When the total was announced, a great cheer would rise from the crowd of staff and volunteers. It was 1998 when we had our first million-dollar day. The news traveled the valley like lightning. Other wineries took notice and began to emulate Silver Oak; focusing more on Cabernet and customer events.

Every now and then we would break out our banjo and guitar and lead a huge communal sing-along. It's how Justin and I first found our connection with each other, and it continued for decades until there was only one musician standing.

On Partnership

Yesterday my friend Wilford asked what great partnership in a relationship meant to me.

Of course, my mind immediately went to my amazingly powerful partnership with Justin. The first thing that came to mind was the shared values that served us as an unwavering foundation. We did not question them or transgress them, and everyone around us knew that.

Our values were the basis for all our decisions and for how we interacted not just with each other, but with all others.

Our partnership was two people standing together side by side facing the world and making our way hand in hand, occasionally steadying or supporting each other when the need arose. This was very different from two people leaning on each other for support. In that scenario, when one person is weak, they can both fall and the relationship crumbles.

As true partners, we were cheerleaders for each other, energetically cheering each other on to victory. We reminded each other of who we were, and what our talents and contributions were in the hard times when we felt discouraged or too tired to carry on.

We calmed each other down when we got overwhelmed or anxious. We turned up the music and amped up the energy when the other began to lag. We brought a wider perspective when the other's focus became too narrow. We helped each other with work and chores when one of us got too far behind. We were so attuned to each other, we knew when to help pick up the load or kick the other one into gear.

We lived in a state of compassion and laughed and cried with each other. Sharing our joy and sorrow made our life exquisite. Justin knew my heart and treated it with the utmost tenderness, as I did his. We each respected the path the other was on and held a flashlight to light the way.

We shared a fundamental focus and orientation to life. We were both passionate and dedicated to the life and business we were creating together. All that said, we never felt a need to have the same interests and talents. In fact, our life was richer because we didn't. Our complementary talents and proclivities helped every project be more successful. I would know nothing about football if I had not watched games with Justin and heard his running commentary. And he would not have been introduced to design, sewing and photography without me.

Our great partnership made all of life better in big and little ways too numerous to mention.

The Heart of Silver Oak

Deep in the center, within the sacred heart of Silver Oak, were love and passion. Within Justin there was a deep devotion to and love of God, for me, our family, for the vineyards, and the wines they would produce. Justin's relationship with God was primary in his life. This devotion began in early childhood and was nurtured by his mother, Edith. She found a way for Justin to attend Garces, a Christian Brother's junior high and high school in Bakersfield, which shaped and molded him through his teen years. The question, "How can I best serve God?" was ultimately answered by his entry into the Brotherhood. Then later, he answered it as a devoted husband, father, and vintner.

Our love and passion for each other was seared by our struggles through the ups and downs of the first five years of our forbidden relationship. The moment Justin decided to leave the Brothers and I said "yes" to his proposal of marriage, our love exploded like a Fourth of July skyrocket, having been tightly contained, then suddenly ignited and allowed the freedom of full expression in every direction. Silver Oak, in all its aspects, and our family life were true manifestations of our unbounded creative love force.

To watch Justin walk through a vineyard was like watching a monk walk the "Camino" on a mindful pilgrimage. The vines knew him and responded to his tender touch and attention. Justin frequently stated that "Great wines are made in the vineyard," and he lived this truth. He had a deep relationship with each vine and the vineyard as a whole. He was not a student of quantum physics, but the holographic universe lived for him in each microscopic cluster within a bud; the structure of a vine, block, and vineyard; the smallest and largest expressions of living holographic systems. The vineyard didn't just exist in the soil, but also in his mind as a whole living system that at best was in perfect balance with its place, its microclimate, the way the vines were pruned and cultivated, and the perfect moment of harvest through to recovery and restorative rest to reawaken again in the spring.

Justin was renowned as a winemaker, but that's not how he thought of himself or his work. Just look at the back label of an early Silver Oak Cabernet and you'll see the title he gave himself: "Justin Meyer, Winegrower."

In his youth, Justin was a fierce competitor, earning him great respect, honor, and a bum knee from a high school football injury. Dedication to excellence and integrity burned in his soul. There was an absolute conviction that he had the ability to make the best Cabernet in the world. This single-minded dedication served him and Silver Oak well, earning us many accolades and undying dedication from our staff and customers. We all lived the dream along with him, carried by his love and passion.

Every year, Justin would say to the cellar crew and staff, "We have yet to make our best Cabernet." He was never satisfied, always striving to make a more perfect wine. That said, he was supremely pleased with the 1997 Cabernets, the last vintage over which he had complete oversight before we sold our half of Silver Oak to the Duncan family in 2001. For him, the dream had arrived at its apex; the consummation of his life's work and his life itself, just three days after the 1997 was released.

Chapter Nineteen

1928 Model A—Spitfire Meyer Trucking

Spitfire Meyer

In my garage there is a 1928 Ford Model A pick-up truck: original forest green and black with solid oak side rails. To a knowledgeable eye, every detail is as true as when the truck came off of the factory assembly line. Green leather bench seat. No seat belts. Rear view mirror with an embedded clock. Wooden-spoke wheels tired in hard rubber. Removable canvas top. Hand-operated windshield wipers. Even the hand-crank starter mechanism is intact and still working, though a battery-operated electric starter has been added to save unskilled hands and wrists from accident when the transmission kicks the hand crank back.

The only other addition to this classic vehicle is a bold black message engraved on the side rails:

"SPITFIRE MEYER TRUCKING"

Justin rarely expressed an interest in having or owning anything. Clothes were a necessary utility. He owned a few precious books, a fly-fishing rod or two, a shotgun to scare away the flickers that pounded holes in the house every spring and fall, and his banjo. We had a wine collection in the cellar below the house. That was about it.

But every once in a while, we would be driving down the road and he would see an old Model A pick-up and his eyes would go dreamy. "I would really love to have a truck like that someday," he would say. Then his voice would go soft, as if he were talking with himself. "Probably too expensive ... Sure would be fun ... Just drive it around the valley ... Maybe someday ... "

I decided to organize a big party at Silver Oak for Justin's 50th birthday. This was not a surprise party, because I wanted his full participation in creating the guest list, menu, and other elements. But I did want to give Justin one big surprise. I called his cousin, Dick Kahler, who was a serious car buff, a great researcher, very well connected in the

Bay Area, and always a willing accomplice to anything fun. Justin and Dick had worked on old cars when they were teenagers together. When I asked Dick if he would help me find an old Model A pickup truck for Justin, he was delighted. To my surprise, it didn't take him long to find one in mint condition in the Bay Area. I drove down, inspected the truck, and wrote the check. Dick kept the truck—and the secret—until the party.

Silver Oak had two massive arched redwood doors that opened into the tasting room. Visitors and guests would enter through the right door only, the left normally remaining fixed in position. Midway through the party, I gave Dick a signal and he took off to get the car out of its hiding place while I quietly unlatched the left door. When I heard the unmistakable sound of an old four-piston engine, I swung both doors wide open and Dick drove the 1928 Model A right into the tasting room where the party was in full swing.

Justin's eyes went wide with amazed delight and the crowd cheered. I will always remember that moment; he was thrilled and so was I. Dick moved over and Justin jumped into the driver's seat. He backed it up and took the Model A for a spin around the winery front entrance. His delight and disbelief lasted for days.

I too got a surprise that evening, because when I bought the truck it lacked side rails. Now it sported not only rails but that striking engraving—and thereby hangs a tale.

Shortly after Justin and I married, he joined his friends Ed Schuh and Dave Nickerson at the corner bar, the Oak Rail, for a drink after work. They noticed a somewhat inebriated patron hanging around the pool table, making foul-mouthed comments that were disturbing to a young couple who were trying their best to ignore him. Justin got up, went over to the intoxicated fellow, and suggested that he settle down and stop offending the young woman. He did not settle down. Instead he followed Justin to the bar and delivered yet another string of expletives.

Justin's account of what happened next was brief. "The guy walked up and started in on me. I don't remember exactly what he said, but the next thing I knew I was throwing him out the door."

Frankly, I thought it was cool that my new husband had stood up for the young woman who was just trying to play pool. It gave me the feeling that if anyone ever messed with me, Justin would step in immediately. Justin, though, was feeling a bit embarrassed about it. Growing up in Bakersfield, he had seen and participated in plenty of fights in bars, schools, and other places. He thought he had left that rough way of being behind him, so he felt sheepish about being involved in a bar brawl in our neighborhood. It was quite a contrast with how people saw him: as a true gentleman who was respectful, polite, and kind to all. (Except drunks, apparently.)

Justin's contrite feelings were not exactly shared by his friend Ed. From then on, Ed dubbed him "Spitfire" Meyer and never ceased teasing him about throwing that guy out of the bar.

Dave Nickerson, who was also in the bar with Justin and Ed that night, was the one who joined with the cellar staff to commission the side rails and engrave them. Today Meyer Family Cellars produces a Napa Valley Cabernet Sauvignon called "Spitfire," in remembrance of Justin's readiness to defend the honor of a lady.

BMW 325i Cabriolet

Traveling North on Highway 101, I come upon a red BMW 325i Cabriolet in the next lane. My heart skips a beat. Could it be? I accelerate and maneuver a bit to get a closer look. Searching for gold pinstripes. No, no pinstripes. Not the car I remember.

The first time I drove a BMW was in Germany, when Justin and I took the boys there to visit the Eckes and tour the wine country. Our souped-up sedan made a strong impression, handling tight turns and autobahn straightaways with equal grace and excitement. Years later, that car was undoubtedly one of two things Justin had in mind when he decided to surprise me for my 40th birthday. The other was the 1928 Model A Ford truck I gave him for his 50th birthday. If he could get a dream car, I should have one, too: a fire engine red BMW 325i Cabriolet tricked out with gold pinstripes and gold wheels. In my humble opinion, you have never (or maybe very rarely) seen a more breathtaking automobile.

Justin bought it, brought it home on a random day in the middle of July, and completely surprised me. I have never received such a perfect and completely unexpected gift. And I wasn't the only one who loved that car. The kids and their friends liked it a whole lot better than the lame blue station wagon I had been hauling them around in. And I found that with the top down it could hold almost as much cargo as the family car.

Eventually, it was time to trade the car in for a later model that had an electric top, and for my 50th birthday Justin bought me yet another new iteration, gold this time. But something about that original red beauty still has a piece of my heart. When I see one on the highway, I just have to get close to it for a few miles and remember the day in July when Justin showed me how generous and loving my husband could be.

BMW 325i Cabriolet

Fire engine red
Gold pinstripes and gold wheels
Black cloth top
Opened to the sun

In the middle of the summer
For no apparent reason
You surprised me
With the best valentine I ever received

I Quit!

Justin grew up in an era when husbands worked and wives were homemakers. So when we got married, I shifted from being a diligent university student to making a home for us on the former dairy farm that soon became a vineyard. I was not used to isolation, quiet, or an empty schedule, and quickly got bored the first winter, after the weather closed in. I read the small collection of classics I found at the local library and volunteered up at Mont La Salle teaching the fifth- to eighth-grade boys who attended the boarding school there. But that was part-time. I wanted something I could sink my teeth into.

So one evening I informed Justin that I was going to apply for a job at the local bank. He gave me an incredulous look and asked, "Why would you want to do that?" Clearly, he was both disappointed and taken aback by my idea of working full-time, but he had a beautiful response: "Well, if you want something to do, I could use your help."

And that's how Justin and I came to work together throughout our marriage.

The first benefit of working alongside Justin took us both by surprise: I no longer greeted him at the end of each day with, "Tell me everything you did today." I was no longer starved for stimulation and information, because we were together, or working separately toward the same goals, all the time.

After an initial awkwardness that always accompanies two people getting into sync with each other, we naturally slipped into a synchronized flow, not unlike our experience cutting and stacking firewood years before or our playing folk music together. It was easy, fun, and fulfilling, as we each naturally gravitated toward tasks and roles that we had the talents and affinity for. Essentially Justin was a production guy, and I had a talent for design, marketing and sales. A perfect partnership.

But every now and then, especially as the winery grew and our systems formalized, I chafed at feeling like I did not get the budget I thought marketing deserved. Opportunities would crop up or a new packaging approach would arise which I could not take timely advantage of because the budget didn't include the money for it. That's when we would get into a power struggle. "Tell me why you can spend tens of thousands on a new pump or press for the cellar and I can't have $5,000 for my department? You buy whatever you want, but I get treated like a second-class citizen!" After some heated and frustrated back and forth, we would work it out—and I would determine to adjust the budget appropriately the next year.

Working together gave us expansive opportunity to talk about strategy, solve problems or mull over an employee challenge. Fortunately, or unfortunately, this usually occurred over dinner, particularly when we were out at a restaurant and didn't have the children with us. Noticing this propensity, we would resolve to not talk about business over dinner. That would hold for a month or two. Then we would slip back into talking shop over dinner again. The truth is, Justin and I loved and were deeply engaged in what we were doing at Silver Oak. And we loved working and working out the challenges and opportunities together. So it often didn't feel like work.

Until I quit.

Twice.

In both cases, I walked out because I felt my business partner was getting a bit too full of himself or too overbearing. Neither departure lasted more than a week and a half. We wouldn't really talk about it or try to resolve the disagreement. We would both just soften a bit and I would feel myself being reeled in by the next enticing piece of work that needed to get done.

The conversation when I came back the second time took a few seconds. I walked into Justin's office to ask him a question. He looked up and said, "I thought you quit."

"Well, I'm back," I replied, and that was that.

I knew why he sometimes got a case of "Boss-itis." All day long, every day, everyone around Justin would do whatever he asked or told them to do. He was a strong, compelling, convincing, and somewhat intimidating leader. It worked well for everyone when he laid down the law and others had clear direction. But Justin didn't intimidate me. When the boss-itis began to spill out of the winery and into our home life, I would nip it in the bud.

"Your attitude may work at the winery, but it doesn't work around here," I'd say.

He would get the message, put his attitude and approach in check, and become lover and father again.

Sometimes people would ask me if I enjoyed certain privileges at the winery, as an owner and wife of Justin Meyer. The answer was no. From the beginning, we were extra cautious not to come anywhere close to exercising a family advantage over other employees or our financial partner, Ray Duncan. In fact, during my close to 30-year tenure at Franciscan and Silver Oak, I was always intentionally undercompensated relative to my position and responsibilities.

I suppose there was one exception: I got to sleep with the boss.

After the Children Left

After the children left home, life changed dramatically and wonderfully. I think we were never fully aware of how deep a responsibility we carried for them, until we were free of it. Now there was no one to get up and fix breakfast for, no one to wonder about late at night when they weren't home.

We quickly slipped into a new, relaxed routine. We woke up with the sun instead of an alarm, and began the day making love. Our passion for each other never seemed to fade, but instead got stronger and more deeply resonant over the years. We had never stopped touching, holding hands, kissing, and flirting like newlyweds. So, as we moved further into middle age, our sexual life blossomed.

Conventional wisdom, usually transmitted in disparaging jokes, did not prepare us for this. We had kind of expected to feel old and relatively disinterested in sex when we reached our 50s and 60s, respectively. I began to wonder who had made up all those silly jokes and why. Given leisure and privacy again after decades of child-rearing, we began to explore each other's bodies and ways of making love we hadn't before. I personally became much more responsive. I truly believe Justin got at least as much pleasure taking me to climax again and again as he got from his own release.

We became daily visitors to that territory of ecstatic spiritual union we first embarked upon more than 30 years before in a single bed in the Olmos' house. Our lovemaking, although at times active and wildly passionate, more often had a quality of stillness, reverence, and timelessness.

Years before, I had bought a book on Tantric sex and had shared some of the suggested rituals and practices with Justin. The idea of sexual union being a path to spiritual awakening was fascinating and appealing to me. Justin, to my deep disappointment, wanted nothing to do with it. It felt foreign and contrived to him. He was also a bit leery of spiritual practices that weren't Catholic. Though he was fairly open-minded in other areas of life, he had residual programming that blocked his access to other traditions—especially eastern traditions. They felt wrong or possibly even sinful to him.

As we spent more and more time in the territory of spiritually rich physical union, I realized we didn't need Tantra. All rituals, mantras, and paths to God are made up by somebody along the way anyway. As we opened more and more to each other and to spirit, we blazed our own trail, and found our own path into the mystic.

Come To Me My Love

Come to me my love
And fill me again
With your sublime
Powerful essence

Kiss me so deep
You touch my soul
With the tip
Of your tongue

Breathe me in
As I inhale you
And we become
One breath

Pull me into you
Closer and closer
Until our boundaries blur
Our bodies becoming one

Together we surrender
Into the mystery
Dive into the stillness
Of ever-expanding silence

Flying like Icarus
Into the sun
Until blinded by the light
We completely disappear

Chapter Twenty

Justin Meyer at Silver Oak Cellars

I Know The Truth

I know the truth. I know the truth about relationships. When I see people struggle, and struggle, and struggle with and within relationships I want to spread my hands wide and yell, "It's so simple! Take heart, open your heart, and get ready for joy!"

Authenticity, transparency, and trustworthiness are vital to great relationships. These qualities take courage, perseverance and practice. I practice authenticity every day. I find that I must be ever vigilant and dedicated to speaking my truth, maintaining healthy boundaries, and showing up over and over and over again in ways that honor my essence. But the rest is easy.

Kindness

When young engaged couples have asked me about a foundational quality of great marriages, I have often replied, "Kindness." They look surprised, so I repeat, "Yes, kindness."

We are so quick to be kind to our friends, yet so quick to be short, impatient, or disparaging with our partners. When we are consistently kind to one another, just imagine how wonderful all our close relationships become. Imagine how our world would be. Polite. Kind. Gentle. Gracious. Thoughtful.

How powerful these sweet qualities are!

Generosity

Generosity is related to kindness, but it is different. Justin grew up poor. It is my perception that such people are generally more generous than people who have more. Maybe it is because when they have a little bit of something, they think they are rich. Maybe it is because they have a keener experience and understanding of need or hunger. At any rate, Justin's generosity always impressed and moved me. When he was a kid, he shared everything special he came by with his a-little-worse-off friend named Larry. Later in life, he would hoist cases of wine on his shoulder and deliver them to the humble Carmelites down the road at Christmas time. He also loved donning his "Santa" outfit of green sweats, white turtleneck and red suspenders to deliver wine all over town to friends and business associates. Justin loved to cook on the weekends for our family and a parade of friends. He was generous with his sense of humor, with his affection, and with everything he had. He was the quintessential provider. Like most men, Justin had toys he loved; his fishing rods and flies, his single engine Cessna 206 and Model A Pickup, his wine collection ... but he wasn't attached to any of it. What he loved was the experience, the richness of life, and the joy of sharing it.

Non-Judgment

The great attraction in judging others is that we get to feel superior. Then, of course, the others get busy judging us. Escaping judgment is impossible. If you think you can achieve perfection and thus escape, think again. Also, take a moment to consider how everyone else feels about so-called "perfect" people—it might cause you to re-think any desire to be perfect yourself.

The easy thing about non-judgment is that it is a "non." When I take a moment to relax and just hang out and watch those around me with curiosity, appreciation, and permission, it is a joyful experience. I find it is easier than I might imagine, and I can let go of the ever-vigilant job of judging.

No relationship can weather constant distain and judgment. Not being judged means I am free to be me and to flourish, expressing my uniqueness. Together we are free to be our unbridled unique selves within our relationships, which, of course, creates the permission and space to be fully authentic. Within this frame of mind, together we can whole-heartedly enjoy all the little things that attracted us to each other in the first place.

These simple truths are the foundation of "fairytale marriages"— relationships that are deeply admired and longed for.

Authenticity, Trustworthiness, Kindness, Generosity, and Non-Judgment are qualities that make life and love a whole lot easier and more beautiful in ways too numerous to count.

Fear of Surrender

Author Gregg Braden says our three primal fears as human beings are fear of "not being enough," fear of surrender, and fear of abandonment.

These fundamental fears seem to hold our minds and hearts hostage and ultimately limit us, keeping us from experiencing the depth of who we really are. Shaky self-esteem, or feeling we are not enough somehow, prevents us from knowing and coming from our authentic power. Fear of surrender, and fear of possible subsequent abandonment, keep us from the deep intimacy we all long for.

In her research on the subject, Dr. Brené Brown discovered that allowing ourselves to be more vulnerable is a key to living a happy life. She produced a lecture series called "The Power of Vulnerability," which I have listened to many times. Brené makes it clear that contrary to what we may think, vulnerability is power, not weakness. It is essential for innovation, creativity, great relationships, and a life well lived.

Spiritual masters from many traditions say that surrender—letting go of our minds and egos, letting go of our fears—is the gateway into bliss: resting in the security of our true nature and true union with the divine and each other. Surrender is so simple intellectually, yet so difficult emotionally. In fact, it seems impossible for many, as evidenced by the despair we see all around us.

I have been blessed with wise teachers and have read books about many wisdom traditions. I have been taught and shown the way with gentleness and patience. I even have had profound moments of insight and experiences that have left indelible imprints on my soul and shifted my perspective and worldview forever. And yet, like almost everyone, I continue to get caught in grief, loss, a sense of separation and a deep longing for intimate connection. I know the destination is already here, it lies in surrender to the love that surrounds me in every moment. And yet it feels so far away at times ... too far to reach.

I know the particular one I long for. Justin is right here with me always. I know the intimacy and power of our connection has actually become stronger with our physical separation. There are moments when our connection is so powerful, so profound, it goes beyond understanding or description. And still, I fall deep into grief and the experience of profound loss and separation when those moments end.

I am ready to end the craziness. I am ready to take the leap ... or maybe it's a descent ... into surrender. Ready to fully let go of my attachment to my human experience of separation and live into my experience of oneness and connectedness. It's the only way out of grief and suffering, the only way into what is real.

The Course in Miracles says. "Nothing real can be threatened. Nothing unreal exists. Herein lies the peace of God."

Love is real.

Our connectedness to each other and all things is real.

My journey is ultimately about becoming a master of the dance between my humanness and my spiritual essence.

Feeling and embracing the very physical, natural experience of loss and grief, the sense of separation, while simultaneously knowing myself as divine essence and feeling the oneness, connectedness to all things. This is the journey of a lifetime. This is the journey of my lifetime.

I Have Courted Grief

I have courted grief
We have walked together
Oh, so many miles

We have danced
Whirling and swirling
Circling 'round each other

We have talked quietly
Hour after hour
Sharing knowing glances

But, up until now
I have
Avoided his kiss.

The time has come
And I approach
Trembling with terror

I catch my breath
And shut my eyes
Suspended in silence

Then I plunge
Deeper, deeper
Falling, spinning

Plummeting into dark
Unutterable depths
Into the murky void

Somewhere there
Falling turns to flying
As Grief and I embrace

We are caught-up
In the undulating
Dance of lovemaking

Up and down, in and out
Faster and faster
Oh, exquisite passion!

A cry rises and bursts
My heart explodes
Ripped wide open

Ecstasy!

Maria Magdalena

There is a painting of Mary Magdalene from around 1530, by Giovanni

Girolamo Savoldo (also known as Girolama da Brescia). A friend who saw the painting sent me a digital photograph of it, with a note saying the woman in the painting reminded him of me.

I took that as a compliment. This "Maria Maddalena" has quite a presence. She gazes directly out of the frame toward us. Her countenance and posture portray intelligence and wisdom, open-heartedness and curiosity. Both artistically and emotionally, she is deliciously captivating.

Most people know Mary Magadalene through the Bible's New Testament. There, she comes across as a passionate, vibrant, deeply authentic woman who is strong and aware enough to give herself completely to Jesus. So much so that she was oblivious to the disdainful reactions of those around her when she lovingly washed Jesus' feet and dried them with her hair.

In the painting, she is at the sepulcher where Jesus was resurrected. There is a profound mixture of emotion in her face—deep grief, surprise, realization, recognition, and something beyond joy. It took me a moment to understand why. When we first look at the painting, we see Mary facing us directly, so the natural impression is that she is looking at us. But when we remember where she is, and what is happening, we realize that her attention is on something—or Someone—else. Her experience is the totality of love and loss bound together in the same moment.

I have experienced this. I do experience this. My life journey through great love and great loss has both deepened me and opened me up. I seem to experience the present moment more fully, more poignantly, and the moment itself seems to hold a mixture of surprise, despair, joy, uncertainty, love, passion, and peace. I feel a deep river within that nourishes my body and feeds my soul.

There are other connections for me with Mary Magdalene besides love and loss. Many people are surprised to learn that there is a gospel of Mary Magdalene. It was found in the 20th century along with other previously lost gospels, known as the Gnostic gospels for the Greek word "gnosis," which means "spiritual knowledge or experience." In the fourth century after Christ, the Council of Nicene rejected these gospels in order to simplify and codify the path of Christianity. The story they preferred featured the gospels of Matthew, Mark, Luke and John, which point to Jesus as God and Savior. The gnostic gospels shed a much different light on the teachings of Jesus of Nazareth. They emphasize Jesus as teacher and exemplar of living an awakened life. We are encouraged not to worship Him, but to become like Him—a much more daunting task then just asking for help in a prayer.

The Gnostic gospels also clearly imply that Mary and Jesus shared an extraordinary love. They may have been married, if not legally then spiritually. Some scholars have theorized that Mary was also the spiritual heir to his teachings because she understood them so consummately. How different Christianity would be today if Mary had taken the lead after Jesus' death, instead of the impetuous and hard-headed Peter.

Like Mary, I was married to an inspiring, spiritually oriented man and leader who had spent his entire adult life to that point dedicated to teaching and spreading God's love. In his 33rd year, Justin hung up his robes and entered a secular life as husband and father. Yet he continued to carry the dedication, zeal, and values that had led him to join the Brothers when he was 19.

Also like Mary, I am constantly conscious of carrying within me an ever-present experience of the ineffable, translated into a million forms of compassion and acknowledgement of our "oneness" embedded in the work that I do. As Mary did, I prefer to work behind the scenes instead of in front of the crowd. This contributes to us being discounted and/or misunderstood. We are powerful nonetheless.

I look at the image of Maria Maddelena again. Yes, she and I are one and the same.

Basket of Cards

The basket is a large oval shape with a strong handle, both basket and handle made of woven strips of oak. It was a gift from A&K Cooperage, the folks who made the American oak barrels we used at Silver Oak for decades. A salt-of- the-earth family that air-dried their oak wood outside in the elements for a couple of years before constructing the finest barrels built in this country. The forests and cooperage are in Missouri where the weather is cold enough to mean tight growth rings in the trees, which translates into great flavor profiles in the barrels. We still buy these Missouri oak barrels for Meyer Family Cellars. Today the cooperage is owned by the Duncan family and is called The Oak, but the barrels are made in the same time-honored tradition.

In that basket is a collection of cards that came to me in the aftermath of Justin's death. I read each of them as they came in the mail or with flowers, then tossed them in this basket. Now, for the first time in 15 years, I take the basket down from its honored place perched high above, overlooking our great room. The cards number about 500. The top layer is covered in fine dust. I quickly find what I am looking for: response cards with a photo of me and Justin on the front and a message of thanks printed on the inside.

After his death, our home began to resemble a florist shop, which smelled heavenly. Sympathy cards arrived by the dozen. Initially, I was determined to write a personal response to everyone, because I felt so much gratitude for every expression and the time friends took to reach out to me with offerings of comfort and remembrance.

It didn't take more than a day or two to realize that writing to each person individually would be a daunting task. I decided to create a card I could send to everyone. The photo on the card came from Gina. It was the last photo of Justin ever taken, the two of us at the picnic table just minutes before his heart stopped. The original photo clearly showed a bright ethereal halo around his head. Perhaps it was some technical effect related to the camera lens, or the film, or the angle of the sunlight. But it did not look technical. I contacted a friend who was skilled in retouching photographs and asked her to remove the halo. I didn't want to freak anyone out with a photo that so obviously looked like Justin's spirit had begun to move out of his body.

The photograph went on the front of the card. Inside I had the printer inscribe Justin's qualities that I had committed to embody going forward in my life. The text also included a note of thanks. When each condolence card arrived, I read it over slowly and mindfully, then I sent a signed response card. Sometimes I added a short note, sometimes not. This proved a good way to express my gratitude and offer a last photo of Justin to those who held him dear.

Like some of the stories friends related at the memorial, I was occasionally surprised by an original story people shared in their cards. Mostly the messages were more personal; sweet words of comfort and encouragement.

I kept them because they were so beautiful and precious. I kept them because they moved me so, with their expressions of honor and tribute. I kept them because I thought that maybe one day, the children and grandchildren might want to read them, and they might get to know their father and grandfather in ways they hadn't before.

Now I am looking at the basket full of condolence notes and I am wondering if I have the courage to begin to read them again after all these years. I am feeling quite content and happy these days. Would I be inviting grief in all over again? Do I really want to open that Pandora's box of uncertainty?

Well, maybe just one ...

Chocolate from an Old Pal

A couple of boxes of chocolate candy mysteriously showed up at my house about a week before a recent Christmas. Tucked between the two boxes was a business card from Bob Fellion of Herdell Printing. This sent me down memory lane to the last time Bob left something at the house unannounced at Christmastime: a bag of fake reindeer poop.

That was in the days when Justin, Ed Schuh and Bob Fellion were in the habit of pulling practical jokes on each other. I remember having breakfast one Christmas morning with our neighbors, the Gleesons, after church. I was nine months pregnant with Matt, and that gave Justin an idea. He called Ed from the Gleeson's kitchen and told him I had delivered the baby that very morning: "A girl, 7 pounds 10 ounces." Justin handed the phone to Gerry Gleeson who kept a straight face—and voice—while confirming the birth.

Then Justin took the phone back and set the hook: "Hey Ed, are you cooking Christmas dinner tonight? You are? Listen, Bonny's in the hospital and I have to stay home and take care of Chad. Could you go to the St. Helena Hospital and bring Bonny a plate of turkey, mashed potatoes and gravy? You will? That would be great! She will be so happy. The maternity ward is on the second floor. Thank you!"

I was choking with laughter as were Barb and Gerry Gleeson. It was hard to keep silent as Justin lured Ed into his trap.

For the rest of the day, Justin and I enjoyed Christmas with 16-month-old Chad, who was old enough to enjoy the tree, the lights and ornaments, and new toys in brightly wrapped boxes. As afternoon turned into evening, we expected Ed Schuh to call and take Justin to task for pulling a prank on him. But the call never came.

Finally, it dawned on us that Ed was not going to admit he had been duped. There was only one thing to do. We bundled up Chad and headed to Ed's house. We arrived just as his young adult kids were leaving. They took one look at us and doubled over with laughter.

Justin, Chad and I made our way to the front door and into Ed's large farmhouse kitchen. After a few lame denials, Ed finally owned up. He and his son Jimmy had generously plated up a Christmas feast and headed to the Saint Helena Hospital. They had followed Justin's instructions, gone straight to the maternity ward on the second floor, and asked a nurse where they could find Bonny Meyer.

"I'm sorry sir," the nurse informed them. "There is no Bonny Meyer here."

"She has to be here!" Ed insisted. "She had a baby girl this morning: 7 pounds 10 ounces."

"I'm sorry sir, there is only one woman here and her name is not Meyer."

Though Ed realized he had been had, he still made an effort to salvage something from the trip to the hospital. Would the nurse like a heaping plate of Christmas dinner? Unfortunately, she could not accept, being an Adventist who did not eat meat. So Ed and Jimmy had returned home with the Christmas dinner plate still in hand.

After all the details were shared, along with some friendly banter and Ed's promise to get even, we left full of Christmas cheer along with a beautifully wrapped plate of turkey dinner.

One of the best practical jokes pulled on us also happened at Christmastime. We returned from a family vacation and found all our patio furniture on the roof of the house. We were sure that the culprit was either Ed Schuh or Bob Fellion. We asked everyone who worked on our property if they had seen any sign of Ed or Bob, but no one had. We accused the two men directly, but they each denied any part of it. Years later, we found out the culprit was Dane, our vineyard manager. His delight in the prank had been doubled by our long-held certainty that someone else had pulled it.

The merry pranksters were not above using others to do their naughty work. One unwitting accomplice was Napa Valley's local radio station, KVON. It's the kind of station that is intimately involved in local life, right down to details such as the elementary school's daily hot lunch selection.

One day in spring, Justin and I called the station and asked them to announce that it was Bob Fellion's birthday. The station was happy to do this, because Bob worked for a company that specialized in wine labels. So he was well known to Valley vintners.

That, of course, was the essence of our plan. Soon "birthday gifts" of wine began to show up in Bob's office. Some were full, but many of them were curiously half empty. By the end of the day he had an office full of wine bottles to deal with. It didn't take him long to figure out who called in the birthday announcement to KVON, but he did bide his time before responding with a practical joke of his own. Half a year later, at Christmas time, we found the "reindeer poop" sitting on the Bonny's Vineyard sign as we drove up our driveway.

To my knowledge, the last practical joke pulled on Bob by a member of the Meyer family was the work of my demure young daughter Holly when she was still a teenager.

This was in the days when magazines promoted subscriptions by offering a few months for free. Holly subscribed to 20 random magazines—all in the name of Bob Fellion. He probably thought nothing of it when the first couple of magazines came, but as they piled up he undoubtedly imagined that Justin was responsible. Eventually, Holly revealed that it was her, not Justin, which made Bob enjoy the joke even more. But I had to wonder: who could possibly have inspired my sweet girl to conduct such a prank?

Chapter Twenty-One

In Maui, Above: Dane Peterson, Margaraet Peterson, Captain Carr, Cindy Moon, Jill Stenner, Bob Stenner.
Below: Justin Meyer, and Laura Blears

Success

People often comment on the remarkable and extraordinary love affair Justin and I enjoyed, adding, with a wistful catch in their voice, that our kind of relationship is incredibly rare. Folks also ask me about the secret of our success at Silver Oak Cellars. How did we create such an iconic winery?

The secrets of our relationship and our business success are simple. They are also essentially the same.

Justin and I began our married and working life together with an abiding admiration and respect for one another. I admired how hard he worked, how he wasn't afraid to step in and do the smallest or most menial task. When he jumped into a ditch to fix a water main, those around jumped in right behind him. He demonstrated his leadership through his practical humility. I admired his integrity and impeccability even more. In return, I felt Justin's love and admiration for me ceaselessly. If I were to speak for him, I would say he admired my can-do attitude, my abiding kindness and compassion, and my emotional intelligence.

Our mutual admiration served us well when there were rough patches. Every now and then Justin or I would inadvertently say or do something that hurt. Our foundational respect and admiration kept us from getting furious with one another or sinking into judgment. While we might feel a bit wounded, the stronger feeling was surprise: "I can't believe you just did that!" Respect kept us on high ground and afforded us the luxury to step back, have a calm conversation, and straighten out the misunderstanding or misstep.

Because this was our steady state with each other, it was natural to extend it to our staff, customers, and suppliers. Each person on our team was unique and important in our eyes, and they thrived at work because they felt respected and appreciated for who they were and what they contributed. It was the same with our winery visitors. I have heard dozens of stories from customers who arrived at the winery just as we were closing. At many wineries, these people would receive a polite but firm request to come back the next day. Not from us. We would invite them in, pour them some wine, and give them our time even if our day had started before dawn.

Embedded also in our marriage was a deep and pervasive generosity. If I could see that Justin had a hard day, I would give him a back rub. He would see that I was occupied with the children and, without any prompting from me, start in on the housekeeping chores I usually did. We wordlessly tag-teamed in the kitchen when cooking for our family and friends, throwing in playful squeezes and kisses in the kitchen.

As with respect, we carried this generosity into our business and community. Justin volunteered countless hours of time and leadership to the Napa Valley Vintners, the American Society of Enology and Viticulture, and the American Vineyard Foundation. I served on school boards and led community 4-H activities. We were active in our church and related to our staff like family—especially when there was a crisis. On two different occasions, an employee didn't show up for work and didn't call. Concerned, we went on a search until he or she was found and, in one instance, taken to the hospital. We were likewise there to celebrate with them. We attended their weddings and kid's graduations, and of course they were always included in celebrating Silver Oak successes.

Wine pricing is one of the ways that wineries "keep score" relative to each other, but we never looked at it this way. We wanted to receive fair value for our hard work, so every year I did a market survey to help me determine the pricing for our upcoming wine releases. Then we purposefully and consistently set our prices a little lower than the other wines in our category. Because both Justin and I grew up with little money to spare, we wanted wine lovers to be able to afford our wines, at least for a special celebration or an occasional Sunday dinner.

Justin and I were always honest and transparent with each other, right down to the simplest things. If one of us asked "How are you?" or "What do you think?" we got real answers. And if the question involved a decision about what we wanted, we did not mess around.

"La Bohème is playing at San Francisco Opera," I would say. "Want to go?"

"No, take one of your girlfriends," Justin would respond. "I'd rather stay home and work in the garden."

Or he would say, "I got an invitation to go salmon fishing tomorrow morning, want to come along?"

"No, I already told the kids I would take them to the park."

This candor went right into our wine. So many wineries bottle and sell every last drop of their wine, as if all of it is at the same level of quality. But we were honest with ourselves: nature doesn't work like that. In some years, in some vineyards or parts of them, the fruit you get is not in peak condition, and once you vinify it, that relative quality is obvious to someone with Justin's experience and expertise. He would not stoop to doctoring weak wine with technical tricks. We took the honest route to high quality: we made about 30 percent more wine than we intended to sell, used only the best of it, and sold off the rest as bulk wine to other producers. No settling for good enough.

Respect, generosity, honesty. That's a good list of attributes to describe the way Justin and I approached our relationship and our business. But there was one more ingredient that I would suggest was equally powerful: fun.

Early on, Justin and I looked at each other in bemusement one evening, acknowledging a surprising reality: We spent more waking hours of the day at the winery than we did at home. We decided that as long as we were going to spend the better part of our lives at Silver Oak, it should feel like fun rather than work.

The light-hearted tone we set gave our staff permission to relax and be themselves. Laughter was frequently heard in the cellar, tasting room, and office. I watched closely to see if this would rub off on all the other people we interacted with: the "glass rep" who sold us our wine bottles, the restaurateurs who put our wine on their lists, the tasting room visitors, everyone. It did. Deke, our company pilot, once said that it was impossible to work for Silver Oak and not feel happy. In thirty years, virtually no one ever left, and Silver Oak became an employer of choice for winery workers up and down the Valley.

Fun characterized our personal life too. When I met Justin, it was in the context of people he knew well, loved deeply, and teased all the time. Teasing and fun were how he showed love. I had my own talents in that area, so we began joking around with each other from our earliest interactions. By nature, neither of us took ourselves too seriously, so teasing didn't make us tense up. If anything, it sparked us to raise the level of humor to something even more outrageously enjoyable.

It was only after Justin died that I had a chance to really look at other businesses with a broader perspective. I was shocked. Most businesses struggle to attract and retain talented people; pay dearly to acquire customers who drift away inexorably; and focus so narrowly on money as the measure of success that it distorts the core business in detrimental ways.

For the first time, I realized that Silver Oak was what is now known as a sustainable business: driven by values more than money, emphasizing people over profits, and achieving phenomenal success because of those choices.

I saw the opposite when I looked at the larger world of business. Values aren't really running the business; desire for growth and increasing profits are. People are more often considered as units of labor than respected for the work they did or their contribution to the business. There is not a generosity of spirit, but rather a pervasive stinginess. The questions are not about maximizing fulfillment or sharing success. They are about gaining advantages over others: getting grapes or wine bottles for less money than they're worth; paying employees less for their work; and charging customers more for wine regardless of the quality.

In the companies I studied, I also observed lots of employee dissatisfaction and turnover. Management seemed only vaguely aware that this was causing a heavy burden on morale and expenses for constant recruiting and training. And when I looked around for the people who were genuinely having fun, I didn't see too many. Certainly none of them were in management.

As an investor today, I look for the kind of core sustainability that we had at Silver Oak. That means employees, customers, and suppliers are all considered essential to making the business succeed. No one is profiting extravagantly, and everyone is enthusiastically loyal. The company's "ecosystem"—a favored term of venture capitalists today— is healthy, happy, and oriented toward success that lasts. In short, the business leader is playing an "infinite game," embracing an expansive vision that will take the company, its people, and culture into the future indefinitely.

Meyer Family Port

It started at the pinochle game held every Tuesday night in the Christian Brothers' "Family Room" at Mont La Salle. Brothers Justin, Tom, Luke, Greg, and Fred would gather at around 7:00 in the evening and play for nickels and dimes until long past midnight. They didn't have to get up for early Mass on Wednesday mornings, so they would stay up late playing cards and drinking Christian Brothers' pot-still brandy and tawny port.

It didn't take too long for Brother Justin to develop an appreciation for port, after he was introduced to it by legendary Christian Brothers' cellar master, Brother Timothy. After a long day in the cellar or vineyard, he appreciated a glass of good port and a cigar as much as a person possibly could.

After leaving Christian Brothers, founding Silver Oak and focusing on Cabernet, Justin never forgot those happy card games or lost his love of port. Thus years later, when Christian Brothers Winery was sold to Heublein, which eliminated the port program, Justin immediately decided to start his own. We bought the Christian Brothers' last cuvée of port made from the grape variety, Touriga Nacional, which has centuries of history and tradition in port-making. Justin knew how to age that wine, blend it with subsequent vintages, and create a California tawny port that rivals Spain's finest. Justin loved his little port project, and I loved designing the bottle—the back label signed by our family like a Christmas card.

Meyer Family Cellars has carried on the family port tradition in creative ways, such as using Zinfandel rather than Touriga Nacional. What hasn't changed is the dedication to producing a great sipping experience at the end of the day or after a meal. Holly has taken the appreciation of port a step further by compiling a collection of 50 ways to cook with it in a book called "Port, the Secret Ingredient." If grilled lamb with port sauce or port-infused dessert truffles fire up your culinary imagination, then get the book, get the port, and get going. Don't be surprised if you are inspired to play some pinochle for nickels and dimes, stay up late, tell jokes, and laugh until your sides ache.

Celebrating the Sale

When we sold our share of Silver Oak to our partner Ray Duncan and his family, Justin was ecstatic. He called his old buddies from Bakersfield with the news, incredulous that a kid from the poor side of town could actually be a millionaire! Money magazine published an article entitled

"Robes to Riches." It was the first time in our lives when we felt really flush. When all your assets are in a vineyard and winery, you are land-rich but cash-poor. So we were always juggling funds to purchase grapes, barrels, and bottles each year; make major equipment purchases; and cover our payroll, benefit obligations and taxes.

The first thing we did when the sale was complete was to make a list of everyone who had worked alongside us for almost 30 years to make Silver Oak such a success. Justin wrote them checks that in many cases were big enough to significantly shift their lives as the sale had just shifted ours.

As the dust cleared, and the business transitioned away from our hands-on management, we felt a huge wave of relief. We no longer had demanding day jobs. So what did we do? We went to Maui, and invited friends and family to join us there.

Among them were Dane and Margaret. Dane was Los Amigos' first employee and our long-time vineyard manager. He had been farming the prune orchard and small Cabernet vineyard when Ray and Jack Novak bought it in early 1972. I met Dane and Margaret later that fall, and we became colleagues and friends in what became the great Silver Oak adventure. We laughed as we recalled how young, optimistic, and undaunted we were then, and how we felt we could do just about anything.

For more than 25 years Dane and Margaret made the drive from the Alexander Valley to Oakville for our monthly wine-tasting dinners. They were always there to help out in tight situations and to help us celebrate. Now they came to play with us at the beach.

A year or two before, Justin and I had taken a snorkeling trip to Lanai. The coral reefs we viewed were breathtaking. I wanted to share this amazing experience with our friends. I suggested to Justin that we charter my favorite sailing catamaran, the Kapalua Kai, for a day trip to Lanai. Justin quickly agreed and I made the arrangements. It was enthralling to be able to write that big check and not care about the cost! We had such a magical day that day. We motored close to the cove that is home to a large pod of spinner dolphins and watched them play all around our boat; jumping, spinning, frolicking with us until we were out of range of their territory. We went to the great deep black wall where hundreds of Moorish Idols live; their white, black, and yellow stripes brilliant against the immense black-green wall. Not far from the wall there were a couple of underwater arches, which some of us swam through using scuba gear. We enjoyed a delicious lunch onboard, hungry from snorkeling, then sailed back to Maui propelled by the afternoon trade winds.

As I look at the photo I took at the end of that day, I see Dane in his burgundy Silver Oak shirt, Margaret below him in her navy top and floppy hat and, Justin in the center, so happy to be surrounded by friends. He is wearing the original Silver Oak crush shirt designed by our son Matt. The back shows a purple outline of bare feet and the words "It's all in the feet." Matt took this quip from Justin himself, who used to say it when people asked him what made Silver Oak Cabernet so special.

As I contemplate this photo from the perspective of today, I have the poignant and heart-wrenching realization that it represents a precious moment in time when Justin was carefree. A few days after this snorkel trip, I was taken to Maui Memorial Hospital in extreme pain caused by a large, previously undiscovered tumor. What followed was dramatic abdominal surgery, months of slow recovery, and Justin's sudden death four months later. If he were sitting next to me right now, he would say, "Well, at least I had a few carefree days there in Maui sharing the sun, sand and sea with our friends before all hell broke loose." Then he would chuckle, always at peace with what was.

Tumor on Maui

I have a large tumor where my left ovary should have been. A few days earlier, I had taken a carefree sunrise bike ride with our friend Koerner Rombauer, from the crater summit of Haleakala volcano down to Paia beach. Something during that ride must have triggered a disruption in my internal organs. The pain has intensified over the past few days and resulted in a visit to the Maui Memorial emergency room. The scan reveals a tumor in my left abdomen. The first tentative diagnosis is ovarian cancer. I know very little about ovarian cancer except that it is quite deadly. Six months or so and you're gone.
Well, that re-prioritizes things.

I had never thought I would be the kind of person to get cancer. I am strong, happy, active, and relatively healthy. But here it is. Maybe the tumor is benign? No one will really know until surgery and a pathology report. Well, one step at a time. I will deal with things and make decisions as they come.

One thing I feel strongly about; quality of life is the most important thing to me, no question. I would rather maximize my comfort and the quality of the life I have left than extend my life a little with the toxicity of chemotherapy. I have seen too much extended suffering in others who made the latter choice. Besides, chemotherapy is basically counter-intuitive to me. I have the feeling cancer represents a failure of the immune system. It doesn't make any logical sense to me to damage an already compromised immune system further with poisonous drugs. Doesn't it make more sense to actually build up the immune system?

But I'm getting ahead of myself. We don't know what it is yet. Wait and see.

I have brought a crochet project with me to the emergency room: a baby blanket for an expectant mother. So I crochet into the night. Morphine and the rhythm of my work calms my mind and helps me enter into the territory of acceptance of whatever is to come.

When Justin arrives the next day he looks worse than I do. Our friend Bill Haywood tells me in confidence that Justin has cried all night long out of concern and grief for what might be coming. As I comfort Justin, I have my first personal experience of something I've heard before: those who love and care for a seriously ill person can go through a serious torment of their own.

This fills me with tenderness and compassion for him. His balance has become shaky, leaving him vulnerable and more dependent. He needs a walking stick when he's on his feet, and he's no longer safe to drive a car. The depth of our relationship, how we are everything to each other, comes into vivid focus. He would be lost without me.

When our children hear I am in the hospital with a tumor they panic. Chad calls. He and Holly are at San Francisco airport ready to buy tickets to Maui, even though they are already scheduled to fly to Hawaii a few days later. I convince them to stick to the plan, that there is no emergency. I change the subject to how much fun we're going to have together. It works.

I stay in the hospital for four days as powerful antibiotics and narcotics are administered directly into my veins to manage the pain and any possible infection.

As my condition stabilizes, the Maui doctors want to discuss surgery to remove the tumor. I propose a different course of action. To reach its current size, the tumor must have been in place for quite some time, so there is no reason to have immediate surgery so far from home. I can wait until I'm back in California in a few weeks. Instead. I ask for medication strong enough to block the pain so I can enjoy the rest of my time in the islands.

But I'm not in denial. I go to see a cancer specialist in Honolulu. He says the tumor will require major surgery with at least a week-long hospital stay, followed by two more weeks of recovery before I can get on a plane to fly home. In other words, my entire Hawaii trip would be a medical adventure if I have surgery now. That confirms my plan to postpone it and have fun with my family.

As it turns out, we have a wonderful time together. But the next time someone proposes a bike ride down Haleakala, the group goes off without me. I stay behind and relax on the beach.

Trying on Heaven for Size

After he turned 60, it was clear that Justin's diabetes was taking a toll. Always a natural and extraordinary athlete, excelling in every sport he embraced, he began to shuffle more than walk; he would trip easily, and took to using a tall walking stick to maintain his balance. His writing became a scrawl, and words would become mildly garbled in his mouth. Doctors at the Mayo Clinic said the part of his brain that governs coordination had atrophied somewhat due to diabetes-related circulation problems.

This was Justin's worst nightmare. From the time I first met him, he always said, "The worst thing I can imagine is to grow old and lose my ability to do things." Now he used a walking stick and a driver. He didn't complain, but I knew he hated that his body didn't respond with the ease, grace and power he had always enjoyed. He also seemed to get tired more easily and became less interested in activities and events he would have been enthusiastic about before.

On our patio there were two large wrought-iron rocking chairs covered in woven seagrass. Justin began to take solace there, rocking gently while looking out over the pool and the vineyards beyond. He spent less time walking in the vineyard and more time planting wildflowers.

A month after my cancer surgery, we traveled with Holly to Italy where we had rented a house for a month. She had studied in Florence the previous semester and this was her chance to show us around. We considered canceling the trip because I was still weak and needed to be transported through airports in a wheelchair. But I figured I could recover just as well in an Italian country villa as I could at home. Besides, friends had made plans to join us there.

During our time in Greve in Chianti, I slowly became stronger: able to walk farther and wrangle small pieces of luggage during excursions to Perugia and Assisi. Justin chose to stay behind in the villa when we journeyed to Assisi. One day, toward the end of our trip, I took a bus to Florence for the day to hand-deliver some of our wine to a member of Italy's renowned Antinori wine family. When I returned, I found Justin deeply shaken. He had fallen in the shower and hit his head. Fear consumed him when he tried to get his bearings again and felt confused, alone, and afraid. His loss of confidence was more significant than the blow to his head, and this changed him. When we returned to the Napa Valley, Justin needed airport assistance more than I did.

In the months that followed, he became more quiet as if watching life from a distance. His main interest was the wine cave that he had conceived of and designed. He would sit on our front porch bench, walking stick in hand, and watch the workmen for hours. At the end of each workday he would slowly make his way over to the cave to examine their progress.

Then at night, after dinner, he would make his way to a rocking chair on the patio and sit there looking up at the stars. After cleaning up the kitchen, I would join him sometimes. But mostly, he would sit there alone, impervious to the cold night air.

Looking at him gazing up at the starry night, I imagined he was trying heaven on for size.

Songs of Justin

Today we will sing songs of Justin
Of dancing eyes filled with merriment
Of hearty laughter, and zest for life
Of embracing everything and everyone

CHAPTER TWENTY-ONE

We will sing sweetly
Of him walking through vineyards
Lightly touching vines
Coaxing them to grow

Tender gentle spirit
In a bear body
Eyes softening
Revealing a beautiful soul

Of his passion for excellence
His need to win
Then his light dismissal
Of accolades and acclaim

His deep reverence of the sacred
Joyful irreverence for the serious
Easy jokes
Careful listening
Distilling everything to essence

Let us sing songs of Justin
Loud and clear
Filled with laughter
Ringing through the air
Rising to the sky

In the evenings
Sitting for hours
Contemplating the stars
Trying on heaven
For size

Let us sing songs of Justin
Sweet voice filling the night air
Melodies of gladness and sorrow
Silliness and sassiness
Thumping the banjo
The Preacher and the Bear

Let us sing songs of Justin
Whose reassuring hand touched us
Whose smile lit up our lives
Whose laughter made us happy
Whose strength empowered us
Whose unpretentiousness inspired us
Whose love is now Everywhere

Justin Died

I have recalled every detail of Justin's death hundreds of times. Maybe thousands. It's the kind of thing that happens with life-altering events—particularly the ones we don't want to remember. For some reason, they have a tendency to come rushing in and hijack our psyche.

I had endured a devastating surgery just four months earlier. A tumor the size of a cantaloupe was extracted from my abdomen along with a sizable portion of my digestive tract. My energy and ability to move about were slowly returning, although my digestive system was still compromised. The diagnosis of cancer was a shock, and it wasn't over. I had decisions to make regarding follow-up treatment when I was strong enough to endure it.

I was feeling just well enough to drive to the mountains to visit our friends Ruggero and Gina for a couple of days. Our first morning there, I called each of our children to let them know we had arrived safely and were doing fine. Matt was at his home in Philo, Holly was in Boston visiting friends, and Chad had just returned to California from his honeymoon. Everyone sounded happy and in good spirits.

We started our day by driving the short distance from the Gigli's home to Grover's Hot Springs for a morning soak in the mineral-rich hot pool. Gina and I stood with our backs to one side of the pool, waist-deep in pleasantly hot water, talking. Ruggero and Justin were chatting on the opposite side maybe 15 feet away. Unbeknownst to our friends, or at least apparently unnoticed, Justin and I locked eyes and held the gaze. We were both filled with a particularly powerful and poignant sense of connection and love for each other that morning. While I half-listened to Gina, time stopped, and everyone and everything around us disappeared, leaving only us.

Then Ruggero turned and suggested it was time to go. His movement broke the spell, and our attention returned to our friends. We all moved then and began to make our way out of the pool.

Relaxed and refreshed, we headed back to the Gigli's house to pack a picnic lunch to take to Lower Blue Lake. The four of us piled into Ruggero's Jeep Wrangler and we headed up to higher elevation. Getting there took us through pine forest and past small high-country lakes. We drove down a dirt road that ran south off Highway 88 past Hope Valley. Ruggero's jeep had no trouble traversing the uneven road up to the lake. Our destination was the picnic area that hugged the shoreline. We stopped at an open site that lay in the dappled shade of pine trees.

Ruggero and Justin began to unpack and prepare lunch. I felt an urge to move and explore, so Gina and I took off for a gentle walk along the lakeside trail. We returned to find Ruggero and Justin drinking wine, laughing and teasing each other. Gina and I were not surprised in the least. It's what they did: tease each other at every opportunity.

The source of Justin's lambasts this time was that Ruggero had forgotten the propane for the camping stove. There was no remedy for this. We had to eat our pasta cold—still delicious because it was made by Ruggero. Nevertheless, the forgotten fuel was rich material for Justin and he used it with almost every bite. "I can't believe you are serving me cold pasta. How could you forget the propane? Have you never cooked outdoors before?"

Not to be outdone, Ruggero teased Justin for not bringing some Silver Oak Cabernet Sauvignon for our lunch. Instead, we were drinking some crummy Zinfandel. At one point, Justin looked at Ruggero and said, "To tell you the truth, I really don't like you, but I keep you as my friend because I like your pasta." Without missing a beat, Ruggero replied, "Well to tell you the truth, I really don't like you, but I keep you as my friend because I like your wine. So we are even."

Well-fed with pasta, wine, and laughter, we cleaned our plates and packed up whatever was left from our lunch and put it in the jeep. After lunch, Justin put his arm around me, holding me extra tight, gripping my upper arm, his fingers going deep. That powerful connection we had felt at the pool rekindled as we sat next to each other on the picnic bench. That hug meant, "I've got you and I'm never letting go." Gina noticed, and took our photograph.

As we prepared to leave for town, Justin rose to go to the restroom and felt a little wobbly. I walked with him to steady him. Ruggero noticed our slow progress, and quickly joined us, taking Justin's other side. But just as we got to the restroom, Justin's legs gave out and he slid to the floor, his back against the wall, laughing at the ridiculousness of his situation. Ruggero knew that Justin could lose his balance from time to time, so he left us there while he finished packing things into the jeep.

I began to get concerned, so I asked Justin his name and address. He answered correctly, which was a great relief to me, then he said, "I'm going to sleep all the way home." Something about it didn't feel right. I left my beloved there sitting on the floor and ran out to get Ruggero to come back and help. When we got back moments later, we found Justin lying on his back, unresponsive.

When people die consciously, they die ... consciously. I knew, even in my shock as I watched Ruggero try to rouse him, that Justin had picked the perfect moment. Our kids were happy and well and in the company of wives and friends. I was on the mend. Silver Oak was thriving and was no longer our responsibility.

Justin's body had seen better days and was failing. Just two weeks before this, we had had a visit from Jack, our dear friend who was a quadriplegic. Justin stood, steadied by his walking stick, watching Jack expertly maneuver his electric wheelchair. I knew what was going through his mind: "I'm not going there. I'm going to find a way out before I end up in a wheelchair."

And so he did, on a sunny Tuesday afternoon by a mountain lake in the company of his wife and good friends.

I sat on the nearby picnic table where I could clearly see everything, caught between an eerie stillness of shock, disbelief, knowing the worst has happened, and a deep desire to honor his sacred passage. Filled with reverence, I stared at him as I barely breathed, knowing his spirit was watching everything from just above his body.

I watched Ruggero administer CPR while internally I honored Justin's passage with every cell of my being. In that stillness, his presence was powerful within me. That's why I became impatient for the CPR efforts to cease: I knew Justin had departed his body, and having me and Ruggero energetically pressing his chest was disturbing the holiness of the moment. But we continued to do so anyway so there would be no regrets. We would do everything we could until he was officially pronounced dead.

Strange as it is to say, that moment was one of great relief. Now I could go to him and tenderly clean his face. As I bent over him I could feel his spirit hovering, watching. I didn't want this indescribable intimacy to end.

Then came the shock of the emergency responder pulling Justin's shirt up to cover his face. I had to stop him just before he slid Justin's body into the ambulance, so I could gently pull the shirt back down, take Justin's face in my hands, and kiss him tenderly, over and over. Extreme unction, the final anointing.

I now realize what a very radically different life began for me the moment Justin died. We had sold our share of Silver Oak what felt like just moments before and had taken a celebratory island vacation. Two months later came cancer, surgery, and a difficult recovery. Then Justin suddenly died. One of these events would have been enough to shift life as I knew it. But all three together meant that the fabric of my life had been ripped nearly in two. Truth be told, the moment Justin exhaled his life force, a lot of life left me too. It would take me more than a decade before I would feel filled with vibrant life again.

Gina sent me the photo she took. There is an unmistakable aura around Justin's head, much like the halo you see on images of Jesus and the saints. It's as if his spirit knew what was coming and was already beginning its journey heavenward.

And he was right. He slept all the way home.

10th Anniversary

The 40th anniversary celebration at Silver Oak Cellars was a grand day. More than 2,400 customers and fans came to sip the 2008 Alexander Valley Cabernet Sauvignon and savor pizza from five different chefs. There were bands playing, visitors had their photograph taken holding an impressive looking six-liter bottle, and watched barrel-makers demonstrate their art. A festive day for everyone.

But for Chad, me, and a group of Silver Oak old-timers, it was a day of bittersweet remembrance. Ten years before, Justin and I had attended a similar celebration for Silver Oak's 30th anniversary. People stood in line under the big white tents to buy their allocation of wine and enjoyed Häagen-Dazs ice cream bars—Justin's favorite. And of course, there was an after-party. It was hosted by Ray and Sally Duncan in their backyard, on the winery property. I got thrown into the swimming pool along with a number of other managers and staff. The Duncan children and grandchildren were all there. The Duncans had purchased our share of the winery from us a number of months before and this was their first major event as full owners, so every Duncan family member wanted to be there.

Two days later, Justin was dead. Our children and I, the Duncan family, the Silver Oak extended family and two thousand friends and colleagues returned to Silver Oak Cellars under the big white tents for his memorial service. That's why it was emotionally complex to see the tents, the people, the wine ... It brought back both a great celebration and the end of my life as I had known it.

I honored the tenth anniversary of Justin's death a couple of days later with a slow walk around Bonny's Vineyard. It reminded me of taking the same walk a year after Justin died, when the children and I threw his remains into the wind above the vines. It seemed like it all happened just moments ago ... and a lifetime ago.

Chapter Twenty-Two

Justin Meyer in front of Silver Oak Cellars

The Monroe Institute

Shortly after Justin died, I began to have lucid dreams of him. These dreams were vivid, highly interactive and memorable. I found them simultaneously startling and comforting. In these dreams, Justin and I typically talked about the kids and what was currently going on in my life. The setting and our conversations always felt very natural. I can still clearly recall the first one. I am walking down a paved path and I see Justin walking towards me. He is dressed in his workout clothes and is carrying his gym bag; clearly on his way to workout. As we approach each other, I express great surprise at seeing him. My first words startle me as I ask: "Justin, don't you know you are dead?" He just shrugs his shoulders; neither assenting nor denying the reality of his existence on a different plane. Only then do I hug him, kiss him, and tell him how wonderful it is to see him. After the hug, we engage in a rather routine conversation about current activities and our children.

I found these lucid dreams comforting as they happened, they were otherwise frustratingly elusive. I could not make them occur at will. I had to wait and hope for another to spontaneously arrive.

Then one day a book by Robert Monroe fell into my hands. The title was *Journeys Out of the Body*. A week or two later I picked it up and began to read. Robert Monroe was a respected radio executive in the 1950s who unexpectedly began to experience regular out-of-body experiences that he termed "journeys." He would lie down for an afternoon nap and shortly after relaxing, he would feel a vibration and find himself floating above his body, bumping up against the ceiling, or stranger yet, going through the ceiling, out the roof, and flying above the neighborhood.

At first, these uninvited experiences made him feel afraid that he was either dying or losing his mind. He consulted a number of physicians who determined that he was not in danger of either dire outcome. One psychiatrist encouraged him to treat the experiences with curiosity and an open scientific approach, by keeping detailed chronicles of his experiences.

I found his story fascinating, particularly his growing ability to direct his journeys intentionally. A striking example was traveling to a different physical location, such as a neighbor's house down the street, and observing events there. He would then contact the neighbors afterward to verify that what he had seen and heard actually transpired. As time went on, he reports, he was able to visit individuals who had died and who resided in a different dimension altogether.

I read Monroe's other books, *Far Journeys* and *Ultimate Journey*, and confirmed that the research institute he founded to study the out-of-body phenomenon still exists. This was not idle research. I wanted the ability to meet Justin more often in my dreams. The first time the Monroe Institute offered a class near my home, I signed up. The workshop began with Saturday dinner and ended six days later, on Friday afternoon.

The 22 participants were an eclectic mix: two from Japan, a teenager, an elderly woman. Three young men who ate only raw food were certain their diet would guarantee them out-of-body experiences. I wasn't convinced, but at dinner I paid close attention to what our trainers ate—a nice, balanced meal—and followed their choices.

After dinner we gathered for orientation. We were instructed in the protocol, process, and use of specialized listening equipment. The trainers had set up a local-area broadcasting system so that each of us could listen to meditation recordings from Bob Monroe, via transistor radios and headphones.

That evening I lay down on my bed and adjusted my headphones. The meditation began with the sound of ocean surf and the comforting, professionally modulated voice of Bob Monroe encouraging us to get comfortable, let go and relax. Our first exercise took us to what he called "focus level 10": the body is asleep but the mind remains awake. I had experience with meditation techniques and this state was not unfamiliar to me.

When the group re-convened later that evening, most people seemed to feel good about their experience. A few participants admitted that they had fallen asleep; they were assured that just about everyone falls asleep or "clicks out" at some point or another, and they should not worry. They also advised us that the subconscious mind hears the recording even if we sleep, so we don't need to experience and remember everything consciously. We were then sent off to get a good night's sleep to the sounds of a recording called "Super Sleep."

Over the next four days we learned to shift our body's vibration with the aid of the "hemi-sync" recordings we were listening to. Hemi-sync refers to the fact that the sound oscillations, or vibrations, we were listening to were designed to synchronize the two hemispheres of our brains, left and right. The goal was to gain access to various states of non-ordinary consciousness.

I was fairly successful, meaning I didn't fall asleep or click out except for very short, inconsequential periods. It was very much like learning to ride a bike; using our recorded "training wheels" we would go to a higher focus level, come back, go a little further, come back again, in a steady progression. We would debrief after each meditation, and it was powerful reassurance to hear other participants describe the same experiences I was having at each new level of consciousness. Apparently I wasn't just making it up.

On the fifth day we were aiming to reach level 21, which Monroe describes as a bridge between physical and non-physical or spirit worlds. I followed the instructions and got myself aligned with the hemi-sync signals, and soon was having the mental experience of crossing a bridge, curious about what I would find there.

Justin.

He appeared directly in front of me, his face just inches from mine, as if he had been waiting at the very border of his world and mine. My heart leaped. In an instant we were embracing passionately and kissing with a fierceness that I will always remember. I was in the territory beyond time. I could stay here with my beloved forever.

I might have too. But at some point, Bob Monroe's melodious voice was there, calling me back to level 1: normal waking consciousness. My immediate instinctive reaction was to tear off my headset. Mr. Monroe could go back to normal waking consciousness without me. But it was too late. The connection with Justin had been broken.

I lay in bed, both sensually and emotionally stimulated and bereft with loss, torn out of a loving embrace with Justin. Slowly another feeling came into my consciousness: amazement. The Monroe techniques worked. I had warned myself that they might not. I had imagined that I would have to take many workshops before I was able to visit Justin in an intentional, lucid way. But I had achieved it in five days. Though I was still in an excited state, now I was filled with anticipation.

At some time in our life, we all have had a lucid dream, or powerful nightmare that feels as palpable as our everyday experience of reality. These guided Monroe meditations were like that. Maybe even more real than "real." Mystics from many traditions would say that these experiences are indeed more real than ordinary life, because our waking consciousness is itself a dream, a dream of separation from divine union with all things.

Now I could experience union with Justin at level 21. I just needed to get back there. So imagine my excitement when I received a graduation package, with a cassette tape of the recording for going to level 21. If the cassette recording was effective, I wouldn't need another workshop. I could travel to the bridge into the spirit world whenever I desired.

As it turned out, I could. Eventually, I did not need the recording at all. I joined with Justin many times over the following months and years, sometimes for wordless comfort and connection and other times for a more ordinary visit to learn how he was faring.

I did take more advanced courses from the Monroe Institute, becoming an engaged and committed consciousness explorer. I have visited, and sometimes aided, other deceased loved ones, including both my parents. I have been guided by unknown wise beings on some of my journeys. I have had innumerable experiences that demonstrate that we are not alone in this life or in the next; as the Monroe Institute says, we are much more than our physical bodies.

Justin Came to Me

Justin came to me yesterday morning. I lay in bed somewhere between awake and asleep, my defenses down, no thoughts of the list of things that needed to be done.

There he was. Completely unexpected. Powerful and pure. He was kissing me. Consuming me. Drinking me in as I was him. It had been a long time since he had come to me unbidden like this. I had forgotten the raw power and immensity of our love for one another. I lay there filled with him. Feeling his embrace, my left hand in the familiar slight indentation on the small of his back, his sacrum, my right hand hugging his neck. We were pulling each other closer, our bodies melding into one another. Eyes closed, holding on for dear life.

And then a third energy filled the room, enveloping the two of us. I had forgotten about this, too. You may have heard references to a "third person" that is created when two people deeply love each other. This being is our union. I had forgotten the size, the tangible substance, the aliveness of our love for each other. The immensity was almost too much for me to take in. Waves of emotion coursed through my body. It felt so natural and familiar, and at the same time so startlingly enormous.

I knew he would not stay long. He never did when he came in spirit like this. And as I felt his energy withdraw I began to grieve, crying out as tears washed my face and sobs wracked my body.

I did not beg him to stay. I never do. I do not presume to understand the mystery of how he comes and goes, the after-life experience he is in now, or the promises he has to keep.

Widows Club

When Justin died, I knew no one who had lost husband or wife. I was so very alone and isolated in so many ways. Now, over 15 years later, a few longtime friends are joining me. And they are seeking me out. They know that I know. I know the journey and can help them navigate the territory of grief and the re-imagining of their lives.

Recently someone I know walked through the front door and into my house calling my name. I was upstairs, slightly alarmed; I wasn't sure who was in the house and if there was an emergency. Having just taken off one of my shoes, I grabbed the shoe and awkwardly trundled down the stairs, one shoe foot, one sock foot.

Steph was standing there a bit wide-eyed and clearly fragile. I suggested we sit at the dining room table and I took a moment to put my shoe back on. This also gave me a few seconds to take a couple of deep breaths and compose myself. When I looked up and into her eyes, she blurted, "How'd you do it?" Her husband had died two weeks before. His aging body had begun to give out about two years before. Bit by bit he had become incapacitated and less vital. In the end pneumonia had taken him home.

I had known this man for a long time, and his passing had left an ache in my heart too. I looked squarely at Stephanie and said, "It's really hard isn't it?"

She shook her head, agreeing and expressing her disbelief at the same time. "It's unbelievable!" she blurted out. "I just want to be with him!" Anguish colored every syllable. I nodded my head, remembering how I had ached to be with Justin after he died. I wanted to die so I could be with him. I wasn't done with my life, but I just couldn't imagine life without him. I would go to bed at night and think: Up. Rise up. Somehow get up higher. I would even reach my arms up toward the ceiling, attempting to reach him.

This is the ache-wracked song of the one left behind. Grief takes us over and slams us onto the floor over and over again. Ultimately, it can tenderize us and soften us into wiser, more openhearted souls. But knowing that doesn't make the process any shorter or any less agonizing. Steph told me she was thinking of simply driving her car into a telephone pole in order to be with her husband. Or at least stop the pain. She gave me a worried look. Was she going crazy, talking about willing her own death? No, I assured her. It is normal for those of us who have truly loved and bonded deeply with another to feel this way. When, in an instant, the center of life is gone, a new meaning, a new purpose must be found for vibrancy to return.

Then Stephanie asked what kept me going; what drove me to choose life instead of death. Before I had a chance to answer, she added, "I think I need to stay around for the grandchildren." I told her about looking into my children's eyes and seeing how frightened they were of losing me after their father had died. Sparing them that tragedy became the original foundation of my recovery.

I began to share with Steph the mysterious signals that seemed to come from Justin after his passing: the pebble flying across the room and landing at my feet, the wall-mounted hairdryer with a mind of its own. I told her of vivid, lucid dreams during which Justin and I had chatted about our children. All of these experiences brought me a measure of comfort, even if it was temporary. I suggested that Stephanie be open to any comfort she might find from considering her husband as still alive in spirit, and might be accessible to her in some way

Her mood immediately brightened, and she revealed that some mysterious messages had already reached her, including something that really caught my attention: an email from an address she did not recognize, with a two-word message: "Justin. Love." She interpreted this to mean that her husband had somehow connected with Justin in some other reality.

I took care to thank her for sharing these experiences. Majority culture in this country somehow teaches us that if we experience these profound and unexplainable events, we should hold them in our hearts and never talk about them to anyone. This, of course, is the first step in losing the experience entirely. Which is crazy because it is so much more helpful and comforting to open to these magical occurrences, talk about them with our friends and family, and normalize the truth that death is a shift into a different dimension, not a hard ending. Connection continues!

Slowly I shared with Stephanie how in my experience, my relationship with Justin had continued to evolve over the years since his death. It isn't easy to explain, but my sense is that we continually help each other to learn and grow. Remaining actively connected means our lives—mine on earth and his beyond—are greatly informed by our different-dimensional perspectives. This sounds much more odd and esoteric than it feels from within. Stephanie nodded, indicating she would consider this as a possibility.

As abruptly as she had arrived, Steph stood up and made her way out the front door. There was a great life celebration later that evening for her husband. The evening was full of music and exuberance as well as that aching feeling when the one who should be there is not. Stephanie was warm and gracious. She clearly enjoyed the music, but I could not help noticing that she did the same thing I had done so many times after Justin died: slip out quietly, fairly early in the evening, and disappear to be alone in her own heart.

Spirit Dust

When my friend Len died it was a surprise. I was unaware that he had succumbed to pneumonia again. The email from his wife Hilary was short and direct: "The work is complete. 4:38 this morning."

So much of what I know about Hilary and Len reminds me of my journey with Justin. The love, admiration and respect between them was obvious. They were as solid as it comes as a couple. They were also solid as individuals; truly actualized people with passions and purposes of their own making. They were continually in an ever-evolving dance, either together or riffing on their own, the other admiring from the sidelines.

A couple of years ago, Hilary was diagnosed with bladder cancer. She underwent procedure after procedure, surgery after surgery, with predicable grace. She was fighting a recurrence of her cancer when Len came down with severe pneumonia; they spent three weeks in the hospital together. He returned home to a hospital bed in the living room and was lovingly tended to by Hilary and Eli, a young caregiver. As Len faded in and out of consciousness, we were all certain he was on his way from this life to the next. Then one day he woke up and looked around lucidly. Eventually, he got out of bed and began to re-engage with the world.

Having miraculously arisen from his deathbed last summer, Len openly told friends and strangers that he was living on borrowed time, drinking in life and savoring every delicious moment even more profoundly and consciously than before. Two and a half weeks ago he was celebrating at my annual Cinco de Mayo party. And now he was gone.

Hilary asked me to support her when Len was cremated, which brought back painful memories of how Justin was turned back into dust. He died up in the mountains and an ambulance carried him away. He was cremated somewhere far from home by unknowing hands. No one there to witness or care as his body was set afire.

Len's body lay just in front of us as I gazed at his beautiful face, feeling fully the luxury and gift of being able to see his countenance one more time. At the perfect moment, I caress his face, kiss his cool forehead, and offer a blessing. We are listening to his hand-picked "transition playlist" while gazing at lit candles that represent his children.

In unison, we know it is time. Hilary motions to the undertaker and Len is moved into an adjoining foyer and readied for the incineration chamber. The chamber door is opened, and Len is rolled into its gaping mouth. Just before the door closes I put my arm around Hilary and she leans into me, our heads together. We know this is the last and final moment we will see Len in recognizable human form. With the push of a button, the transition is initiated. Hilary separates herself, ready to face life transformed. Corporeal couple to spirit couple.

In a few days, someone will hand Hilary a box containing Len; a box of sandy dust. When I received Justin's remains, I took them into our wine cave cut into a hillside and bathed myself with them so I could feel Justin on my naked body one more time. Only Hilary will know the ritual she will enact with Len. It will be their sacred secret.

Someday, I too will become spirit dust. Hopefully, my children will throw me into the wind over Bonny's Vineyard as we did their father, a year to the day after he died.

The Alchemy of Grief

Transforming the base metal of our loss and grief into a healing fire within us brings us alive in new ways and lifts up those around us.

My friend Deb just called me and was barely able to talk. She lost her beloved dad two months ago. One month ago, she slipped on some ice and cracked some of her back vertebrae. A relatively new man in her life showed up beautifully in response to both tragedies; supporting her with strength, generosity, compassion, and grace. Her back is healing in a brace, and she is feeling better every day. Now she has just received another blow. Her new gentleman friend, away on business, has had a fatal heart attack. In a heartbeat, he is gone.

At the core of deep loss is the loss of our imagined future. This applies to all loss; the imagined future with the same colleagues we have worked with for the past 23 years, our imagined experience of never-ending physical capacity and health, or our imagined time with loved ones. Deb is sobbing over her hopes for what might have been. She deeply feels the loss of her imagined and planned-on additional time with her father; she is a stranger in her own body due to the back brace; and she will never know the possibilities that her budding relationship with John held for her.

The peace of God lies within knowing that nothing real can be threatened. This is a core teaching from a set of spiritual lessons known as The Course in Miracles. Love and a felt sense of connection are eternal and cannot be threatened or harmed. This experience of connection beyond physical form has saved me. It will save Deb too. She is a student of The Course in Miracles and these are the times when she will be well-served by remembering and embodying these principles.

Sometime in the middle of the night, Deb will catch a glimpse.

She will feel the presence of her father, her friend John, the memory of wellness. These inner experiences will support and save her like they saved me.

"Nothing real can be threatened. Nothing unreal exists. Herein lies the peace of God." — *The Course in Miracles*

Chapter Twenty-Three

Bonny Meyer

Anemia

Five years after the cancer surgery that preceded Justin's death, my oncologist's office called me in for an appointment. It was not long after my bi-annual CT scan. I was deeply concerned that the scan had revealed another tumor, so I asked my friend Holly to come along. But my fears were unfounded. In the oncologist's opinion, the cancer was gone for good. I could stop the CT scans and stop seeing him. We could relax our vigilance. Holly and I left the office so jubilant we went out and had a margarita at a local bar–before noon.

It was wonderful not to have cancer hanging over my head for the next few years, even though I knew that idea was a convenient self-delusion. Once you have cancer, you are more likely to end up with another diagnosis than the general population.

When I started having severe leg cramps and alarming shortness of breath after minimal exertion, I went to my doctor. He checked my heart, which seemed fine, and then sent me to the lab for a blood test. The next morning, I received an alarming summons: Get to an emergency room as soon as possible. Instead of taking my friend Verna out to breakfast for her birthday, she followed me to the hospital. There I learned that I had a hemoglobin count of six and my organs had begun to shut down for lack of oxygen.

Now the doctors went looking for the cause, and they found it in my small intestine: a tennis-ball-sized tumor that had been hemorrhaging blood for so long that my bone marrow lost the battle to produce enough new red blood cells.

Once again, I had to be cut open so an errant mass could be extracted from my body. At 4:15 in the morning, a nice Ukrainian phlebotomist extracted two vials of my blood, to see if I can safely withstand surgery. I lay in bed, wide awake, marshaling my strength. This time all the white coats thought the tumor resulted from a different type of intestinal cancer, not the rare endometrial stromal sarcoma I had before. Personally, I hope it is a recurrence, because then I have some familiarity, some relationship with what has been growing and going awry within. I faced that cancer before, even though I had a near-death experience. I can do this again.

A Less Than Ideal Patient

A week and a half after surgery, I got my wish, sort of. The cancer was a recurrence of endometrial stromal sarcoma. Now my doctor wanted to start me on a drug designed to extract all the estrogen from my system.

This is a protocol commonly used for breast cancer patients for a limited period of time. I did not have breast cancer, and my ovaries had been removed two decades ago. I had depended upon estrogen supplements for normal hormonal functioning since then. But the doctor was recommending that I strip estrogen out of my system. So in what way was this a good idea?

I could tell from the look on his face that I was not being a model cancer patient. It didn't help that Paul and I knew each other socially. So I reasoned with him gently rather than just refusing. I am weak, I said. Recovering. My blood count is still quite low, and it will take months to normalize. I've just had surgery. I really don't need another assault on my body.

He handed me the prescription and asked me to consider taking it. I got it filled and then, at home, read the detailed literature I was given at the drug store. In small print, I saw that the drug in my hand is known to potentially increase the risk of endometrial cancer—the cancer that nearly killed me nine years earlier. My jaw dropped. I went to the internet and read further. Confirmed.

Weeks later, I made a return visit to see Paul. He was pleased to see I was recovering from surgery, slowly but surely. Of course, he asked if I was taking the anti-estrogen medication. His face fell when I told him no. He really wanted to help, but he didn't know how. It wasn't fair to expect that he would know about every form of cancer, particularly a rare one like I had. But that still left me without any certainty.

Because in reality, Paul wasn't the first well-meaning doctor who had advised me to do something dangerous after surgery. The previous time I had a tumor removed, the doctor had advised full-torso radiation to kill off any cancer cells that might remain after surgery. I had made the difficult decision to refuse that treatment because of the certainty that it would burn my body both inside and out. So imagine my surprise when the doctor who performed the latest surgery casually mentioned that it was a good thing I had not had radiation previously. I immediately asked him why. Because, he said, the radiation scarring on my internal organs would have made it impossible to find the tumor he had just removed, which was hiding in a loop in my intestines.

Rarely do physicians readily and honestly tell you the full truth regarding potential side effects. I was grateful that this one had just affirmed my choice years before to refuse radiation. It certainly strengthened my decision to refuse a drug that could increase my risk of more cancer. But I felt alone, forced to make complex medical decisions on my own. I wanted a supportive team who would take a more holistic approach to my ongoing cancer misadventure.

Marital Status: Widow

\When I registered to see a gynecological oncologist at the medical center of the University of California at San Francisco, the intake form had many questions with multiple-choice boxes to fill with the appropriate answer. One was for marital status. I stared at it. I wasn't single. I wasn't married. That meant the right category for me was ... Widow.

I don't care that it has been over a decade: This never gets easier. "Widow" sticks in my throat and stabs my heart, leaving me feeling like I'm hanging out there in space, a third-class citizen. No relationship, no sense of belonging to anyone. Not to mention the increased medical risk and the worried look on the physician's face as he or she does the medical math: widow times cancer times three equals a low likelihood of survival.

Widows and widowers don't do well in our society. We are typically forgotten and alone. Our married friends, more comfortable socializing with other couples, quickly and easily forget to include us. And who wants a fifth wheel anyway? It creates an unbalanced dynamic. So, the couples get together with other couples and leave us behind.

Home alone, we learn to deal with our loneliness and lack of connected social life. But sickness and disease are another thing altogether. It can be deadlier and carry more risks for us. I used to have a loving partner, now I feel so much more bereft and physically uncared for. I am not held, tended to, and nurtured in the same way as before.

Simple human touch is miraculously healing. Frequent casual backrubs or sleeping in a lover's arms are denied us. No nourishing daily lovemaking, kisses and hugs. And we suffer for it. We fail to thrive. Thus, the physicians' dread of working with us. They know our marital status is like a disabling social disease on top of the physical one we present them with.

I wish there was a silver lining somewhere.

There isn't. All lies naked within the initial terrible question and response.

Marital Status: Widow.

Chapter Twenty-Four

Silver Oak Cellars Partners, Ray Duncan and Justin Meyer

Letting Go

Holly wants to learn to play the banjo, like her father. So I pack up the long neck banjo Justin painstakingly made by hand some 50 years ago, along with some instruction and chord books from the same era. I throw in a copy of Pete Seeger's "American Favorite Ballads."

Another letting go. You don't know you are holding onto things until you feel the heart tug when they are asked for, or you discover, for some other reason, that it is time for them to leave your keeping.

In some mysterious way, Holly asking for Justin's banjo does not come as a surprise. It seems to be the season for letting go. On the occasion of his 37th birthday, I gave Chad the gold crucifix Justin had worn for years. This crucifix, originally a gift from me, has been a deep and precious memento and symbol. I wore it along with one of Justin's old T shirts a lot in the early days and weeks following his death. It holds his energy, and wearing it has comforted me deeply in times of need. I last wore his crucifix two weeks before Chad's birthday—on the 10th anniversary of Justin's passing. It felt good, familiar, solid, and heavy thumping on my chest as I circumnavigated Bonny's Vineyard in front of our house where we had thrown his dusty remains. At the end of that day, I knew it was time for Chad to have it.

Then I knew it was time to let go of a gift I had received from Justin: a BMW convertible, antique gold exterior, a Harman Kardon music system, 330 cc engine (which undoubtedly contributed to more than one speeding ticket), and heated seats so I could cruise comfortably in cold weather with the top down. When I bought a fuel-efficient hybrid, the BMW started collecting dust in my garage. It took a while to realize that it was my experience of the car I wanted to keep, not the car itself. So I let go of my sweet sporty joy ride.

Forty years after I married Justin, some experiences are so fresh it seems like they happened yesterday. On our wedding day he dressed in black and white, a classic look. His eyes were aglow. They were the deepest, brightest blue, sparkling with life and love.

He was nervous, and when he took my hand at the altar it was shaking and damp. We knelt there before an equally nervous priest; he couldn't remember if he had blessed us already, so he did it again. The parish pastor who was supposed to officiate had taken ill at the last minute, and his replacement had just returned from a leave of absence. How interesting; the juxtaposition of Justin leaving the service of the church and our marriage being officiated by another who was just returning.

I remember the friends and flowers and the mariachi band. I remember taking up my guitar and performing a couple of final numbers with a college folk group I had played in pubs with. I remember being showered with rice, my parents glowing with pride, and my father's going-away kiss.

Much more than all these memories, I am filled with a resident calm and deep gratitude for all the years of caring and loving in a beautiful relationship. From that day, 40 years ago, I have felt held by Justin, 30 years physically and emotionally, followed by 10 years of energetic support. I continuously experience love transcending physical presence; as it continues to grow and evolve despite even dimensional separation.

I haven't always felt comfortable about my ongoing spirit connection with Justin. I received differing opinions from people over the years about what was appropriate and in the best interest of the person who has passed on. For example, there is the Buddhist stance that we need to leave the person alone and withdraw all emotional ties. This is necessary so the departed can move forward in their spiritual progression. At the other end of the spectrum is the Hawaiian idea that everyone is fed by an uninterrupted flow of connection and communication. Traditional Hawaiians often have daily conversation with their grandparents and loved ones who have died and say they receive wisdom and perspective that they can feel in their minds and hearts.

Over time, I have settled into a middle ground. Most of the time, I keep a respectful distance, wanting the best for Justin's spirit always, and leaving him unencumbered by my human presence and energy. That said, I feel a powerful, unbroken connection as if there is a delicate golden cord connecting us always. When I pay attention, I can feel him just behind me or just beyond my line of sight. Then, on occasion, I take a deep dive. I drop into the meditative state I learned at the Monroe Institute and my spirit flies in his direction. Sometimes, I land directly in front of him and the experience is powerful and profound. Other times I am not able to reach or "see" him and I am disappointed, but not distressed. I figure that either he or I are not in the right state of consciousness to connect. There will be another time.

At the end of this day of our 40th anniversary, I will close my eyes and allow my spirit to soar. If circumstances are right, the experience will be exquisite.

Celebration on the Mont

When my friends Pat and Dick celebrated their 50th wedding anniversary, they chose to do it where they met: the Christian Brothers' monastery where I taught school and Justin entered the religious life and then later learned to make wine. The winery itself is now under a long-term lease to another commercial wine company. The massive oak and redwood aging tanks, along with the cement fermenters, have been replaced with modern stainless steel. But in my mind's eye, I can still see Brother Justin in worn work pants, Ben Davis work shirt with a zippered front opening, and taped-up tennis shoes, proudly showing me the cellar.

I walked into the sunny central courtyard before the anniversary party. It had been some years since Brother Timothy's passing, but his rose garden looked well-tended by new hands. I glanced over in the direction of the boys' school. The monastery itself looked and smelled the same. Polished floors, open colonnades. Someone was even playing organ music in the chapel. Timeless.

I gravitated to the group of old friends who used to work in the winery or manage vineyards for the Brothers; Jerry, the PR and marketing guy; Russ, the accountant; and Rollin, who worked closely with Justin as vineyard manager. Rollin, a stellar viticulturist, still works as a vineyard consultant for my next-door neighbors. Old stories were tossed around, bringing chuckles and smiles to lined faces. They were all there with their wives, each, like Pat and Dick, having celebrated 50 or more years of marriage.

Dick had been Christian Brothers' champagne maker at Greystone years ago. Pat had been the winery secretary. She was one of the few who knew of the secret romance between young Brother Justin and a college coed at the university. She was the one who picked up the mail and periodically handed him thick hand-addressed envelopes with a Davis postmark.

Justin—Why did you have to go so soon? I would have loved another 20 or 30 years with you. But I dare not allow myself to yearn for this. My heart would break all over again.

Christmas Caroling Party

The first Christmas after we married, Justin and I wanted to go caroling. We had been singing together for years, and there's no better season for singing than Christmas. But we were not in the city of Davis anymore. We lived in the countryside, with no neighbors near. So we called up some friends, piled into someone's car and headed into town. Armed with empty wine glasses, we went to the homes of people we knew. We targeted friends who worked at Christian Brothers or were growers. We rang the doorbell, sang a few songs, and demanded entrance and a glass of wine. After making the circuit for two or three hours we were full of wine, cookies and Christmas cheer

We did it again the next year. And the next. That year Jack Novak, who owned Spottswoode Estate, drove us in his van. His enthusiasm for the music was robust; his equal or greater enthusiasm for the wine was a little worrisome. We were relieved when we all arrived home safe at the end of the night. Our friends Dave and Barbara expressed a desire to bring their young children the next year. What could we do that would be just as much fun, but a little more child-friendly and safe?

Then the following August of 1975, we bought Franciscan winery the week Chad was born. By December, the tasting room was up and running and looking very festive. We decided to invite all the carolers and "carolees" to Franciscan to sing. I had been so busy with a brand-new baby and getting the winery open for business that I knew I could not manage to bake cookies for the crowd that would be coming. So we decided to provide wine, brandy, and apple cider and invite everyone to bring cookies. We raised the roof with song that year and everyone loved being there and singing together.

So the caroling party evolved: from wandering revelers to a party at Franciscan then to the great room in our newly-remodeled house in

1980, two days after Holly was born, with a 25-foot Christmas tree that brushed the rafters.

The tree is smaller now. We have new song sheets that Holly updated with her graphic design talents. She also refinished our traditional reindeer wine bar, which had gotten a little shabby after decades of caroling parties and being stored in the garage in-between. Dave Ruane now leads us on the baby grand without the benefit of music since he has all the songs memorized, adding as many flourishes as he can get away with.

Every year some of the original people come, like the Dettman family did this year. And every year someone new comes. This year it was Carole and Wilford. The experience of tree, candles, and a hundred voices singing carols in harmony brought tears to Carole's eyes and exuberant joy to Wilford's heart. They have vowed they will come every year for the next 40!

Ray Duncan

Ray Duncan was the man who, over a dinner of barbecued steak on an outdoor picnic table, smoothly pivoted from offering Justin a job to forging an equal partnership in a new winery. His flexibility, courage, and vision made Justin's dream of a path-breaking, cabernet-only winery come true.

More than four decades years have passed since that conversation. For the first 30 of those years, Ray, Justin, and I were in close partnership creating Silver Oak Cellars. Ray was about as good a partner as anyone could hope for. He was kind and generous and brought a perspective to our business choices and directions that was invaluable. He also knew that he did not know anything about the wine business, so he left us completely alone to make wine, promote it, create events, and design packaging and messaging. Basically, we had complete freedom, backed by his financial collateral. That allowed us the confidence and ability to move along a path of our own making, at a speed far faster than we could have managed on our own.

Ray also became a friend. He was generous with shared experiences we probably would not have had otherwise. We spent a week on his sailing yacht in the Mediterranean visiting the Balearic Islands, then later wandering about the San Juan Islands and the Caribbean, sightseeing and snorkeling. We slid down beautifully groomed mountains at his ski resort, Purgatory, and were his guests at The Lodge at Vail.

When Justin died, Ray said he had lost his best friend.

Our families never really melded because his kids were 15 years older and lived more than a thousand miles away. But Ray's twins came to spend the summer with us when they were 12, working as "cellar rats" learning the wine business from the bottom up. These early experiences served them well later on when the Duncan family purchased our half of the winery and they took over total ownership and management of Silver Oak. David, the youngest Duncan, has done a marvelous job of leading Silver Oak forward into a new era while honoring all of the values that grew this great business and great Cabernet.

When Ray died after long illness, it was a sad day for every Silver Oak alumnus. Together, he and Justin discovered a partnership that changed Napa Valley, and American wine, in ways that have reverberated for generations.

Maui Boys

I have often talked about Maui as a haven, oasis, and escape—a place of happy times and happy memories. But there were times when it was not so carefree. One was after Justin died. Another was when Bill Haywood succumbed to cancer.

Sweet, generous, funny, wise Bill, who took over my kitchen and cooked for everyone after Justin died, and who helped me find solid ground when I felt lost and adrift as a new widow, has died. We all thought he would be with us longer, but then what would that mean for him? More chemotherapy? More pain and struggle? More sleepless nights and exhausted days? So he slipped away quietly before I had a chance to fly to his side for a last hug and sweet aloha.

Bill's friend, Wayne Cody, known to many as "The Mate," had died some months before. His heart stopped and was re-started after what should have been a routine surgery. He struggled, mostly unconscious, for months. Soon after he slipped into a coma, his sister Jill arrived from New Zealand to sit with him in the hospital. Day after day, week after week, she was there. She was there to watch for any hint of change and encourage the slightest flutter of eyelids. Jill's devotion was unlike anything I have ever witnessed. The Mate's eventual passing was an escape from his severely damaged body that could no longer contain his ebullient, playful spirit.

Bill, 6'5", and Wayne, 6'2", became friends working together at Kimo's in the early days of the now famous Lahaina restaurant. They worked hard and they played hard. While Jill was on Maui tending to her brother, Bill and I and others in our circle spent an evening celebrating her birthday. This, of course, included recounting the jokes people played on each other. As always with Bill, we spent the evening laughing until the tears came streaming down our faces. I have never met a funnier man.

The day after her brother died, Jill was sitting on his front porch just after nightfall. She looked mauka—inland, up to the mountains—and saw some lights twinkling in the near distance. She blinked a couple of times to clear her vision, but the lights were still there. As Jill watched the lights, she remembered telling Wayne how much she loved twinkle lights at Christmastime. Maybe this is a parting gift from him? She saw that they were in a circle in the sky not too far above. After a little while they faded, and Jill went back inside wondering to herself. The next evening the lights reappeared as dusk faded into night. This time Jill gathered her courage and walked up the small distant to where they were so that she could stand right underneath. This time the light display was accompanied by the unmistakable fragrance of a pine Christmas tree. She smiled, knowing that this was the most magical gift Wayne could possibly give her. Standing there looking up, surrounded by light, Jill felt comforted and knew all was well with Wayne. She stood there for a long time until the lights faded into the night sky.

The evening Bill died, I was home in Oakville outside enjoying dinner on the back patio with Mary Kay and Pat who had both spent time with me and Bill during one Maui trip or another. They knew he was struggling with cancer again and that I was thinking about him. I had put Hawaiian music on the stereo and was feeling very sad, which was curiously the opposite of how I usually felt listening to Keola Beamer playing slack key guitar. As we were finishing our meal, three butterflies appeared from nowhere. They fluttered around us then left. Mary Kay commented, "Looks like Justin and Wayne are out for a spirit flight with Bill." I thought to myself, "Too soon for that." Then I received the message Bill died that evening. Mary Kay was right after all.

The spirits of my loved ones are real and accessible to me in dreams and meditations. This gives me solace and comfort in times of grief, though the grieving remains. I miss their physical presence and sharing life with them. I long for the imagined future that I know we will not share. My heart aches every time I think of Bill gone.

I flew to Maui for Bill's memorial where more than 1000 people gathered to celebrate his life. Bill's ohana—family and close friends, spent the day "talking story," relating the many crazy good times we all had together. The central ceremony was the classic tribute to a Hawaiian waterman. Hundreds of surfers and paddlers went into the waters off D.T. Fleming beach. A minister and family members were in the middle of this aquatic assembly, offering words of love and prayer. A helicopter passed overhead dropping flowers, mine among them. The spectacle and symbolism took my breath away. It was fitting for this larger-than-life man whose love for everyone was matched by the love they returned to him. Our prayers and goodbyes became one with the ocean and rose to heaven.

Early the next morning I pulled on my bathing suit and tucked into it a plastic bag full of beautiful purple-pink rose petals. Then I walked slowly down to the water's edge, the sand cool as it cradled my feet with each step.

Before sunrise, Kaanapali Beach was serenely peaceful. I entered the water one slow step at a time, a fitting pace for the ceremony I was entering into. When I was far enough out that I was partly standing and partly floating, I remained there quietly watching light from the rising sun flash on small ripples playing across the water's surface. I kept my head above water, feeling the turquoise ocean embrace and hold me. More than anything I wanted to be held by these men: Bill, Wayne, and Justin. This salty embrace was their only way to hold me now.

I carefully unzipped the bag just a little and extracted three petals, one for each of these beloved men, and watched them as they were slowly carried away. When those three were out of sight, I took out five more, the number of my family before Justin died. I watched them travel a short distance then released a few more petals, the beautiful pink-purple blending perfectly with the color of the morning sea. Sometimes I let go of a pinch of velvet petals, sometimes I released them one by one, all the while half standing, half floating, my toes brushing the sandy bottom. Pretty soon a long trail of rose-colored flower petals extended half a mile north, carried there by the morning tide. I spoke in my heart to the men

I held there, "I am honoring you, Bill; you, Wayne; and you, my beloved Justin, blessing you all as the ocean carries my prayers and aloha nui loa out to sea."

After what seemed like a long while, with a strong sense of finality, I released the last rose petal. Now I alone remained. Time passed without reckoning. The sun eased up into the sky. The rose petals continued their tidal journey out to sea.

When I turned back toward the beach, there were people now. A snorkeler adjusted his face mask and dove in. A swimmer stroked past me. A woman called out to me, "What are those things floating in the water?" A hesitation. "Oh, they're flowers!" Her voice sounded delighted.

When I think of Bill, Wayne, and Justin together, my heart is filled to overflowing with the memories of years and years of laughter. All three of them easy-going, jovial, and funny as hell. With these two men gone along with Justin, I felt that the playful heart of Maui had also changed for me. Yes, I have treasured friends there still, but no remaining larger-than-life men who loved, laughed, and teased each other in a way that brightened the lives of everyone around them.

Sometime later, I emerged from the sea and walked up the beach before turning back for a last look. The river of rose petals was barely visible. This expression of love and release of grief would remain with me always.

Chapter Twenty-Five

Bonny & Justin Meyer, Bonny's 50th Birthday

Great Lovers

We held hands. Whenever we were next to each other our hands were clasped together, or one hand was on the other's thigh. There was an abiding attraction and connection that ran deep, compelling us to touch.

When Justin died, everyone wondered how I would recover because we had been so close, so intimate. That journey was arduous indeed. The more frequent comment was and still is about how rare our relationship was. I have already written earlier in this book about respect, generosity, and honesty as foundations of our relationship. With time I have also come to see authenticity, courage, and vulnerability as qualities of great relationships.

Justin and I never hid who we were from each other, or tried to be someone else for each other. We never intended to date in the first place, so neither of us ever stretched to create an impression that might diverge from our authentic selves. We certainly had different tastes; he liked watching football and I liked to read on the weekends. We were always our own persons and chose each other for who we were, not what we might become.

Justin was one of the most courageous men I have ever known. He persevered through childhood and adolescence with two alcoholic parents. He recovered from childhood polio, going on to excel in football, basketball, and baseball, and leading his teams to victory throughout high school though his father never attended a game. Justin was class president his senior year. He made the truly courageous decision to devote himself to God and service to others when he was 19 years old.

Yet this physically large, robustly energetic, charismatic leader was also a vulnerable human being. I believe this grew out of his monastic training. Living as a Christian Brother novice and monk required humility, obedience, and self-reflection. I am convinced that his 15 years as a monk softened him and taught him to be introspective, open, and questioning life rather than mindlessly forging ahead.

Many a night Justin would bolt out of bed, taken by a dream, pull on his shorts and grab his shotgun. I would usually awaken and stop him before he got through our bedroom door, assuring him there was no one there to cause us harm. This primal protection energy that moved within him gave me the absolute certainty that Justin would protect me and our children, no matter what. Justin, likewise, knew I would support and protect him through the many less dramatic occurrences of everyday life.

All this sounds sober and serious, but I can tell you that laughter wove through our daily lives endlessly. We teased, we flirted, we played all the time, no matter what. There was a lightness of being that permeated our individual orientations to life and was carried forward into our relationship with each other. If all the above are the skills or characteristics of great relationships, laughter is its saving grace. We had about as many challenges, difficult moments, and scary moments as anybody. Making jokes about being able to cover the Franciscan winery monthly lease payment, the awkward way I moved from wheelchair to bed after ankle surgery, the big stick Justin leaned upon in his final years—this constant movement toward the lighter side all served to bring ease and perspective to the challenging experiences of our lives.

Whenever I consider the possibility of inviting another into my life and home, I know that easy laughter will be an essential ingredient.

Sweet Connections

After years of soul-wrenching elation and devastation as Justin and I connected in spirit and then separated—or so it felt—we have evolved a sweet and stable spirit relationship. The dramatic swings of emotion have given way to an abiding supportive connection. Although I sense keenly that I support Justin, on some level it feels that I receive even more from him.

All I need do is quiet myself, breathe deeply, close my eyes, and I feel myself enveloped in his strong arms from behind me, his big bear paw hands coming together and resting over my heart. I take another deep breath, and I feel safe in his supportive and comforting embrace.

Then I listen.

The words come as I open my heart, feeling safe and confident they are his and not mine. His messages are always consummately loving, with a small element of surprise. These messages are clearly not my habitual self-talk or mind-based strategizing and problem-solving. His words are a salve to my wounds and aloneness rather than solutions to business or personal challenges. Like the sage that he is now—he is more likely to point out an obvious loving approach, then let me figure out the details.

My connection with Justin is never intrusive and always available. He is always there when I quiet myself to hear him. It is no longer necessary that I purposefully connect using the Monroe meditation techniques, though that is always an option. I find it expansively comforting to know he is always with me. I am relieved to no longer be experiencing the wild swings of emotion that accompanied our passionate and ecstatic spirit-blending during the earlier years of our physical separation. Much like the mature love connections my happily married friends are experiencing, our coming together is marked more by constancy and sweetness than explosive passion.

So tonight, as I drift off to sleep or maybe tomorrow morning as I awaken, I will allow my breath to generously fill my breast, open my heart and allow myself to be embraced by Justin's ever more powerful and expanding love.

Living Boldly

The pledge I made to honor Justin by being more "genuine and generous, living boldly with personal integrity, unpretentious self-confidence, and joyful humor" thrust me into leadership in ways I would not have taken on otherwise. I have lived boldly internally and externally; charting new territory and dedicating myself to blazing trails in consciousness and the world of impact investing.

Justin's passing triggered the establishment of multiple trusts for me and our children, funded with the proceeds from selling our half of Silver Oak Cellars. So I suddenly had fiduciary responsibility for a large asset base, but was a novice investor still in a fog of grief. So I relied on financial professionals to invest the assets. Once the fog cleared and I began to live more boldly, I came to understand that the investment portfolio I was responsible for was estimably balanced. It was also consummately boring.

I realized that I was much more engaged and excited about the innovative non-profits my family and I had funded than by the stocks and bonds we were invested in. About that time, I attended an event of the Global Philanthropic Forum at Stanford University to learn more about what was happening in the philanthropic world and be introduced to other exciting non-profits.

But as I sat there in the balcony, overlooking the crowd on the main floor and stage, I had the overwhelming feeling that I didn't belong. The room was filled with leaders from mega-million and billion-dollar foundations who were effecting significant change in the world. I watched in awe as Bill Clinton took to the podium and talked about what his foundation was accomplishing. My little family fund was tiny compared to these behemoths. Our donations were not going to cure AIDS or eliminate malaria worldwide.

But then I thought about a small investment I had made in a company that cleaned contaminated dirt. The strategy behind this company was bio-chemically scrubbing the contaminated earth from harbors and rivers, which cleaned up those waterways. Government contracts for this service produced the return on investment. In that moment, I realized I could invest in other socially beneficial companies like this one. I could convert my very balanced, very boring portfolio into a dynamic investment program to make the world better while still fulfilling my obligation to realize a financial return for the family trusts.

That was the moment I made the leap from being a conventional follow-the-herd investor to being a dedicated impact investor. Today I am invested in over 60 social venture companies. Some of these are private investments, some are held within private funds. I am invested in yet another group of beneficial companies through meticulously chosen public market stocks and stock funds. Together with these companies, we are making it faster and cheaper to install solar panels and timberland is being conserved and managed ecologically. We are educating children in some of the poorest places in East Africa, Liberia, and India. We are producing healthy, organic, fair-trade foods. Books are being shared, exchanged, and sent where there are none. Restorative agriculture and land management is producing better and better soil and food simultaneously.

As a result, my investing is generating much more impact than my philanthropy ever did—or could.

In 2004, when I determined to see how much good I could do with my investing, this was called venture philanthropy. It is now commonly called impact investing. That term, however, is confusing and misleading. All investing has impact: good, bad or indifferent. What I do is invest in companies and strategies that are designed to solve environmental, economic, and societal problems, making things better than they were before. The latest industry descriptor is "regenerative investing." By virtue of the fact that I was one of the first to have this idea, I am now considered a pioneer in regenerative investing.

From the moment I uttered the words, my pledge to live more boldly has taken on a life of its own. It has molded me and led me in directions and taken me places I never would have planned or embarked upon. My life is so much richer now for having made this commitment. My tribute to Justin has been a great gift to myself.

Alchemy

At some point, I came to realize that alchemy is all around me. I had thought of alchemists as medieval, long-bearded chemists who labored in dank laboratories attempting to turn lead into gold—one tiny flake of which would cure every manner of disease. Then I had chance conversations with some friends of mine who turned out to be alchemists. I just had to understand the concept correctly.

Alchemy is the transmutation of an ordinary substance into an extraordinary one. Wine, the world I've lived in for over 40 years, is a classic example. Break or crush a grape and fermentation begins almost immediately because of the yeast on the skins of the grape. The wild yeast naturally turns the grape juice into wine. Grapes grow wild the world over. Cultivating a vineyard with care, on the other hand, is a science and an art. Further transforming beautiful grapes into fine wine is alchemy.

When I take money, the ordinary stuff of commerce, and invest it as a regenerative investor into a company that makes the world better, I have transmuted that money into solar energy, low income housing, or schools in Kenya. This, too, is alchemy.

Certainly, my love affair with Justin challenged and molded both of us in ways we could not have imagined. We were worked, melted, and transformed by the fire of our love into a strong creative force that ultimately birthed a beautiful family, a successful winery, and extraordinary Cabernets.

Once I understood alchemy, I began to see it all around me.

And then I saw it deep within me. I have been broken open, fermented and fined like a precious wine by great love, deep grief, and recurrent cancer. My heart has been distilled into a golden substance that has healing power for those who are ready to receive it. And my wish is that you may discover an alchemical journey that awakens the magic that already lies within you.

Afterword

Bonny Meyer
Photo by Gabriela Hasbun/The Forbes Collection

Afterword

The stories of three men who felt they were broken and incapable of loving are what moved me to write this book.

In the process, the unusual showed up.

From the moment I began, I entered a time warp. No sooner had I written a couple of stories from decades ago did parallel experiences arise in the present. Time bent back upon itself. I found myself living in an uncanny vortex of recurring life experiences.

I wrote about grief and was plummeted into grief. I wrote about cancer and found myself in the throes of a recurrence. I wrote about the anguish of being in love with someone who is not available, and a complicated love affair appeared.

I don't know how to fully explain or understand this. Maybe it is just an expression of how our deep longings and lessons remain constant. They appear to be woven through time but are with us in the precious present all along.

Some people say we all live parallel lives, but for the most part we are unaware of it. Parallel planes of consciousness are one explanation of how distant healing works or how two scientists thousands of miles apart can come up with the same discovery simultaneously. Time is not linear, they say, but instead is holographic.

All I know is that I found myself living in a circular soup of poignant experiences that occurred in the most curiously synchronistic fashion. Sharing my stories and reflections is my gift to you so that you may see within yourself the possibility and path to an extraordinary relationship, and how great relationships can create and grow a beautiful business and a beautiful life. Each is inextricably intertwined with the other, and each offers life-giving energy and passion to this trinity. I shared my grief journey so that you can know the transformative power of grief and the comforting truth that spirit and relationship extend beyond death and physical form.

I wish you exquisite passion and the courage to hold it. I wish for you the experience of loving someone so much you are burned until you are no longer recognizable, emerging as a burnished spirit bright with inextinguishable inner light.

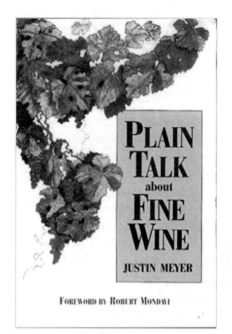

Plain Talk About Fine Wine

This is an easy to read classic wine appreciation book that contains all the basics of grapegrowing and winemaking, the history of wine and other alcoholic beverages, wine tasting along with abundant permission to trust your own palete. Features over 20 illustrations and cartoons.

Available at www.bonnymeyer.com

Port: The Secret Ingredient

This beautifully bound and illustrated cookbook features over 50 recipes that feature port and an essential ingredient. Growing up in a winemaking family, Holly Meyer developed an appreciation for Port and food. She combined the two to offer up delicious dishes that will delight every palete.

Available at www.bonnymeyer.com

Biblioghraphy

Family
Meyer, Justin, *Plain Talk About Fine Wine*. Napa, CA. Meyer Family Enterprises. 1989

Meyer, Holly. *Port: The Secret Ingredient*. Self-Published, HCM Designs. San Franisco, CA, 2011.

Relationship
Brown, Brené, *The Power of Vulnerability*
https://www.ted.com/talks/brene_brown_on_vulnerability

Brown, Brené, *The Power of Vulnerability*: Teachings on Authenticity, Connection and Courage, Audio CD Set: Sounds True, 2012

Carter, Steven, *Getting to Commitment: Overcoming the 8 Greatest Obstacles to Lasting Connection* (And Finding the Courage of Love), New York, NY, M. Evans & Company, 1998

Lerner, Harriet, *The Dance of Intimacy: A Woman's Guide to Courageous Acts of Change in Key Relationships*, New York, NY, Harper & Row, 1989

Schnarch, David, *Passionate Marriage*, New York, NY, W.W. Norton & Company, 2009

Spirituality & Emotional Intelligence
Jamplosky, Gerald, *Forgiveness: The Greatest Healer of All*, Hillsboro, OR, Beyond Words Publishing, 1999

Jampolsky, Gerald, *Love is Letting Go of Fear*, New York, NY, Celestial Arts, 1979

A Course in Miracles, Mill Valley, CA, Foundation for Inner Peace, 1976

Grief

Didion, Joan, *The Year of Magical Thinking*, New York, NY, Vintage Books, 2005

Greenspan, Miriam, *Healing Through the Dark Emotions: The Wisdom of Grief, Fear, and Despair*, Boston, MA, Shambhala Publications, Inc. 2003

Tatelbaum, Judy, *The Courage to Grieve*, New York, NY, Harper & Row, 1980

SARK, *Glad No Matter What*, Novato, CA, New World Library, 2010

Zunin, Leonard M. and Hilary Stanton Zunin, *The Art of Condolence: What to Write, What to Say, What to Do at a Time of Loss*, New York, NY, HarperCollins, 1992

Afterlife

Alexander, M.D., Eben, *Proof of Heaven: A Neurosurgeon's Journey into the Afterlife*, New York, NY, Simon & Schuster, 2012

Elder, Paul, *Eyes of an Angel: Soul Travel, Spirit Guides, Soul Mates, and the Reality of Love*, Charlottesville, VA, Hampton Rhodes, 2005

Kagan, Annie, *The Afterlife of Billy Fingers: How My Bad-Boy Brother Proved to Me There's Life After Death*, Charlottesville, VA, Hampton Roads, 2013

Giesemann, Suzanne, Various works

Monroe, Robert, *Journeys Out of the Body*, New York, NY, Doubleday, 1971

Monroe, Robert, *Ultimate Journey*, New York, NY, Doubleday, 1994

Monroe, Robert, *Far Journeys*, New York, NY Doubleday, 1985

Moorjani, Anita, *Dying to be Me*, New York, NY, Hay House, 2012

Steiner, Rudolf, *Staying Connected: How to Continue Your Relationships with Those Who Have Died*, Gt. Barrington, MA, Anthroposophic Press, 1999

Strieber, Whitney and Anne, *The Afterlife Revolution*, San Antonio, TX, First Walker & Collier, Inc, 2017

Acknowledgements

I want to thank Thom Elkjer who I initially approached to ghost write this story. He wisely looked at me across the table in a small Boonville café and said, "This is a spiritual journey and you have to do it." He was right. He became a most encouraging writing coach, and when it was time, a brilliant editor. Working together we laughed and cried much as we explored my life experiences as a metaphor for the Great Human Condition. A spiritual journey indeed.

Thank you, Mary Kay Bigelow, Karen Sperling, Hilary Zunin, Cindy Moon, Jeff Vander Clute, Sandie Sedgbeer, Kimberly Cameron, and Esther Dungan for reading the manuscript and sharing your impressions, thoughts, and wisdom. Esther, you kept me sane and precise with your Word expertise, editing, and help with research.

Thank you, Dr. Jerry Jampolsky and Dr. Martin Weiner for being powerful mentors and friends.

Thank you to Mary Kay Bigelow, who was my talking partner for critical passages in this book. You understand the anatomy of extraordinary relationship better than anyone I know. Thank you for your precious friendship.

I am grateful to my daughter, Holly Meyer, for her beautiful book layout, Rich Bolen for his photo restorations and cover photographs, and Charles McStavick for the cover design. To Sandie Sedgbeer, Beth Grossman, and Carina Sammartino for help with the logistics of publishing and getting the word out.

I am forever grateful to my sweetheart Justin and my family for all the learning, laughter, and love.

Invitation

I invite you to share your stories of the magical ways your loved ones showed up after they died. We typically don't talk about these experiences in our culture, but it is nourishing and healing to do so.

You can send your stories to me at
Bonny@BonnyMeyer.com

Photo by Rick Bolen

About the Author

Bonny Meyer began thinking and writing about the nature of love when she was fifteen. She met Brother Justin shortly after she turned eighteen at his 29th birthday party. They spent that evening playing music together igniting the love affair that changed their lives and ultimately spawned Silver Oak Cellars.

Napa Valley vintners, inspired by the extraordinary success and reputation of Silver Oak Cabernets, focused more and more on that variety. Today, Cabernet is considered the king of the Napa Valley red wines with some bottles commanding as much as $1,000. Its flavor profile displays a wide variety of black fruits, including currant, cherry, and plum, often showing notes of spice from American or French oak barrel aging. It pairs beautifully with robust red meat dishes such as game, lamb, aged steaks, cheeses, and love.

After establishing and growing Silver Oak and the unexpected death of Justin, Bonny devoted her attention to addressing world environmental, social, and economic challenges by financially supporting social ventures. She has been acknowledged by Forbes Magazine and the financial industry as a pioneer of impact and regenerative investing. After years of encouragement to write about their love affair, she decided to share the story of how she and Justin met, fell in love, and created a business and wines infused with their values and love for one another.

Bonny lives in the old redwood farmhouse surrounded by Cabernet vines in the middle of the Napa Valley where she and her beloved Justin raised their family.

www.BonnyMeyer.com